The story goes...

Nico ter Linden was born in 1936 and studied theology in The Netherlands and the United States. After working as a prison chaplain in Alkmaar and a hospital chaplain in Nijmegen, in 1977 he became minister of the Westerkerk in Amsterdam, where he remained until 1995. His biblical sermons brought him fame, and he became a newspaper columnist and television broadcaster as well as writing many books. In 1995 he retired to devote himself to full-time writing and began on *The story goes...*, which became a bestseller on publication in the Netherlands in 1996. More than 150,000 copies of the first volume, on the stories of the Torah, have been sold, and more than 80,000 of the second volume, on the Gospels of Matthew and Mark, which appeared in Dutch in 1998. Both were published in English by SCM Press in 1999 as *The story goes... The stories of the Torah*, and *The story goes... Mark's story and Matthew's story*. Three further volumes after the present one are planned and will also be published by SCM Press. A volume on the 'Latter Prophets' will appear in 2001, to be followed by volumes on the 'Writings', including Job, Proverbs and the Psalms, and on the works attributed to Luke (the Gospels and Acts) and John (the Gospel and the Book of Revelation).

Nico ter Linden

The

story

goes...

3

THE STORIES OF

JUDGES AND KINGS

SCM PRESS

Translated by John Bowden from the Dutch *Het verhaal gaat... 3. De verhalen van Richters en Koningen,* published 1999 by Uitgeverij Balans, Amsterdam.

0 334 02797 7

This edition first published 2000 by
SCM Press
9–17 St Albans Place London N1 0NX

SCM Press is a division of SCM-Canterbury Press Ltd

Typeset by Regent Typesetting, London
Printed in Great Britain by
Biddles Ltd, Guildford and King's Lynn

CONTENTS

Please note

The asterisks in the text refer to the list of sources and quotations at the end of the book.

1

WITH THE TORAH INTO THE LAND

JOSHUA 1

And it happened, after the death of Moses, the servant of the Lord, that the Lord said to Joshua, Moses' servant: 'Moses my servant is dead. Now then, arise, go over the Jordan here, you and all the people, to the land that I shall give the children of Israel.'

This is a story of the exiles, the kind that they told one another by the rivers of Babylon, centuries after Moses' death. The children of Israel were then *out* of the promised land again. What had gone wrong? It was as if the holy land could no longer bear its inhabitants and had spat them out, into exile.

Prisoners by the rivers of Babylon, the people of Israel reflect on their past. Those who do not learn from the past are doomed to repeat it.* How did they actually end up in the promised land? Why were they driven out of it? Was it because they hadn't put into practice the ten words which Moses received from on high? And if they now convert, turn to the Torah again, will they get a new chance, may they then return into the land?

And what if they never see their land again? Does the promised land only lie over there, in distant Canaan? Can't it also be *here*, or wherever they might end up? Isn't the promised land wherever the ten words take form? Isn't the Torah, according to rabbinic wisdom, their 'portable fatherland'? The Lord God didn't just begin things for Canaan, but *in* that one small land for all the earth. God's love first goes out to the children of Israel, but *in* them to all human children.

Far from home, Israel's prophets began to reflect on the past. The prophets weren't clairvoyants, they weren't soothsayers; they were speakers of the truth. They try to look at the world with God's eyes and bear witness to their discoveries. They do that in story form and in so doing make use of fragments of history and old sagas, myths and legends.

They add new narrative material to it, often wisdom acquired by bitter experience, and they bring all these stories together in the prophetic history which in the Bible took form in the books of Joshua, Judges, Samuel and Kings. Israel called this collection *The Former Prophets.** Really it's just one long lesson in religion, which begins with the entry into the promised land under the leadership of Joshua and ends with the people at long last being driven out of the land again.

It's a *prophetic* book; it doesn't offer any history in our sense of the word. In reality the wandering Hebrews infiltrated the land over a period of many decades to find a place here and there. The walls of Jericho, which in the story fell in the time of Joshua, were already lying in ruins centuries before Moses' death. The kings of the north and the south, Adonizedek and Jabin, who are said to have suffered a devastating defeat at the hands of Joshua, are back on the battlefield, alive and well, in Judges, the next book of the Bible. In other words, the wars which are described here in all their cruelty depict the battle between good and evil.

The stories about Joshua form the beginning of these writings. Joshua. His name means *God liberates.*

And it happened, after the death of Moses, the servant of the Lord, that the Lord said to Joshua, Moses' servant: 'Moses my servant is dead. Now then, arise, go over the Jordan here, you and all the people, to the land that I shall give the children of Israel.'

Why does Joshua have to be told that Moses is dead? Doesn't he know that? Of course he does. But he has to realize that with Moses' death a period has come to an end. The prophet has completed his task: he has given the people the Torah. Joshua will not be a second Moses. Another task awaits him. He has to cross the Jordan with the Torah and take possession of the land. There under the leadership of Joshua the children of Israel will have to live from the Torah, and please God the children of God will do that in such an infectious way that all Gentiles, all *goyim*, all over the world, will follow them in doing so.

'Every place on which the sole of your foot shall tread, I have given to you.'

So the land is not to be trodden thoughtlessly. Remember at every step that you take: this land is *given, given* to us. The earth isn't ours, the earth is the Lord's and can be received only as an inheritance.

'Joshua, be strong and mighty. The book of the Torah may not depart from

your mouth; meditate on it day and night. The Lord is with you wherever you go.'

Joshua told the people that they must make ready to depart. *'In three days we shall cross the Jordan.'*

Can it be that the narrator is making a mistake? After all they *are* already in the land; surely the Jordan flows straight through the land?

Yes, but in this story the river doesn't form a frontier on land but a frontier in time. Moses is dead; a new time is dawning. The Jordan flows between the Torah and the Prophets; the river marks the transition from teaching to practice, from doctrine to life. Now it's time for the Torah to take root and flourish. In three days the people will cross over to take possession of the land. In Israel's stories, when things take a turn for the better, when God's blessings come, it's always *on the third day*.

The part of the land that lies to the east of the Jordan was already occupied in Moses' days: the tribes of Reuben, Gad and Manasseh settled there.* But they too must cross the Jordan with Joshua. 'Remember the word that Moses the servant of the Lord spoke to you: the Lord your God grants you rest and gives you this land. Your wives, your children and your cattle may remain in the land on the other side of the Jordan that Moses gave you. But you shall go at the head of your brothers and help them until the Lord has also granted your brothers rest and they too have taken possession of the land that the Lord your God shall give them. After that you may return to the land beyond the Jordan that Moses, the servant of the Lord, gave you.'

Joshua calls on Reuben, Gad and Manasseh to show brotherly solidarity. The Torah teaches that the *one* land and the *one* God are there for the *one* people. There will be no rest for Reuben, Gad and Manasseh until *all* brothers have found their place in the land.

In these stories Israel's prophets have in view not just the land of Israel, *erets Yisrael,* for that one land stands for the whole *erets,* God's wide world. As long as one brother people has still found no rest on earth, the promised land has not yet been realized. One people or no people. One land or no land. One world or none.

'Joshua, as we have listened to Moses, so we will listen to you. May the Lord be with you as he was with Moses. Anyone who resists your command and does not listen to your words must die. Be strong and mighty!'

The words spoken by the Eternal One to Joshua – *be strong and mighty* – are here addressed to him by the brothers from beyond the Jordan.

They will enter the land at the head of the people: they will go before in brotherly service. Anyone who is unwilling to be his brother's keeper is unworthy to live here. Anyone who realizes at every footstep that this land is given by God will find his destiny here.

2

IN RAHAB'S INN

JOSHUA 2

Joshua, the son of Nun, secretly sent out two spies. 'Go and view the land, especially Jericho.'

In this story Jericho stands for the whole land, for all walled cities which together form the closed society of Canaan. It seems an impregnable fortress. In the story the spies are to do no more than view the city of Jericho, but in so doing at the same time they will have seen the whole land. On returning from the city they will therefore report that the Lord has given *the whole land* into Israel's hands.

Joshua sends out two spies, and not twelve, as Moses once did.* But in this story these two are in fact mentioned twelve times, so the narrator leaves no doubt about it: all Israel views all the land. However, there is a difference between the perception of the spies then and the spies now. 'The people is strong, the cities are walled, giants dwell in them,' they reported at that time. By contrast Joshua's spies return full of good cheer. Why the confidence?

They derive it from the faith of a woman. An easygoing pagan woman, who ran an inn on the walls of Jericho, at the periphery of society. Sometimes she shared her bed with her guests. Her independent position gave her more freedom than other women, and she could make her own choices. Rahab. Her name is derived from a verb which means *make room, be open*. In this story she does her name proud by being open to Israel's God. With her faith she gives a new future to a wavering people.

'Go, view the land, especially Jericho.'

They went, and came into the house of a woman, a prostitute; her name was Rahab; they wanted to stay there.

Their arrival hasn't remained unnoticed; it has immediately been reported to Jericho's king. 'Men came by night, sons of Israel, to spy out the land.'

There's a knock on the door of Rahab's house. 'Open up!'

Rahab quickly hides the men under the flax that is lying out on the roof to dry.

'Open up! Where are those men? They've come to spy out the whole land.'

'Where are those men? They came here, I don't know where from, and when the gate was about to be closed, they went away again, I don't know where. You mustn't ask too many questions in my business, you understand.' The king's soldiers do understand. 'But if you're quick, you can still catch them up.'

The soldiers set off in pursuit in the direction of the Jordan, where the fords are. The city gate is shut behind them. No more spies can enter. But how are those two going to get out again?

Rahab hurries to the roof. 'You can come out now, they've gone.'

With shaky legs the men creep out from under the flax. What has moved this woman to risk her life for them?

'I know that the Lord has given you the land.'

She knows it! She doesn't know precisely where these nocturnal visitors have come from, far less does she know where they're going, but she does know that the God of Israel is Lord, and that this God has in mind a land where the children of Israel can dwell. *'We have heard how the Lord dried up the waters of the Reed Sea before you when you came out of Egypt, and also what you have done to Sihon and Og, the kings of the Amorites on the other side of the Jordan, how you smote them with the ban. We heard it and our heart sank and everyone's courage failed, for the Lord your God, he is God in the heaven above and on the earth beneath.'*

This pagan woman is indeed familiar with the Torah of Israel. She knows by heart the song that Moses sang at the Reed Sea.* Rahab is like a prophetess, she can foresee by looking back on Israel's history. For just as Sihon and Og were smitten with the ban, so of course the king of Jericho will be smitten with the ban, and as the waters of the Reed Sea had to yield before Israel, so too the waters of the Jordan will part. What she has *heard* with her ears about Israel's past she knows she will *see* in the future with her own eyes. So she gives the two spies from Israel a lesson in faith. *'The Lord your God, he is God in heaven above and on the earth beneath.'*

That too is a saying of the great Moses.* The story-teller just wants to say that this Rahab, a marginal figure in her own land, belongs at the heart of the people of God. What makes you a daughter of Israel isn't your origin or your social status, but listening to the Torah.

'But swear to me by the Lord,' said Rahab, 'that as I have had compassion on you, you will have compassion on my family. Give me a sign, a sign of trust, that you will leave my father and mother alive, and my brothers and sisters and all who are theirs.'

'We vouch to you with our lives. If you are silent about our encounter, then we will have compassion on you when the Lord our God has given us the land.'

Rahab let the men down the city wall from the window by a rope. 'Flee into the hills, so that your pursuers don't find you. Stay in hiding for three days, until the soldiers have returned. Then you can go.'

'When we come into the land, tie this scarlet cord to the window by which you let us down. See to it that your father and mother, your brothers and sisters and all who are theirs are with you in the house. We shall ensure that no evil befalls them.'

The scarlet cord will be like the blood smeared on the doorposts of the houses of Israel when the angel of death went through Egypt.

Soon Israel will be standing before the walls of Jericho. The walls will fall. But Rahab and her family will be spared. Israel is open to the woman who was open to Israel. From her window hangs a scarlet cord, waving in the wind. An age-old sign of easy virtue. Now a sign of deliverance and trust.

3

PASSAGE THROUGH THE JORDAN

JOSHUA 3 AND 4

'What happened next?'

The exiles look at the story-teller questioningly. They hardly dare believe that there was more to come and still is more to come. Who knows, the pagans here in Babylon may be right when they claim that life is an endless cycle of rising, shining and setting. Does it go anywhere or does it go nowhere? It can well be just like the wind. 'It blows from the south, it turns to the north, and round and round it goes until it blows from the south again. And everywhere the water flows through the river to the sea, but it never fills the sea; time and again the water keeps flowing through to one and the same sea.'*

Listen, the story-teller is telling his story. It's a story from the time when Israel set out to enter the land. Perhaps this story can comfort the people in captivity.

Early in the morning Joshua set off from Shittim and went to the Jordan, together with all the children of Israel. There they spent the night. The officers went through the camp. 'As soon as you see the ark of the Lord your God and the priests who carry the ark, leave the place where you are, and go at a respectful distance behind the ark, then you will know the way. For you did not go along this way yesterday or the day before yesterday.'

It's a new, unknown way which leads to the promised land, a way which you find only by looking at the ark and following the Torah.

'When you get to the edge of the water of the Jordan, then stand still there.'

The Jordan is called *The descender, the flowing-down-stream*. This river flows and flows to the sea; it did so yesterday and the day before yesterday, and of course it also does so today. Or does it?

8

'It shall happen that as soon as the soles of the priests' feet rest in the waters of the Jordan, that the waters of the Jordan will be cut off; the waters which flow from above, they will stop like a dam.'

Just as *in the beginning*, God will divide the waters from the waters and make room to live. Just as at the Reed Sea, God will make a way for his people straight through the water of death. The miracle of the creation and of the exodus will happen again at the entry.

As soon as those carrying the ark came to the Jordan and the priests' feet touched the water, look, the waters which flowed down from above stood still; they rose up like a dam, and the people went across, opposite Jericho. The priests stood still, those who were carrying the ark of the covenant; they stood there immovable in the river bed, in the midst of the Jordan, and all Israel went across.

Where God's will is, there's a way: the priests' feet stand still and the waters also stand still. The eternal course of nature is interrupted so that the word of God can be fulfilled. A new time dawns.

And it happened as soon as the people had crossed the Jordan – Reuben, Gad and Manasseh went out before their brothers – that the Lord said to Joshua, 'Choose for yourselves twelve men from the people, one man from each tribe, and tell them to take twelve stones, from the middle of the Jordan, from the place where the priests' feet stand unmoving, and bring them to the other side, to the camp where you shall spend this night.'

Joshua chose twelve men from the people and they did as Joshua had told them. Joshua said to the priests who were carrying the ark, 'Come up out of the Jordan.' And it happened that as they lifted their feet from the sandy bed, the waters of the Jordan flowed back to their place; they again flowed along past the bank, just like yesterday and the day before.

It was the tenth day of the first month when the children of Israel came out of the Jordan, three days before Pesach, the Passover meal with which Israel commemorates the liberation from Egypt. They camped at Gilgal, *Stone Circle*, on the eastern boundary of Jerusalem. Joshua set up at Gilgal the twelve stones which they had taken out of the Jordan. 'When your children ask later, "What do those stones mean?", tell them, "Here Israel crossed the Jordan on dry land. The Lord dried up the waters of the Jordan until you had crossed, as the Lord did with the Reed Sea, so that all the people of the earth shall know how strong is the hand of the Lord and so that you shall be in awe of him all your days."'

Parents must teach their children to ask, 'Father, why is this night different from all other nights?'

Then the priest of the house can tell the Passover story of the exodus: 'My child, we were captives in Egypt, but the Eternal One brought deliverance and gave us the Torah.'

'Father, what do those stones mean?'

'I shall tell you, my child. After a long journey through the wilderness we came here through the Jordan by God's grace to live in the land with the Torah.'

And when the children who are born in exile ask you what kind of story this is, then tell them: 'My child, our temple is destroyed, the ark has been lost, but our God is the same yesterday and today, the Torah is still a light on our path. If we again venture with our God and are faithful to the ten words, belonging together like those twelve stones in the Stone Circle by the bank of the Jordan, then a new time will dawn for us, too. Perhaps the promised land will come... here. A land without God becomes wilderness, my child. The past teaches us that. But the past also teaches us that a wilderness with God becomes land.'*

4

PASSOVER IN THE LAND

JOSHUA 5

Joshua fit the battle of Jericho, Jericho, Jericho,
Joshua fit the battle of Jericho,
And the walls come a tumbling down.

What were they thinking about, the black slaves of North America, when they sang this negro spiritual? Were they thinking about a Jewish man of a long time ago who conquered a city? Why did that song touch them so deeply? And why are we still moved by this song today?

There's something eternal about it. It sings that the world's miracles aren't yet finished and that we must never despair. It isn't a war song, but a processional song for those in chains who pray with their feet and who dream of living as free men and women in a free land. Nothing will stop them; the walls which rise up before them will fall, one by one.

Soon we will be told that the walls of Jericho fell, and did so at the command of the Eternal One himself. Apart from Rahab and her family, all the men and women and children of the city were killed with the sword, including the oxen, the lambs and the asses. Streams of blood flowed through Jericho's streets.

This isn't an *event* in war, it's a war *story*. However, for present-day readers it is and remains complicated that these ancient writers tell us a story about liberation, peace and justice with bloody pictures which they take from the battlefield. So we constantly have to do a bit of translation, for what is there isn't there, Jericho isn't Jericho and the walls aren't city walls. We aren't given a historical account of an episode from Israel's national history; we are told a prophetic story from Israel's history of faith. The illiterate slaves of the cotton plantations understood that very well, and simply by singing, they joined the children of Israel, in that great journey through time and through the lands, away from slavery towards the promised land.

See them go, the children of Israel, straight through the Jordan, behind the ark. God knows the way. *It was the tenth day of the first month.* In three days it will be Passover.

The story-teller has thought that out nicely: in this way his story about the entry is a mirror image of the story of the exodus. It began with the slaves in Egypt celebrating Pesach, the feast of liberation, and then they went straight through the waters of the Reed Sea. Now they go through the waters of the Jordan and then celebrate Passover in the land of God on which they've just set foot in freedom.

Who may celebrate Pesach? Those who belong to the people of God. So not those who are uncircumcised. The men and boys who were born in the wilderness haven't yet been circumcised. That must happen as soon as possible, now.

Originally this circumcision was a transitional rite to adulthood, a sign by which a youth was accepted into the circle of men. In Israel it has become a ritual by which after your birth you're accepted into the circle of the people of God.

The men must go under the knife. *Joshua made flint knives and circumcised the sons of Israel at the Hill of Foreskins.* A strange thing to do just before a military operation, but it must be said once again that this is no military operation anyway.

Then the Israelites celebrated Pesach, the evening of the fourteenth day of the first month, the first Passover meal in the land given to them by God, 'Father, why is this night different from all other nights?' 'I can tell you that, my child. We were slaves, but one fine night the Lord liberated us and brought us to this land flowing with milk and honey.'

On the morning after Pesach they ate of the produce of the land, unleavened bread and roasted grain, on that very day. And the manna ceased; that morning they ate of the produce of the land.

The manna which served them as food during their wandering through the wilderness is no longer needed. The exodus is now really over. Egypt is finally past time, *home at last, free at last.**

However, they aren't really 'inside'. The land has indeed already been given to them, but it still has to be possessed. How?

It's night. Joshua is lying in his camp; he's worried, the walls of Jericho are high.

And it happened that Joshua opened his eyes and look, there was a man in front of him, a drawn sword in his hand. Joshua went up to him, 'Are you one of us or one of our adversaries?'

'I am neither. I am the commander of the Lord's army.'

Joshua prostrated himself reverently. 'What has my master to say to his servant?'

You would expect the commander of the army now to give his orders for the battle. But what does this master say to his servant? *'Take your shoes from your feet, for the place on which you are standing is holy ground.'*

This is an echo of the words which Moses once heard on Mount Sinai near the burning bush, when God called him to bring the people of Israel out of Egypt. Later Moses would receive the Torah on this holy mountain. At that time he was not allowed to go up immediately. 'Be careful about going up the mountain, Moses; whoever touches the mountain will surely die. *Only when the ram's horn sounds a long blast may you go up the mountain.'*

Jericho too is holy ground, which cannot be trodden without reverence. Take your shoes off, this land is God's, and only those who are utterly convinced of this may enter it. And you can enter it only by God's grace; it is the Eternal One himself who gives access to the land of promise. 'Joshua, as I was with Moses, so I shall be with you.'

It is this promise that the man in the night portrays, in a vision which Joshua receives to encourage him, now that he is setting off to take possession of Jericho.

Jericho closed the gate, the city was closed to the children of Israel; no one could go in and no one could get out.

How does Joshua get in? By surrounding the city and starving it out? By ramming the gate? No, Jericho will be given to Joshua. By faith he will be able to take possession of the land. Faith can move mountains, knock down walls.

The Lord said to Joshua, 'Look, Jericho, the king and its mighty heroes, I give them into your hands. Go round the city with all your warriors, once. Do that for six days. Seven priests must bear seven ram's horns before the ark. On the seventh day you must go seven times round the city while the priests blow on the rams' horns. Then it will happen that on the long blast of the ram's horn, when you hear the sound of the horn, the whole people will let out a loud shout of joy. Then the walls will fall down and the people will climb over them, each one straight ahead.'

The people have just celebrated Passover, Pesach; after seven times seven days, on the fiftieth day it will be Pentecost, the Feast of Weeks. The children of Israel will celebrate that festival in the land. The Torah which Moses received from on high when the ram's horn had sounded loudly will be carried in over the fallen walls of the city when the ram's horn sounds a long blast. The Torah will show the children of Israel the right direction and teach them how to live in the holy land.

For example, they will have to keep counting. Just as every seventh day is the sabbath, so every seventh year will be a sabbath year. Then the land must lie fallow – what grows by itself is for the poor – debtors must be let off, slaves freed.* And after seven times seven sabbath years there follows the fiftieth year, *the year of jubilee,** so called after the ram's horn which is blown then. In the year of jubilee the children of Israel are neither to sow nor reap; they are to eat without having sown, just as in the first year in Canaan. In that year land sold because of poverty will also return into the possession of the original owners. Then each person will again be able to sit in his own vineyard and tie his ass to his own fig tree. Always after seven times seven years the distribution of the land returns to what it was under Joshua, so that great differences in possessions are prevented. For really the whole land is God's, the earth is the Lord's; we are here only as guests.

Israel tells of a dream: the walls between free men and slaves, between rich and poor, fall whenever the ram's horn sounds a long blast. Among the pagans the bold own half the world and the rich have the rest. May it be in Israel that the priests set the tone and show the way to a world of justice and righteousness.

5

THE WALLS FELL DOWN

JOSHUA 6 AND 7

Joshua, the son of Nun, summoned the priests. 'Bear the ark of the covenant. Seven priests must bear seven ram's horns before the ark of the Lord.' And to the people he said, 'Go out, go round the city, and let the advance guard go out before the ark of the Lord.'

And so it happened. Seven priests bore the seven ram's horns before the face of the Lord; they went out and blew on the trumpets. The ark of the covenant went after them.

Joshua commanded the people: 'Do not utter any cry of joy, do not let your voice be heard, let no sound escape from your lips until the day when I call to you, "Shout for joy!" Then you must shout for joy.'

So the ark of the Lord went round the city, once. After that the Israelites returned to the camp to spend the night there.

Early in the morning Joshua arose, and again the priests bore the ark of the Lord. The seven priests who bore the seven ram's horns went out in front of the ark. So they went and blew the trumpets. Again the Israelites went round the city, also this second day, After that they returned to their camp. This they did for six days.

And it happened on the seventh day that they arose early in the morning, as day was dawning, and they went round the city as before, but now seven times. When they had completed their circuit for the seventh time, the priests blew the trumpets. Joshua called to the people, 'Shout for joy, the Lord has given you the city.'

And it happened that when the people heard the sound of the trumpets, they uttered a loud shout of joy; the walls of the city fell down and the people climbed over the walls, each one straight ahead.

They conquered the city and smote with the ban everything that was in the city, men and women, children and old people, along with the oxen, the lambs and the asses, with the edge of the sword.

And to think that this massacre took place once again *at the Lord's command.* How are we to read such a story?

Well, in the first place as a *story.* Just as in fairy tales the wicked witch is cruelly destroyed, to the great delight of the children, so in this story the whole of Jericho is put to the sword. Both kinds of story show how evil is punished and good triumphs. With his story the story-teller wants to depict a spiritual battle which has to be fought time and again, because 'paganism' constantly lies in wait for us human beings.

The story-teller of the time has no difficulty in making the inhabitants of Jericho the model of the corrupt world of the pagans, a world where for example people want to earn the favour of the gods by killing their firstborn children or using them as the foundations of a house or gate.* It is a world at which the Eternal One shudders and which as far as he is concerned must be exterminated root and branch. However, let Israel beware of complacency! That's why the story-teller began with the story of Rahab, a daughter of the pagans who made room for the Torah, and that's why he goes on to tell of a son of Israel who tramples on the Torah.

So a holy war *in a story* is not a unholy war *in history.* It's a story full of prophetic self-criticism on the part of the exiles. For why did Israel ultimately not succeed in the land of Canaan? Why were they driven out of it? Because – the prophets tell us – we made alliances with paganism, because alongside the God of the Torah we accepted the gods, the idols, the ideologies of Canaan. The prophets can only see the exile as the harvest of what people have themselves sown. This happens if you squander your spiritual heritage. The people of God should have made short shrift of the gods of the *goyim,* the pagans. Now they've become a snare for Israel.

'How different it was in the days of Joshua,' sighed the exiles. 'Then our ideals were still intact, and there was a great fight against paganism...'

But even if we know that the fall of Jericho isn't about Israel's national history but is a theological narrative, the narrator's picture of God can still disturb us. Fortunately another quite different image of God emerges in other stories of Israel. The story of Jonah is a nice example of this. Jonah has to summon the great city of Nineveh – which just like Jericho stands for the world of the peoples – to be converted. Jonah proves to be a stubborn prophet who delights in the threatened destruction of the city, whereas his God is concerned to preserve it, *all these people and animals, so many.'*

In Jericho the people and the cattle fall to the edge of the sword. The two spies have taken Rahab and her family to a safe place well beforehand. Rahab stands for all those who are not of Israel but who belong to Israel. Then the city goes up in flames.

'The silver and the gold that you find,' Joshua had said, 'all that is made of copper or of bronze, shall be holy before the Lord, it shall belong to the temple.'

There is one son of Israel who can't resist temptation; he steals part of Jericho's gold and silver and hides it in his tent. Achan is his name, the son of Carmi the son of Zabdi the son of Zerah. For three generations he has been rooted in the people of God, but earthly treasures lead him into temptation. This evil too will be exterminated root and branch, it's a cancer that must be cut out before it spreads over all the people. Along with his family, Achan, the son of Carmi the son of Zabdi the son of Zerach, is stoned and burned. He is a son of Israel, but he doesn't belong to the people of God. Rahab is accepted into the community as a daughter of Israel.

Then Joshua swore an oath: 'Cursed before the Lord's face be the man who rises up and rebuilds Jericho. If he lays its foundation it shall be at the cost of his firstborn. If he puts its doors back in the gate, his youngest child shall atone for it.'

As far as Joshua is concerned, Canaan's oldest city, a symbol for all Canaanite culture, has no future. Woe to the man who wants to rebuild Jericho. Just let the remains stand as a memorial to the dead and as an eternal admonition to the living. And if your children later ask, 'What do these ruined stones mean,' say to them, 'I will tell you, my child.'

6

JOSHUA BIDS FAREWELL TO HIS PEOPLE

JOSHUA 23 AND 24

Joshua is old and full of days. He was Moses' right hand in the long years when Israel went through the wilderness. After Moses' death he went before the people through the waters of the Jordan, behind the ark of the Lord. He saw the walls of Jericho fall and he made the people inherit the land. Every tribe, every family has received a piece of Canaan as an inheritance; the independence of all is guaranteed by that. Joshua instituted free cities, places of refuge for those who unintentionally committed homicide, cities of asylum to avoid blood vengeance. Joshua also founded the levitical cities, distributed here and there over Canaan. Unlike the other tribes, the priestly tribe of Levi will possess no land: the earth is the Lord's. It is the priests who must keep that sense alive in Israel. In their levitical cities they are to give form to Israel's faith through liturgy, service and instruction, and hand it on to a subsequent generation.

Joshua has fulfilled his task and feels his end approaching. Once again he gathers his people around him, not as a general who is bidding farewell to his troops but as a priest who wants to impress on his people that they must remain faithful to God. It is under the oak of Shechem, from of old a holy place, that Joshua calls together his people.

Father Abraham built an altar under this tree for the Eternal One whose voice he had heard on the other side of the river.* 'Go out of your land...' He went, away from the gods of sun and moon. Later matriarch Rachel also left that land on the other side of the river. But she didn't dare to entrust herself completely to Israel's God; secretly she also took her own household gods with her. Only after she had gone a long way did she bury the gods with Jacob's help, here, under this tree.* So this is a special place for Joshua to bring the sons of Israel together, *the elders and the heads of the tribes, the judges and the scribes.*

Except that that's impossible! Joshua can never have brought these people together like that, since they didn't live at the same time. The elders and the heads of tribes, they're the village councils of early times, the people who gave leadership to semi-nomadic farmers when they were settling down. The judges and the scribes are the highly educated people of later times, from after David's monarchy. You never get these two groups under one tree, there are centuries between them. The story just won't do.

Or won't we do for the story? Because it's actually very thoughtful of that story-teller in distant Babylon to bring together those two groups, the old and the modern, the illiterate and the literate, the Israel of all ages, under this tree in precisely the way he does. What Joshua has to say in farewell is intended for all the people and applies to all times.

'I have grown old and full of days. With your own eyes you have seen what the Lord your God has done to the peoples. It is the Lord your God who has fought for you.'

The sons of Israel under the oak tree of Shechem know that the Lord has taken their side. That was never clearer than at the battle of Gibeon.* The enemy mustered his forces and attacked, but Israel, which apparently had no chance, stood firm. They would certainly win the victory if the sun didn't go down so quickly. Would victory yet escape them?

'Sun, stand still on Gibeon!', cried Joshua. 'And you moon!', he cried afterwards, for just imagine the sun standing still but the moon going on! And Israel's God, Lord over sun and moon, made the sun stand still above Gibeon until the enemy was defeated. *The longest day.*

'See, I am going away today, I am going the way of all the earth. Know then with all your heart and all your soul that of all the promises that the Eternal One made to you, not one has remained unfulfilled. But as God gave you the good, so he will also bring evil upon you if you break the covenant and serve other gods. Then his anger will be kindled, and you will be driven from this good land.'

'So we were warned,' the prophet in Babylon means to say, driven as he is from the good land, 'and we still are.'

The people of God have assembled. And whether it's semi-nomads and farmers or scribes and judges, whether they're sitting in Shechem or in Babylon, whether the man of God is called Joshua of Jericho or Joshua of Nazareth, all through the Bible and down the centuries this one question keeps resounding. Whom will you serve, whom will you choose, God or the gods, Israel's Lord or mammon?

Time and again the sons and daughters of Abraham and Rachel confess: 'We want to break with the gods, so may the Lord help us at every step into the land.' And time and again this detachment is difficult for them; the fear of venturing alone with God is great and human strength is slight.

'Now, fear the Lord and serve him in simplicity and faithfulness. Break with the gods that your fathers served on the other side of the river, and with the gods of Canaan. Choose today whom you will serve. I and my house, we shall serve the Lord.'

'Far be it from us to abandon the Lord,' the people replied, 'we will serve him, *he* is our God.'

'You are not in a position to do that, he is a holy God. It is intolerable for him if you bow before other gods.'

'We know it, but still, we will choose God.'

'Are you aware of what you are saying, and can you really answer for your choice? You yourselves are witnesses that you are choosing the Lord.'

'We are the witnesses of this.'

'Then remove the alien gods from your midst.'

'We would not have it otherwise; we will hear only God's voice.'

The children of Israel promised solemnly to preserve the inheritance that they had been given and not to become assimilated to the inhabitants of the land. Long before Abraham and Rachel appeared here, this oak tree in Shechem had been a holy place of the Canaanites, where the forces of nature were worshipped. It was at this place that the people of God, as they bade farewell to the dying Joshua, again became aware of their calling and renewed the covenant that isn't rooted in nature. Again it will set in motion a history of liberating salvation and binding law.

And it happened that Joshua, the son of Nun, the servant of the Lord, died, one hundred and ten years old. They buried him in his inheritance.

7

EHUD, THE MAN WHO WAS LEFT-HANDED

JUDGES 2 AND 3

After Joshua was dead and buried, the sons of Israel returned to their dwellings, each to his inheritance, the land that he had acquired. They had been witnesses to the great deeds of God and long outlived Joshua. Then they too died.

A following generation arose, a new generation, which knew nothing of all this; they knew neither the Lord nor the works which the Lord did to Israel. They did what was evil in the eyes of the Lord; they abandoned the God of their fathers and went after other gods, the gods of the peoples round about. They bowed down before Baal and before Astarte and in so doing offended the Eternal One.

Baal and Astarte stand for a culture in which the god of power and possessions is worshipped, for a world in which the rich live at the expense of the poor. The power is in the hands of the king, of the great landowners and the generals, while the priests of the land sanction this godless system with their blessing. Only Israel's prophets vie with one another in declaring that you cannot despise God and his commandments with impunity. Whoever leaves the way of salvation is irrevocably heading for disaster.

The wrath of the Lord was kindled against Israel, he gave them into the power of those who plundered them, of their enemies round about. The hand of the Lord was against them for evil, as the Lord had sworn to them, and they were in great distress. Then the Lord raised up judges to liberate them from the power of those who plundered them.

God will not *continue* to be angry. When the Eternal One sees the children of Israel in such distress, he repents. Then the Lord on high adds a new deed to the great deeds of the past. Then suddenly down below there arises a man who is seized with the spirit, a champion of God who sets right what is crooked, a judge.

21

The second book of the prophetic history that the exiles in Babylon composed from old traditions and popular stories is about these judges. About Hebrew heroes, about brave men of God and also about an intrepid woman, colourful figures who make us laugh and cry in turn.

Those were turbulent times in Canaan. Nomads and semi-nomads were settling in the open territories between the walled cities. They were joined by a group of Hebrews who fled from Egypt under the leadership of a certain Moses, which gradually penetrated the middle of Canaan. They nestled in the land between the cities, where they suffered under the nomads from the wilderness in the east who at times when food was scarce came on raids, and from the Philistines who had settled on the west coast. These last had a new technology; they could forge iron, a knowledge which gave them much power and which they therefore carefully kept to themselves. In league with the cities, they exploited the farmers and shepherds of the hill-country until they had had enough, and the scattered tribes in the hills mustered their strength to free themselves from their oppressors.

In those days there was no king in Israel, and everyone did what was good in his own eyes. A new generation which had not been involved in the entry under Joshua and which lacked that call in this life became more and more alienated from God. *The children of Israel continued to do what was evil in the eyes of the Lord and the Lord made Eglon, the king of Moab, strong against Israel.*

It's always the same old story in this book of Judges, the stories are told according to a fixed framework: Israel goes after other gods, the Eternal One become angry, he punishes them with a superior enemy, the people cries to heaven, the Eternal One shows mercy and sends a judge. Rest returns.

In this story it is the king of Moab who attacks Israel, king Eglon, *Little Bull. He gathered the sons of Ammon and Amalek, set out, smote Israel and occupied the City of Palms.*

Like a mad bull Eglon has gone the way of Joshua, over the Jordan; the City of Palms has already fallen. That must be the city of Jericho, but the story-teller can't use that name; in his story the city is in ruins.

Israel is defeated and has to pay tax to the foreign ruler, for eighteen years. *Then the children of Israel cried to their Lord and the Lord raised up a liberator for them, Ehud, the son of Gera, the Benjaminite, a man who was not right-handed.*

And that for a man from the tribe of Benjamin, *son of the right hand*!

Ehud made himself a sword, double-edged, a short sword. He girded himself with it on his right hip, under his clothes. What does he have in mind?

Ehud has to appear at the palace, in Gilgal, where under Joshua the waters of the Jordan gave way. There he and his people have to pay tribute for the umpteenth time to king Eglon. The little cattle farmers, shepherds and smallholders have to toil for their daily bread and then in addition pay high taxes to the fat bull Eglon from Moab! *For Eglon was a very fat man.*

Ehud and the sons of Israel enter the palace; a rapid search of the left hip tells the guard that Ehud has no sword hidden. After paying the tribute Ehud sends his people back home; he doesn't want them to incur danger.

'I have a word for you, your majesty, a word in secret.'

'Silence!', called the king. The servants understood what he meant by that and left the room, the *cool chamber*.

Ehud went nearer. 'It is a word from God, your majesty.'

Eglon rose from his seat.

Ehud quickly put his left hand out to his right hip, drew his sword and stuck it in Eglon's fat belly, so that it went right in, hilt and all. And the fat closed around the hilt, for Ehud left the sword in the belly, it stuck out from behind.

Ehud quickly bolted the doors of the room and made his escape via the gallery. The king's servants came and found the door shut. Strange. *'The king must be relieving himself in the cool chamber.'*

The servants waited and waited; the king was taking a long time, just as he also sat at table a long time. Finally they got the key, opened the door and found their lord, soaked in his own blood, dead.

By then Ehud had already escaped to the hill-country of Ephraim. 'Follow me, for the Lord has given Moab into our hands.' The sons of Israel came down behind Ehud and occupied the fords of the Jordan. They let no one through. In due time they defeated Moab, and no one escaped. The land found rest again.

Century after century the story goes the rounds. 'Do you know that story of Ehud, the man who was left-handed?' It isn't a subtle story. But the Swiss theologian Karl Barth revived it again at the time of the Third Reich. That was in the days when another servant of God, Dietrich Bonhoeffer, was preparing for the murder of a tyrant in Germany.

8

THE SONG OF DEBORAH 1

JUDGES 4 AND 5

When Ehud had died, the children of Israel continued to do what is evil in the eyes of the Lord. The Lord delivered them into the hands of Jabin, the king of Canaan, king at Hazor.

How can that be? King Jabin suffered an annihilating defeat under Joshua, and Hazor went up in flames.* The tyrant and his city, have they risen again?

They have risen again. That happens with tyrants; they keep rising from the dead. It's like a cartoon in which a flattened cat later springs up again cheerfully to continue its pursuit of the mouse. And no child says that such a thing can't happen. It's a story, and hush, it's so exciting…

The king of Canaan is Jabin, a great landowner who protects his estates with his iron chariots and horses. A certain Sisera is at the head of his army.

The children of Israel cried to the Lord, for Sisera had nine hundred iron chariots, with which he oppressed the children of Israel for twenty years.

What can Israel set against that? Prophecy! The king of Canaan knows about violence, Israel knows about justice and righteousness. See who wins.

Deborah, a woman, a prophetess, the wife of Lappidoth, judged Israel in those days. She sat under the palm of Deborah between Ramah and Bethel, in the hill country of Ephraim.

Just as the left-handed Ehud confronted king Eglon, so now Deborah confronts the king of Canaan. Ehud and Deborah both have something to do with the word of God, God's *dabar*. 'I have a word for you, O king, a *dabar* from God,' we heard Ehud say. Deborah, as her name bears witness, is also entrusted with God's *dabar* and she too adds deed to that word. Deborah's name also has the sweet sound of the word for *bee*. Isn't doing the Torah sweeter than honey?*

The king of Canaan besieges the children of Israel, and in their distress they turn to Deborah under the palm of Deborah, the holy tree where this judge pronounces justice. 'Deborah, get us our rights!'

Must she, a woman, go to battle? Isn't that rather the task of Barak, the son of Abinoam from Naphtali?

'Barak, you must go up to Mount Tabor. Thus says the Lord, the God of Israel: take ten thousand men of the sons of Naphtali with you and of the sons of Zebulun, and I, the Lord, will send Sisera to you, the leader of Jabin's army, to the brook Kishon, with his iron chariots and his men. I give them into your hand.'

Barak is intimidated. He can't think of such a mission. His name means *lightning*, but unlike Deborah, he doesn't do his name justice. He isn't a brilliant man, more a worrier: 'If you go, Deborah, I shall go. If you don't go, I shall not go either.'

'All right, Barak, I shall go with you. But know that for you no glory shall be laid aside. The Lord will deliver Sisera into the hands of a woman.'

Deborah arises and goes with Barak, the battle commences. We are told about it in two ways, in prose and in poetry. We hear little about the fight itself, for Israel's Lord does the work, more than Israel's warriors. That's how freedom fighters quite often look back on their guerrilla campaigns.

If the Lord had not been on our side,
let Israel now say,
when men rose up against us,
they would have swallowed us up whole.

So the psalmist was to sing*, and so sang Deborah before him. Israel remembers her song, the Song of Deborah. It's one of the oldest protest songs in the world, and too good not to quote here. What the prose story says about Deborah and Barak can be found between the lines of the poem:

Listen to the song of Deborah:
Praise the Lord. Israel let its hair hang loose,
the people went willingly to battle.

The men have let their hair grow: that's a symbol of freedom and a sign of their unbridled fighting spirit. They've sworn that they won't have their hair cut until the enemy has been defeated.

You kings, prick up your ears,
illustrious lords, listen,
I sing, I sing for the Lord,
before him I play my stringed instrument,
before the God of Israel.

The great lords have been warned, Israel has a word for them, a word from God. Marvellous things are about to happen; that is the will of the God of Israel, who has already been talked about earlier:

Lord, God of Israel,
when you went out from Seir
and advanced from the fields of Edom,
then the earth quaked,
the heavens dropped,
the clouds dropped with water.
The hills shook before the face of the Lord,
even Sinai quaked before Israel's God.

The illustrious king of Canaan has to do with liberated slaves who are resolved not to let themselves be enslaved again. They've come out from Egypt, through the south, Seir and Edom. Everything has to give way and everything did give way. On Mount Sinai God has given his Torah to show his people the way, and what was set in motion then continues. What applied in those days, applies just as much in the dark days of now.

In the days of Shamgar, the son of Anat,
in the days of the woman Jael,
the ways were forsaken.
Those who had to travel
went by circuitous byways.
Country life stopped in Israel,
it stopped,
until I arose, Deborah,
mother in Israel.

The judge Shamgar had once defeated six hundred Philistines with an ox goad.* But who is Jael? Is yet another woman involved?

The roads of the land are unsafe, and those who have to travel opt for side roads. There is no law in Israel, trade is stagnating, country life has stopped. Until Deborah arises, a mother in Israel, a woman who forges together the dispersed tribes, a judge who creates room in oppression.

> People chose other gods,
> then there was dissension in the gates.
> Has anyone seen one shield or lance
> on forty thousand Israelites?
> My heart goes out to the leaders of Israel,
> who are devoted to the welfare of the people.

They barely have weapons, the Philistines have the monopoly of the iron industry. What can Israel do against such superior power? Iron can only be countered with iron, but they don't have iron. Who raises his voice?

> You who ride on white she-asses
> and who sit on carpets,
> you who go along the ways,
> bold to do so.
> Where does one still hear talk about the deeds of the Lord,
> the righteous deeds done to the country people,
> if not among those who carry water at the drinking places?

How wealth has alienated the rich from God! May God grant that Israel's shepherds keep the Torah, the countryfolk, the poor. They are closest to the source.

> Then the people of the Lord went down
> to the gates.
> Wake up, Deborah,
> wake up, wake up, express it in a song!
> Arise, Barak,
> seize the one who holds you captive,
> you son of Abinoam from Naphtali.
> And go down, you who hear this,
> together with the nobility.
> And you, Lord, go down with us.

The people gets moving and assembles in the gates of the city-states: 'Deborah, get us our rights! Sing your song, Deborah, your song of oppression and resistance, give us new courage. Go before us in the faith that God will secure our rights.'

'Barak, go to battle.'

'Only if you go with me, Deborah, not otherwise.'

'All right, Barak, I will go with you.'

There they go.

9

THE SONG OF DEBORAH 2

JUDGES 4 AND 5

There they go.

> *From Ephraim they come, behind Benjamin,*
> *from Machir come down the commanders,*
> *those who bear the staff from Zebulun.*
> *The rulers from Issachar are there,*
> *together with Deborah,*
> *and with Barak in their footsteps.*

But where is the tribe of Reuben? And where is Gilead? Where are Dan and Asher, the tribes by the sea?

> *In Reuben's clans*
> *there was much reflection,*
> *but finally they remained with their animals,*
> *idly listening to shepherds' songs on the flute.*
> *Gilead remained quietly sitting*
> *on the other side of the Jordan.*
> *And Dan, why did you remain by your ships?*
> *Asher too kept quiet by the coast,*
> *lay down beside a bay,*
> *while Zebulun put his life at risk,*
> *and Naphtali on the heights of the battlefield.*

Zebulun and Naphtali had to pull the chestnuts out of the fire; Reuben and Gilead just sat there and didn't lift a finger while their brothers were in need. Dan and Asher looked after their trade interests among the sea peoples, they felt themselves excused.

The battle begins.

The kings came and fought,
they fought, the kings of Canaan,
by Taanach at the waters of Megiddo,
they got no silver pieces as booty.
From heaven battle was joined,
the stars from their courses,
they fought against Sisera.
The brook Kishon swept the enemy away,
the age-old brook, the brook Kishon.
Go forth, my soul, with strength –
Then the horses' hooves hammered,
with the galloping, the galloping of the horses.

It's like the exodus from Egypt: heaven fights for the tribes of Israel. The oppressed who rise against their oppressors find the Lord on their side. They work harmoniously together: the guerrillas wait patiently until God makes it rain and the river bursts its banks; the Eternal One sends a cloudburst. The chariots of the enemy can suddenly no longer move or turn; their warriors, as though pursued by lightning, try to get away. The battle was won.

But why wasn't the city of Meroz involved?

A curse on Meroz, says the messenger of the Lord,
a curse on its inhabitants,
for they did not come to the help of the Lord.

The Lord could well have used some help, but whole tribes remained away while their brothers and sisters are fighting. That's how it was and that's how it is.

The warriors of Canaan try to get away; their commander Sisera jumps from his iron chariot and flees on foot in an attempt to reach the tented camp of Heber the Kenite, a man from a tribe akin to Israel, but allied through a treaty with the king of Canaan. He hopes to be safe with him.

In the opening of the tent stands Jael, Heber's wife. 'Come in, my lord, come in to me. Don't be afraid.'

Sisera is at the end of his strength and falls down in the tent dead tired. Jael covers him with a cloak.

'Give me some water to drink, I'm dying of thirst.'

Jael pours milk into a bowl, gives Sisera a drink and covers him up again.

'Go and stand in the opening of the tent, will you? If anyone comes and asks, "Is anyone here?", then say, "No one is here."'

Jael sits in the opening of the tent, Sisera falls into a deep sleep, his mouth wide open. She hesitates for a moment; hospitality is highly prized in her land. But this is a man who violated all rights. Jael takes a tent pin, takes a hammer, creeps up on Sisera, knocks the peg down his throat, the pin slips through, into the ground, and Sisera dies. An 'iron' warrior is felled with a wooden pin, by a woman.

The next moment, Barak is standing before the tent, chasing Sisera. 'Is anyone here?'

'No one is here.' Jael gives the answer Sisera asked her to. 'Look, the man you are seeking.'

> Blessed is Jael among women,
> wife of Heber the Kenite,
> blessed among the women in the tent.
> He asked for water, she gave him milk,
> she gave him cream in a precious bowl.
> She stretched out her hand to the pin,
> her right hand to the workman's hammer,
> she smote Sisera, pierced his throat,
> split his head.

So Deborah sings her song. She is a mother in Israel. Jael too is a mother; she gives birth to a dead man and in so doing bestows new life on Israel.

> Between her feet he sank, he fell, he lay,
> between her feet he sank, he fell,
> driven into the ground.

Over there in the royal palace the woman who gave life to Sisera between her feet, his mother, is waiting. She impatiently expects the return of her son and the presents that he has plundered for her. What is taking him so long?

Through the window she peered and lamented,
Sisera's mother, looking through the lattice:
why is his chariot so long in coming,
why does the rattle of his chariot delay?

Her serving women, made wise by experience, think that they know why the men are so long in coming, for what do men do when they've conquered the enemy? Doesn't Sisera's mother know that, how on such a day there is dividing and gambling away?

The wisest among her noblewomen gave answer,
and she herself also gave answer to her own question:
'Of course, first they are finding and dividing the booty;
and then, a girl for every chap, for every fellow,
perhaps even two;
and Sisera is getting fine linen,
fine coloured linen for home,
to adorn the neck of his mother.

The rattle of Sisera's chariot is never heard again, and his mother's neck is not adorned with fine linen but with a mourning garment.

So shall all perish,
all your enemies. Lord!
But those who love you
shine as proudly as the sun.

Then the land had rest for forty years.

10

THE CALL OF GIDEON

Gideon hit out, he threshed the wheat in the wine press. His name is *'the Hewer'*.

Threshing in a wine press? Yes, where else? If he did it on the threshing floor on the hill, where the wind separates the chaff from the grain, he would easily betray himself. The Midianite was again in the land, for the seventh time in seven years, along with Amalek and the other plundering camel nomads from the east. Hardly was the grain in the field when they turned up again and plundered the harvest as far as Gaza. They were a pest, like a swarm of locusts which strip the land in the twinkling of an eye. The Israelites had to look on as they came to get food for themselves and for their cattle. Their lives weren't safe, and many stayed in hiding with provisions in holes and caves and in the mountain fortresses. Their complaint arose to heaven, but it was just as if God had no ears to hear them.

If only the Lord would send another judge to drive out these accursed Midianites, thought Gideon. Is this the land our fathers dreamed of, on the way in the wilderness? It's as if we're still in Egypt. Perhaps it's even worse, for in Egypt God heard his people's cry for help and came to their aid. Now God seems deaf.

What did that prophet say who came along recently? 'It isn't that God doesn't listen to *us*,' he said, '*we* don't listen to God. Yes, we act as if we keep the sabbath well; we say our prayers; by the fire in the evening we tell one another the stories of Abraham and Moses and Joshua, but we no longer know the spirit that inspired them. Their trust in God has become alien to us. We cling to Baal, the god whose name is written with the letters of the verb *have*, and not, like the name of our God, with the letters of the verb *be*.'

The prophet knew how to put it!

'Remove these strange gods from your midst, then our God will certainly hear your prayer. Think of all the farmyards where I have also seen an altar standing to the Baal.'

It was as if when uttering this last sentence the prophet was looking Gideon straight in the eye.

That evening Gideon was sitting with his father in silence in front of the house. 'What did you think of that man?' Gideon finally asked. 'I don't know,' said his father, 'I don't know.'

Weary from the business of threshing the wheat in the winepress and weary of brooding on the ways of God and man, Gideon lay down to sleep.

When he opened his eyes an angel was sitting under the oak tree. 'The Lord is with you, Gideon, you mighty hero!'

Truly, that's what this angel said. Is he by the right oak tree? Gideon a mighty hero? He doubts everything, God and his father and himself, the faith of Israel and belief in Baal.

'The Lord is with us, did you say that? In that case why must all this befall us? Must I infer from the violence of the Midianites that the Lord is with us, in this devastated land? Where then are his wonders? What are we to make of those old stories, that God liberated us from Egypt? We're living now. Why did God help us only then; why doesn't he send us a Moses or a Joshua now?'

'And if God were to send you? You must go, Gideon, and liberate Israel from the grip of Midian. You can do it, you have the strength.'

'How must I liberate Israel? You must have made a mistake, I'm a son of Manasseh, Israel's poorest tribe, and moreover I'm the youngest at home.'

Gideon is just like Moses, when God called him at the burning bush. He too came up with one objection after another. God certainly often chooses people who don't think that they're suitable; then he looks among the last instead of among the first.

How did Moses finally dare to do it after all? With the promise of 'I am with you' in his ears and with that sign of God, the vision of the burning bush, before his eyes. So the angel knows how Gideon must equip himself.

'I am with you, Gideon. And be honest, deep in your heart you've known all along that you must go. And you also know that you cannot serve two masters. Don't hesitate any longer, go! You will defeat the people of Midian as if it were one man.'

'Lord, if I have found favour in your eyes, then give me a sign that you are the one who is speaking with me. Be so good as not to go from here before I return to you to give you my gift.'

Hospitality requires him to prepare a meal for his distinguished visitor, as Abraham once did at the oaks of Mamre.

'I will go on sitting here until you return.'

Gideon hurried inside. He prepared a kid and unleavened bread. He put the meat in a basket, and the broth in a pot. He carefully carried his gifts outside, to the oak. The angel was still there!

'Take the meat and the broth, Gideon, and put it on that rock there. Then pour the broth over it.'

Gideon did so. Then the angel of the Lord stretched out the staff that was in his hand and touched the meat and the broth with its point. Fire rose up from the rock and consumed the meat and the loaves.

The next moment the angel was gone, gone to heaven in the fierce flame which shot up from the rock. The Lord had accepted Gideon's offering. Would anything be impossible for this God? Gideon felt how the fire of God was burning in him.

Marvellous! Gradually he found himself won over in the vineyard to his call, to the fantasy of the Other. He even began to believe that he wasn't as he thought he was, and that he would become what the Other saw in him: a mighty hero.

11

A BOWL FULL OF WATER

JUDGES 6.22-40

Gideon was again alone. Awe seized him. 'I have seen the angel of the Lord, must I now die? Woe is me!'

Strange, Israel makes a mortal speak on familiar terms with God, as a friend speaks with his friend, just under an oak tree, and the angel waits patiently until a meal has been prepared for him; this is in a sense a domestic story of house, garden and kitchen. But in Israel's experience this same God is also an awe-inspiring mystery. The God who gives you breath is also the God who takes your breath away. He is a God who is to be found among human beings, but at the same time he is enthroned above the roof of our thought. Who will see God and live? A human being cannot even look at the sun.

'Woe is me,' exclaimed Gideon, 'have I seen the angel of the Lord face to face, that I must now die?'

But the Lord said to Gideon, 'Peace be with you, Gideon, do not be afraid. You will not die! *Shalom!*'

Then Gideon built an altar there in his yard. And he called that place *The Lord is peace*. That altar still stands there to the present day, in Ophrah of the Abiezrites.

By building this altar he declares that this place is the property of his God, as father Abraham did when he had reached the promised land. 'This is God's land.' Now Gideon understands very well why that itinerant prophet had so fiercely attacked Abraham's children who had an altar for Baal in their yard and a sacred pole for the goddess. And he now knows for certain that at that time the prophet had been looking him straight in the eye.

And it happened that night that the Lord said to him, 'Gideon, take a bull from your father's herd, a bull seven years old, and pull down your father's altar to Baal. Hew down the sacred pole that stands next to it. Then build an altar to the Lord your God, at the top of this stronghold, take that bull and offer it up as a burnt offering. Use for this the wood of the pole which you have hewn down.'

Gideon *the Hewer* has to go to hew for his Lord. He's in a quandary. What will his father think when he sees the altar of Baal in fragments? Must Gideon break with his father Joash and with his father's house? And the local men, the heads of tribes and the elders, what will they say? They will throw him out. How then can he recruit from their midst the men to go to fight against Midian?

At the same time Gideon is also filled with the thought that you must obey God rather than man. He keeps hearing the words that the angel said to him: 'You've known all along what you must do, Gideon. So do it. I will go with you.'

Gideon's resolution was firm. How will he ever be able to be a judge in Israel if he has not first given his own house and home to God? Gideon will raze his father Joash's altar of Baal to the ground. He will build a new altar, an altar to the Eternal One. On it he will offer a bull which is seven years old. He will do all this. And he will do it *by night.*

The next day the men of the neighbourhood discovered that the altar of Baal in Joash's yard had been destroyed, the pole hewn down. Fear seized the heart of the villagers; the vengeance of Baal would fall upon them. Who could have done this?

Then the truth came to light: Gideon had done it. Death to Gideon!

Of course our mighty hero had cut down more than just that altar and that pole; he had overturned the existing order. With the sacrifice of that bull he had sent up in smoke the balance between the religions which had been achieved with so much difficulty. 'Joash, that son of yours, bring him outside. He must die, he has destroyed the altar of Baal and hewed the sacred pole in pieces.'

Joash looked at his angry fellow villagers. His son had done what he had not dared to do. Gideon had listened to the prophet of God. Joash was proud of his son. But how was he to bridle the anger of the people?

'Do *you* want to carry on Baal's dispute for him? If Baal is god, let him fight for himself; it's his altar that has been destroyed. Is the Baal a god who has to be freed by you? Surely liberation is the work of gods, not of human beings?'

The Baal was silent. Gideon didn't have to die.

A short time later Israel's enemies gathered and camped in the plain of Jezreel, ready to attack. The spirit of God seized Gideon; he blew the ram's horn and sent messengers to Manasseh and Asher, to Zebulun and Naphtali. 'Brothers, come out of your hiding places, let's go up together.' They came, the brothers, they came; in Gideon's voice they heard the voice of God. But when they were preparing for the battle Gideon was seized with fear. Did he really have to go to battle? Surely liberation is the work of gods, not of human beings? Why doesn't God do it himself? 'Lord, if you really want to free your people by my hand as you have promised – look, I am laying a fleece of wool on the threshing floor. If there is dew only on the fleece and the land around is dry, then I shall know that you will liberate your people by my hand.'

The next morning Gideon got up early: there was dew on the fleece and the land around was dry. Gideon wrang out the fleece with his muscular arms: a bowl full of water!

Gideon still didn't feel certain of his cause. Has he only been kidding himself? A fleece holds moisture for a long time, the sun makes the dew on the land disappear quickly. 'Don't be angry, Lord, if I address one more word to you, but can you also do it the other way round? Can you also make it so that the fleece is dry and there is dew on the land?'

And so God did that night: only the fleece was dry, and there was dew on the whole land.

12

GIDEON'S GANG

JUDGES 7

Early in the morning they got up, Gideon and all his warriors. They camped opposite the men of Midian, by the spring of Harod. *The spring of trembling.* Who wouldn't tremble in the face of such Midianite supremacy?

The Lord said, 'The men who are with you, Gideon, are too numerous for me to give Midian into their hand. I am afraid that after a victory they will boast only of their own power. *My hand has freed me,* I can hear them already shouting it in their over-confidence. Therefore say to the people, whoever is in fear and trembling, let him return from the hill-country of Gilead.'

Twenty-two thousand men returned, and ten thousand men remained.

The Lord said, 'It is still too much, Gideon. Make your warriors go down to the brook; there I shall sort them out for you.'

Gideon made the people go down to the brook.

The Lord said, 'Whoever laps the water with his tongue like a dog, you must separate from the men who go on their knees to drink.'

There were three hundred who lapped like a dog, and the rest fell on their knees to drink.

Then the Lord said to Gideon, 'With the three hundred who lapped I shall liberate you and give Midian into your hand. Let the rest go home.'

Three hundred men returned to the camp; they had no more than food and their rams' horns. Can you win a war with that? What a strange army this is, and what a strange general, who neglects his arms and on the orders of his God thins out his followers rather than increasing them! Is it surprising that Gideon can't get any sleep that night in the hill-country of Gilead? All those others are now at home, while he is lying by *the spring of trembling,* surrounded by the men of Midian. Can he really trust that God will give him the victory? 'Whoever is in fear and trembling, let him turn back,' the Lord had said. Did that apply only to his men? Why hasn't he, Gideon, also turned back?

'Gideon, get up.'

A voice in the night.

'Get up, Gideon, go down to the camp of the Midianites, I have given them into your hand. If you are afraid and would rather not go alone, then take young Purah with you. Listen carefully to what the men there are saying to one another, you can draw strength from it.'

Together with Purah, Gideon went down in the dark. Vaguely he saw in the distance the enemies' tented camp with all its warriors and with camels as numerous as grains of sand by the sea. 'There are many of them, Purah, there are many of them.'

'Yes, sir.'

'Do you see that tent there, at the edge of the camp? We're going there.'

Why did he choose this tent and not the tent next to it? Purah didn't know and probably Gideon didn't know either.

There was the sound of voices in the tent, soldiers who also couldn't sleep. Gideon crept close, put his ear to the canvas and heard what one Midianite soldier was saying to his friend. 'I had a strange dream! I saw a barley loaf, a big round barley loaf; it rolled from the hill to our camp, reached our tent, knocked against it, and the tent collapsed. That bread turned the tent completely upside down.'

'Then I know very well what you've been dreaming of,' answered his mate. 'You've been dreaming of Gideon's sword, no mistake about that. Gideon, the son of Joash, that man of Israel. God has given us into his power. I wish that you had had a different dream.'

No millstone shatters Midian, no horse's hoof or wagon wheel, but a barley loaf. That simple soldier is a good interpreter of dreams. The barley loaf is Israel, which lives by grain, and the tent is the nomad from the wilderness who lives on plunder. The bread that he wants to plunder becomes his downfall.

And it happened when Gideon had heard the dream and its interpretation that he bowed in worship. Rid of his fear, he returned to his people. A nightmare for the Midianites was a saving dream for Gideon. 'Men, get up, the Lord has given Midian into our hand.'

Has given. It's all settled.

Gideon divided his men into three groups of a hundred, and gave each one a ram's horn in his hand and an empty jar. There were empty jars enough in the plundered land. They had to keep a torch hidden in each jar.

'Pay attention to me, and do what you see me doing. When I blow the ram's horn, you must also blow the ram's horn, each in his place, around the whole camp. Then cry out, "For God and for Gideon."'

None of the men found it strange that Gideon mentioned his name in the same breath as the holy name of God.

The men spread themselves out in the darkness of the night and looked for a place for themselves on the hills round about. Hardly were they standing at their posts – it was the beginning of the middle watch of the night – when look, Gideon appeared there on the edge of the camp. He blew the trumpet and immediately they too blew their trumpets and they broke the jars in pieces. With their left hands they waved their torches, and with their right hands they blew the ram's horn. 'To the sword, for God and for Gideon!'

To the sword? Did they have swords then? They had their hands full of the torches and the trumpets. Where were the swords?

The swords are over there in the camp. In panic there and drunk with sleep, everyone flees in a different direction and in the ghostly light each takes his mate as the enemy. In their deep fear and confusion they strike at one another. Gideon and his men simply perform a *son et lumière* show in the hill-country of Gilead; meanwhile Midian cuts itself to pieces. The camels look on in bewilderment.

13

AFTER THE MIDIANTITES

JUDGES 8.1-21

Some of the Midianites had escaped the slaughter and taken flight. Gideon summoned the help of the men of Naphtali, Asher and Manasseh to pursue them. In particular he had his eye on Zebah and Zalmunna, *Sacrifice* and *Shadow*, the kings of Midian who had once killed Gideon's brothers on Mount Tabor. He also sent messengers to the hill-country of Ephraim: 'Go down to the Midianites, cut them off at the Jordan as far as Beth-barah.'

The Ephraimites cut them off and Midian's commanders Oreb and Zeeb were arrested. *Raven* and *Wolf*. If they aren't robbers! *Raven* met his death at the *Raven's Rock*, and *Wolf* in the *Wolf's Hole*. The Ephraimites proudly showed the severed heads to Gideon, just as a gamekeeper shows his master at the castle the dangerous wild animal that he has shot. But even before Gideon was able to praise them for their action, they expressed their discontent, offended because they hadn't been involved earlier in the struggle against Midian. 'Why didn't you call us, Gideon?'

Gideon remained calm and generously gave them the recognition that they asked for: 'Don't think that I, a farmer's son from Abiezer, have done so much more than you. Now take the wine in our area: isn't the late vintage of Ephraim better than the whole wine harvest of Abiezer? Everyone knows that. Just as everyone also knows how, after we had made a beginning on the destruction of Midian, you of Ephraim put the crown on the work by making *Raven* and *Wolf* a head shorter.'

That helped.

Zebah and Zalmunna, the kings of Midian, had seen an opportunity to go over the Jordan; Gideon and his gang set off in pursuit. After an exhausting journey they reached Succoth. 'Will you give my warriors some loaves, they're so weary,' asked Gideon.

'First try and get hold of those fellows, and then come back to us,' said the men of Succoth, afraid of reprisals from the Midianites. Brotherhood in Israel is hard to come by.

Gideon is furious. 'Do you know what I shall do when I've caught up with those kings and come back here to you? I shall thresh your bodies with thorns and thistles.'

The Hewer certainly knows what threshing is. His words don't sound particularly judge-like. Must we then be disturbed that Gideon's legs can't bear the weight of leadership? Of course, Succoth isn't prepared for brotherly service, but wouldn't Gideon do better to strive for reconciliation than to threaten with thistles and thorns?

On goes the pursuit of Zebah and Zalmunna, now to Peniel. 'Have you a bit of bread for us?' asked Gideon.

The people of Peniel also rejected them wretchedly. Are these the brother people who solemnly promised Moses that they would be in solidarity with the tribes that were going to live west of the Jordan?* Gideon swore that on his return he would also wreak vengeance on Peniel; he would not leave one stone of the tower, the pride of the city, standing on another.

Meanwhile the Midianites had already got a bit further. With a tremendous effort Gideon and his men were able to catch them up and defeat them. Zebah and Zalmunna were taken prisoner and carried off.

'Look,' said Gideon to the men of Succoth, 'here are the kings of Midian for whose sake you scorned me; I was to come back when I had caught them.' And promptly the leaders and elders of the city were scourged by Gideon with thistles and thorns. They might count themselves lucky with this punishment, for he put the men of Peniel to death; they lay lifeless alongside their fallen tower. Can it be that Gideon is going to play God?

In a bookshop in New York I once found a wooden statuette of Gideon, ram's horn and all: *Gideon, the shy warrior.* And indeed that's how it began, with this bashful farmer's son and his fleece on which the heaven dropped dew. But now where is the meekness of before? Has Gideon so quickly forgotten who gave him the victory in the plain of Jezreel? 'For God and for Gideon!' The arrogance has won out over the meekness; the son of Joash preens himself like a star; he's turned things round: for Gideon and for God.

Gideon had the kings of the Midianites whom he had taken prisoner appear before him, bound to their camels. 'Do you still remember those men whom you killed on Mount Tabor?'

'Those men, lord, they had some radiance about them, they had the kingship in them. They were like you.'

'They were my brothers, they were sons of my mother.'

Those brothers had something princely about them, the same royal radiance as Gideon, if we may believe Zebah and Zalmunna. Gideon readily accepted their flattery; it was just as if Israel already had a king! And what does a king do? A king decides on life and death.

'You hounded my brothers to death. Had you not done that, I would have left you alive. Jether, stand up and kill those men.'

Gideon wants his oldest son to take vengeance on the murderers of his father's brothers. But Jether hesitates to do so. *The young man did not draw the sword; he was afraid, he was only a young man.*

Jether still has a lot to learn, but Zebah and Zalmunna know the rules of the game. War is war, blood vengeance is blood vengeance, you kill as a man and you die as a man: 'Gideon, why don't you yourself stand up and kill us? As the man is, so is his strength.'

Gideon stood up and killed them. He put in his bag the golden crescents which were on the necks of their camels.

14

GIDEON'S END

JUDGES 8.22-35

Then the men of Israel said to Gideon, 'Rule over us, you and your son and your son's son, for you have freed us from the power of Midian.'

The old rivalry between the brothers has again built up and the people threaten to fall apart into camps. Now that brotherhood is shaky, couldn't kingship offer a solution, a strong man, a ruler who knows what is needed? And then let his son also be king, and his son after him; then we shall see the end of anxieties at a stroke and for years to come. *'Rule over us, you and your son.'*

'I shall not rule over you, my son shall not rule over you, the Eternal One shall rule over you.'

'Isn't that well said by Gideon? The people offers him the hereditary kingship, but the shy warrior refuses: only the Lord is Israel's king.

Or is Gideon no longer so shy? Why doesn't he immediately deny quite forcefully that he is the one who redeemed Israel from Midian's power? Gideon isn't the liberator of Israel; the judge is simply an instrument in God's hand. And that is precisely why Israel has no king, because it knows from its neighbours that very soon such a person begins to play God. Moses already warned against this in the Torah: they go beyond human measure, they take to themselves many wives, they accumulate silver and gold.* Be aware of what you're beginning!

But surely Gideon isn't beginning; after all, he's clearly rejected the people's request. If only that were true! Gideon says the opposite of what he means. Just like a market trader, who in a courteous oriental way says that he's giving you the object as a present but means that you must make an offer. Gideon says that he doesn't accept the kingship, but in so doing he is opening the negotiations, for they can certainly sell the kingship to him. 'Let each of you give me a golden ring from his booty.' It was tribes from the east that they had plundered, people who like to wear gold.

'That we will gladly do,' exclaimed the people. They spread a cloak out on the ground, and each threw on to it a golden ring from his booty. The weight of the rings amounted to seventeen hundred gold shekels, quite apart from the crescents, the earrings, the purple garments which the kings of Midian had worn, and quite apart from the chains which had sat round the necks of their camels. What did he want with all that gold?

Gideon wants to make an *ephod*, an idol, with it. What has happened to the Gideon of old? Faith always begins – and revives – when someone confesses that he isn't God. That was the strength of the shy soldier of old, that he still knew meekness, that he didn't seek himself in arrogance but his Lord. However, Gideon has gradually lost his sense of a calling. The one who won so many victories, over himself and over Israel's enemies, ends with a defeat. 'I am only an ordinary young man from Manasseh, the poorest tribe of Israel, my father's youngest son' – that's how it began. And it ends with his going beyond human measure; he can't resist the temptation to take the crown and listens to a voice from within which whispers in his ear that he must vie with God: 'Why still so shy, warrior?'

At the height of his fame Gideon wants to go even higher, and then he falls. Having begun as an iconoclast, Gideon bows his knees to the gods whom he initially challenged. Blinded by the desire against which Moses had already warned, he begins to gather gold and silver and many women. The shy warrior is dead.

Seventy sons were born to him, and by a slave girl in Shechem he had another one, Abimelech, a name which clearly came to Gideon through a deep longing: *My father is king.* And that although once he had still cried out so proudly, 'I shall not rule over you, my son shall not rule over you, the Lord shall rule over you.'

Gideon has set up on his own. What still binds him to God? The simplicity and the wonderment has disappeared, all reverence is gone, the dreams, the visions, all that heavenly dew has evaporated. Did Gideon still have the fleece from of old lying somewhere, the sign of grace with which it all began? Called to judge the Israelites, he goes before them into evil. In so doing he has sown the seed of new idolatry and new disasters.

And Gideon, the son of Joash, died at a good old age and was buried in the tomb of his father Joash in Ophrah of the Abiezrites. And it happened that when Gideon had died, the children of Israel turned away. They went whoring after the Baals. They no longer thought of the Lord their God, who had saved them from the hand of all their enemies round about.

15
JOTHAM'S FABLE

JUDGES 9

The sons of Israel didn't honour the memory of Gideon, God's passionate fighter, equipped only with a ram's horn, a torch and an empty jar. They didn't appreciate the much good that Gideon did for Israel; the injustice that he also did became established: the people went whoring after the Baals. So the Israelites followed Gideon in his weakness instead of in his strength.

As his lawful heirs, Gideon's seventy sons form a kind of oligarchy in the ancestral residence of Ophrah. His seventy-first son, Abimelech, *My father is king*, that young man with the ominous name, fathered by a concubine in Shechem, hardly counts at the palace. They think it better for him to stay in the provinces. Slighted, the 'bastard' returns to Shechem, where he turns to his mother's brothers. A man can hardly do without brothers; if need be you choose them from the bad sort. 'What do you prefer, that seventy men rule over you or that one man rules over you, a man of your own flesh and blood?'

The brothers fall for it and talk about it with the other citizens. Shouldn't they opt for the authority of just one man, Abimelech? 'Let Abimelech be our king.'

The inhabitants of Shechem hand over to Abimelech, who is filled with rancour, seventy silver pieces from the temple of Baal, as if with this divine gift they were paying a price for each of Gideon's sons who were to get the worst of it over there in Ophrah. Abimelech hires an army of thieves and vagabonds, goes off to his father's house in Ophrah and slaughters his seventy brothers, *on one stone.*

No, not *all* his brothers: the youngest son, the seventieth lad, Jotham, can hide and escape the bloodbath.

Abimelech is welcomed into Shechem with the sound of trumpets and – it cannot be said more nicely than in Hebrew – *then they crowned My father is king king.* They do that under the sacred oak of Shechem. This is at the very spot where Abraham built his first altar to the Eternal One in the land of promise, where Rachel together with Jacob buried her household gods, and where Joshua renewed the covenant with Israel's God. Under the sacred oak of Shechem *My father is king* is crowned king. What chutzpah! No blessing can rest on that.

The first to see that is Jotham, Abimelech's half-brother, who has escaped the massacre. He goes to the top of Mount Gerizim, raises his voice and cries: 'Listen to me, citizens of Shechem, then God will listen to you.'

There's something royal about him, this Jotham; the good that Gideon did dwells in his soul.

'Listen to me. The trees were going to choose a king. They said to the olive, "We want to anoint you our king." The olive tree said, "Must I then give up my oil that gods and men honour in me, and go and lord it over the trees?" The trees asked the fig tree, "Come, be king over us." But the fig tree said, "Must I then give up my sweetness and go and lord it over the trees?" They asked the vine, "Come, be king over us." But the vine said, "Must I then give up my juice which delights gods and men, and go and lord it over the trees?" Then all the trees turned to the thorn bush: "Come, you be our king." The thorn bush said, "If you will truly anoint me as king over you, then come, shelter in my shade. If not, then a fire shall go out from this thorn bush which will devour the cedars of Lebanon."'

This fable expresses the sorry experience of a people which has known centuries of caprice and oppression. Whatever among human beings wants to make itself great, often emerges from smallness of character. The olive tree, the fig tree and the vine stand for the true nobility of the land. Aware that the kingship will only lead them to exalt themselves, they turn down the honour. The other trees are seized with fear. There must and shall be a king. So why not the thorn bush?

If only they hadn't chosen the thorn bush. It bears no fruit, it's useless, a windbag which offers what it can never give: shade. You can be wounded by it and it's dangerous in another sense: its dry wood easily catches fire and in a moment sets the whole land ablaze.

'Citizens of Shechem!' Once again Jotham raises his voice on the top of the hill. 'Have you elected Abimelech king in trust? In so doing have you done justice to Gideon and to his house? My father fought for you, risked his life to liberate you from the power of Midian! And what do you do?

You have rebelled against my father's house, you have killed his sons, seventy men on one stone. And Abimelech, the son of his slave girl, you have made king because he is your brother. Well then, be happy with Abimelech, and he will be happy with you. But know well: fire will go out from Abimelech which will swallow up the citizens of Shechem. And fire will go out from the citizens of Shechem which will swallow up Abimelech.'

After these words Jotham fled and took refuge in Beer. He kept silence from then on. What had to be said had been said.

Things went badly with Abimelech and with Shechem; Jotham had foreseen that well. *The Lord sent an evil spirit between Abimelech and Shechem.*

Complete anarchy prevailed; the Shechemites plundered the caravans which went by, and on the prompting of one Gaal there was even a rebellion against Abimelech, who was living elsewhere, trusting in his agent Zebul. The people caroused like anything, and bowed down before Baal. *They went out into the field, they harvested from the vineyards, they trod the winepress, they celebrated festivals, they came into the house of their god, they ate and drank and cursed Abimelech. 'Who is Abimelech that we should serve him?'*

Zebul passed all this on to Abimelech and told him when and where he must go and lay ambush to overcome the rebels. When king Abimelech went to battle against his own city, the rebel Gaal saw him approaching from the city gate. 'Look, over there, people are coming down from the hilltops!'

'No, you're mistaken,' said Zebul, 'you're taking the shadows on the hills for men.'

When Gaal saw that the shadows from the hills were indeed men, it was too late. The Shechemites met with a cruel death, the city was razed to the ground and Abimelech strewed it with salt. In this way he made it barren and uninhabitable.

Abimelech continued his punitive expedition and went to the nearby Tower of Shechem. That city had had no part in all this, but Abimelech was unstoppable. The inhabitants of the Tower of Shechem fled hastily into the cellar of the temple of Baal – their god would save them. Abimelech and his men cut branches from the trees, put them on the vault of the cellar and set it all on fire. The people perished in smoke and flame.

Fire had gone out from the king-thorn bush, as Jotham had already foreseen in his sermon on the mount.

It still wasn't enough. Abimelech also wanted to teach the city of Thebez a lesson. The people of Thebez fled in panic, men and women, into the towers, shut the doors and climbed up on to the roof. Abimelech approached; he also wanted to burn the people of Thebez with fire. Then a woman threw down a millstone, on top of Abimelech's head. Abimelech collapsed and called to the young man who bore his weapons, 'Draw your sword and kill me, otherwise they will say that a woman killed him.' The young man ran him through and the king died. He did not die by a woman's hand; that shame was spared him.

The evil that he had done had come down on his own head. *With one stone!* On one stone Gideon's seventy sons were put to death; with one stone, a woman, the Battleaxe of Thebez, had avenged their death.

When Abimelech's men saw that their king was dead, they went their way, each to his home.

There was no longer a king that they could follow into evil.

16

JEPHTHAH'S DAUGHTER

JUDGES 10 AND 11

The children of Israel continued to do what was evil in the eyes of the Lord. They served the Baals and the Astartes, the gods of Aram, Sidon and Moab, the gods of Ammonites and Philistines. They abandoned the Lord, and did not serve him.

It's becoming monotonous, but that's how it is: again the people runs after strange gods, seven in all. And because despite everything God continues to love Israel, he continues to be angry. He gives them into the hands of the Philistines and Ammonites; all the Israelites who dwell beyond the Jordan are oppressed by them. And when their tormentors cross the Jordan once again to enslave Judah, Benjamin and Ephraim, they just don't know what to do. They cry out to the Lord, 'We know it. We have sinned, we have turned our backs on you, turned to the Baals, have mercy on us.'

But the Lord said, 'Have I not delivered you from the power of Egyptians, Amorites, Ammonites, Philistines, Sidonians, Amalekites and Maonites, when they oppressed you and you begged me to have pity?'

From how many hostile peoples has the Lord already freed them? From seven in all, and has Israel learned anything from this? It's always the same old story. And while an enlightened spirit can mockingly say of the Eternal One that it is his job to forgive,* at one point there's an end to it, if Israel keeps ogling paganism. *'I will not go out to free you. Cry rather to the gods whom you have chosen, let them get you out of your distress.'*

'Lord, we know that we have sinned, be gracious to us just once more, we beg you.' And they abjured all the strange gods in their midst and served the Lord.

And God allowed himself to be persuaded; he couldn't help showing mercy and sent help quickly to Israel, his child in need. He no longer wanted to be angry; he wanted to save what could be saved.

Who could help the Eternal One with that on earth, who could be Israel's new judge and liberate the people from the hands of the enemy? The Ammonites were encamped in Gilead, and the Israelites took up their positions opposite them. Who could lead the people in the battle?

The elders of Gilead had someone in view: their brother Jephtah. Now he wasn't quite their brother; he was really their half-brother. Jephthah was the son of a prostitute, a bastard to whom they had once shown the door: 'You shall have no inheritance in our father's house.' Jephthah was thrown out, this illegitimate child; only guilt and shame were to be his inheritance. He had sought refuge in the land of *Tob*, the land where life is *good*. At least, for someone like Jephthah. He had become a robber leader over a gang which was making things unsafe there, the kind of people who can do excellent service in a war. They've nothing to lose; they're afraid of no one, and in hand-to-hand fighting they're both skilful and ruthless.

Jephthah didn't know what was up when his brothers arrived in Tob. What did they want of him? 'Jephthah, there is no warrior in the land like you. Why don't we let bygones be bygones? Come over and help us.'

'You've always despised me, just as contempt was also my mother's fate. And now you come to me in distress?'

'Once again, Jephtah, let bygones be bygones. There's nothing that we would like better than for you to be our leader in the battle against the sons of Ammon. And even after that you must be our leader, head over all the inhabitants of Gilead.'

Jephtah saw that this was *tob*. Now he could wipe out the shame; he, the leader of Gilead! 'Do you really mean it, that if I go to battle against the sons of Ammon and the Lord gives them into my power, from then on I shall be leader of Gilead?'

'We promise that, Jephthah, the Lord is our witness.'

Jephthah decided not to go into battle immediately; first he made an attempt at diplomacy. The Ammonites disputed with Israel a piece of land that Moses had occupied after the journey through the wilderness. Here they were stirring up a piece of history more than three hundred years old. According to Jephthah, their argument failed on all sides. He argued that the Ammonites had lost the land long before Moses appeared on the scene. Jephthah seemed to have a thorough knowledge of the Torah.

However, all this toing and froing got nowhere; it was a ritual dance. Then the spirit of God came upon Jephthah; if Ammon didn't want to listen, it had to feel. Jephthah and his men prepared for battle; there was much honour to be won on the battlefield.

But what if he lost the battle? Jephthah was seized by doubt and fear. It wasn't fear of death, since he had often contemplated that. It was fear of being rejected by his brothers after another defeat; the second time would be even more painful than the first. 'O God, if you give the sons of Ammon into my hand and I get back from the battle, I promise that I will give to you as a sacrifice what first comes to meet me from my house.'

A what belongs before the what. *What?* Has Jephthah thought about it, *what* that what could be, or *who* it could be?

'O God, if you... then I will...'

God was horrified. 'Is he talking to me? He doesn't know me very well, he's confusing me with the god of the Ammonites.'

Battle commenced, Jephthah inflicted a defeat on the Ammonites and returned victorious from the battlefield. As soon as his daughter heard the happy news that her father was on the way, she went out of the house and danced to meet him with drum and tambourine. 'Father, how splendid that you... but what is it, aren't you happy?'

Jephthah tore his clothes and broke out in a lament. 'Woe is me, my daughter, you've brought me low, you're making me so unhappy.'

Whereas it was *he* who was going to make *her* unhappy.

'Woe is me! You've brought doom upon me. I made God a promise that I would give to the Lord as a burnt offering what first came out of my house to meet me. I can't go back on it.'

Why not? In the Torah Israel is adjured in every way not to offer any son or daughter to the gods. Must she die as a virgin, may she know no lover?

'Father, if you've made a promise to the Eternal One, then you must keep that promise. It is the Lord who gave you the victory. I ask of you just one favour: give me two months to go into the mountains and bewail my virgin state with my friends.'

She will never be a bride; her friends will not accompany on her wedding day as bridesmaids. So let them be with her when she tells them plainly the way that she has to go. She is a model daughter. Unfortunately she knows no other God than the God of her father.

'Go, my daughter, go.'

And it happened at the end of two months, that she returned to her father, and Jephthah accomplished in her the promise that he had made. She had never had intercourse with a man.

A special custom arose in Israel from her stay in the mountains: *from year to year the daughters of Israel sing a refrain for the daughter of Jephthah the Gilead, for four days.*

The friends of Jephthah's daughter must have begun this, meeting every year to commemorate their dead sister. Without knowing it, they created a significant ritual here.

A man will have to leave his father and mother before he is in a position to attach himself to his wife – as the creation story teaches – and of course the same also applies to the woman. Such a departure is complicated, and good friends are indispensable for a young person. Both boys and girls need rituals, rituals of transition.

For four days in the year the fathers and mothers of Israel can't say much about their daughters. Then their daughters go into the hills to commemorate the tragedy which took place in the house of Jephthah, and to reflect on their approaching departure from the home in which they have grown up. They long to go and yet are afraid, and it is very difficult to find a place for the competing feelings. A host of stories* and a selection of songs can help them here. When they're back home again, of course they don't want to say much about it.

17

SHIBBOLETH

JUDGES 12

Are we mistaken if we think that things keep going wrong with Israel? Gideon conquered his enemies but he lost himself. He couldn't withstand the seductions of wealth and the lure of the crown, and his son Abimelech was even less successful.

Jephthah, too, isn't a judge whose name is written in gold in the book of Israel. Under his leadership brotherhood in Israel was hard to find. Just as in the time of Gideon, the Ephraimites again begin to kick up a fuss; again they come, offended, to complain that they've been left out. 'Jephthah, why did you go out against the sons of Ammon without calling on us to go with you? We shall send up your house in smoke and fire!'

The tormentors! As if Jephthah hadn't already had to suffer enough from smoke and fire. Had they perhaps wanted to share in the booty? In that case let them say so clearly.

'Why didn't I call you? I cried out for you, but although you knew that we were in distress, none of you so much as lifted a finger. All alone I risked my life and defeated the Ammonites. You can't swallow that so you threaten me with murder and burning. I'll show you!'

Jephthah won't be mocked; everyone who has heard even one story about how things used to be in the land of Tob knows that.

So good and pleasant can it be
*when brothers live in unity.**

So sings Israel, but now that song can't be sung, for all goodness and love has gone; the sons of the same house get in one another's hair. Jephthah and his men emerge from the battle victorious, and occupy the fords of the Jordan, thus cutting off the fleeing Ephraimites. The defeated brothers fall hopelessly into the trap.

'Are you from Ephraim?'

'Why do you think that?'

'Say *shibboleth*.'

They can't say it, those people of Ephraim, just as foreigners can't say *Scheveningen* as the Dutch do.

'Say *shibboleth*.'

'*Sibboleth*.'

Their speech betrays them, and with that one word they've immediately spoken their last word: those who say *sibboleth* are immediately slaughtered. Jephthah has never believed in half measures.

Peace is a long way off, brothers of the same house murder one another, a people goes under in mutual hate and envy. Is there no powerful leader to be found who can bring unity into divided Israel? If there is, he must be a passionate man, not a brute who is himself going to play God, not a weakling who falls for gold and women. Can't such a person arise? For what if the children of Israel go on doing what is evil in the eyes of the Lord?

18

THE BIRTH OF SAMSON

JUDGES 13

The children of Israel continued to do what was evil in the eyes of the Lord and the Lord gave them into the hands of the Philistines, forty years.

Will it never stop? The people hopes and prays that God will send a liberator who will put an end to the rule of the Philistines, but he hasn't yet come. Can't God send someone *now* in order at least to make a beginning?

And it happened: a man from Zorah, from the tribe of Dan, his name was Manoah. His wife was barren, she had not given birth. The angel of the Lord appeared to her and said, 'Look, you are barren, you have not given birth, but you shall become pregnant, you shall bear a son. So take care: drink no wine or strong drink and eat nothing that is unclean. For look, you will become pregnant and bear a son. No razor must come on his head; a Nazirite of God he shall be, from his mother's womb. He shall make a beginning of freeing Israel from the hands of the Philistines.'

And it happened... When these words appear in the Bible you must always take note, for then something is really happening, then something is going to happen from God in the impotent, barren Israel. When the future is at risk, barren matriarchs begin to bear sons. Then Manoah's wife once again gives the people a judge, a Nazirite of God.

And it happened... an angel of the Lord appeared to Manoah's wife while she was working in the field, and as unexpectedly as he appeared, he disappeared again. What had he really said? Would she give life to a son? Yes, that's what she had heard him say. He shall be a Nazirite, a man who dedicates his life to God.*

The woman ran home to tell Manoah what had happened to her. *Rest* is his name. He's a kind of Joseph of Nazareth, a man apart. Rembrandt, who understood well where the evangelist Luke found the inspiration for his story about the birth of Jesus, therefore drew Manoah as an older man and his wife as a Madonna.

'Manoah, I've had a wonderful experience. A man appeared to me in the fields, he looked like a messenger from God, awe-inspiring. I didn't ask him where he came from, he didn't tell me his name. "You shall become pregnant and bear a son," he said. "So drink no wine or strong drink, eat nothing of what is unclean, for the boy shall be a Nazirite of God, from his mother's womb to the day of his death."'

In worship Manoah stretched out his hands to heaven. 'O Lord, may the man of God whom you sent come to us again and teach us what we must do with the boy who shall be born.'

A Nazirite of God, that's someone who must keep alive the sense that Israel is called to be the people of God and that there's a difference between clean and unclean. Israel must be a holy people. Will it be Manoah's son who reminds Israel of its vocation? But how do you become a Nazirite? 'O God, will you come once more?'

Manoah's prayer was heard: God sent his angel a second time, again to the field where Manoah's wife was working. Once more she rushed home. 'Come quickly, Manoah, the man of God has appeared again.' She ran back, Manoah after her.

'*Was it you who came to the woman?*'

Why does he say *the* woman and not *my* wife? Is that peasant language? No, that's the language of faith. For the story-teller isn't so much concerned with the spouse of one Manoah, but rather with a *woman of Israel*, God's barren beloved. This is about Israel as the – apostate – bride of the Lord, and about the heavenly bridegroom who indefatigably continues with attempts to win his beloved for himself.

'Was that you who came to the woman?'

'It was.'

'When the word that you have spoken is fulfilled, what needs to be the guidance for the young man and what will the work be that he must do?'

'Let the woman pay heed to everything that I have told her. She may not eat of the fruit of the vine, she shall not drink wine or strong drink, she shall not eat what is unclean. Let her pay heed to all that I have commanded her.'

Manoah falls silent. He asks himself anxiously what the boy must do and the angel answers by saying what *they* must do. Her son is to make a beginning on liberating Israel, but *they* must make a beginning by dealing with their son in purity. The wife must herself live as one who is dedicated to God. This mother in Israel shall be a living warning against all intoxication and stupor which makes a human being lose sight of God and his neighbour. In this Manoah will have to stand by her side. He needn't be anxious about his son. When the time is ripe, the boy will know what he has to do.

'Can you stay a while? We would so like to prepare a kid for you.'

Manoah isn't very quick on the uptake. Either he's already forgotten that an angel of God has come down to them, or he's forgotten that angels don't live on goats but on the wind.

'I can stay for a while, but your food I shall not eat. If you want to prepare something, offer it as a burnt offering to the Lord.'

Manoah prepares the burnt offering. 'What is your name?,' he asked. 'When the word that you have spoken is fulfilled, we want to honour you with a gift.'

'Why do you ask me my name? My name is *Wonderful.*'

Manoah has again asked too much. How could a mortal of flesh and blood who lives on food and drink know the Eternal One by name? There is only one gift with which Manoah and his wife can honour their creator: a life in the service of the Eternal One.

Manoah took the kid and the food offering and offered this as a sign of their devotion to the Lord. Then something *wonderful* happened before the eyes of Manoah and his wife: the flame arose from the altar and the angel of the Lord went up to heaven in the flame. Manoah and his wife saw it and fell down in worship, their faces to the earth.

The man of God didn't appear again, but Manoah finally understood that it had been a messenger of the Lord. 'Now we shall die, wife, we have seen God.'

'What makes you think that, Manoah? Don't be anxious. If the Lord had wanted to kill us, he wouldn't have accepted a sacrifice from us, he wouldn't have shown us all this; he wouldn't have let us hear all this.'

The woman bore a son and she called his name Samson. *Sun child.* Did the song of Deborah perhaps run through her head, that she gave her child this name?*

So shall they all perish,
all your enemies, Lord.
But those who love you,
will be as proud as the sun.

The boy grew up and the Lord blessed him. The spirit of the Lord began to fire him. Samson radiated power. No razor ever came upon his head; his bright golden hair was like the rays of the invincible sun.

19

WHAT IS SWEETER THAN HONEY?

JUDGES 14

'Tell us about Samson,' someone asks. 'Yes, Samson, that's nice,' exclaims another.

The children of the exiles in Babylon want to hear another exciting story before they go to sleep.

'Shall I tell you about the angel who came to his mother?'

'No, you must tell how he was so dumb as to betray his secret to this woman from the *goyim*, but how he killed all those Philistines.'

The children want some malicious pleasure, and that's quite understandable; they've a lot to put up with. Perhaps one day the Babylonians will get their come-uppance, just as the Philistines once did.

The fathers and mothers tell the story. They tell about Samson, and in so doing they tell about themselves. Surrounded by pagans, they too have a secret that they may not betray. Just like Samson, their children must not marry the children of the *goyim*, for then God will have lost his people; then Israel will dissolve like a drop of ink into the great sea of the world. They are prisoners here, chained, just like Samson, but Samson had a wonderful power which kept him going. He always got into a fix, but he always got out of it again. Although Samson was destined to be a Nazirite of God, he did everything that God had forbidden. But God remained faithful to him. Samson made a beginning of liberating Israel from the hands of the Philistines, so that the people could again dwell in freedom in Canaan. Would the exiles also be able to experience that?

Samson went down to Timnah. It was difficult for the sun child to find the way up in his life. His father and his mother were worried about all the mischief he got up to, but what could they do? He wanted to live it up, and how can a young man do that at home? Samson went down to Timnah, where the girls are.

'*Philistine* girls,' his mother warned. 'Isn't there one among the daughters of your brothers in Israel? Why are you after a woman from the *goyim*? It will only lead to trouble.'

Samson didn't care. 'Girls are girls,' he said, 'what does it matter if the woman of my dreams happens to be a Philistine?' Or is Samson just looking for an excuse to cause trouble?

Samson went down to Timnah to marry a Philistine woman, and there was little that Manoah and his wife could do but to accompany their sun child to the wedding. Samson went on a mile or so in advance, since he desired his bride so ardently. Already he saw in the distance the vineyards of Timnah, when suddenly a young lion sprang out at him roaring.

Heroes have to kill lions, that's fitting. A lover can't just enter the vineyard of love; first he has to slay a dragon or a lion; only then may he marry his princess.

Then the spirit of the Lord seized Samson and he tore the lion apart as one tears a kid, with his bare hands. He said nothing to his father and mother.

A few days later Samson went to look at the corpse, and lo and behold, there was a swarm of bees in it and quite a lot of honey. This dead body teemed with life, it buzzed and it sang. Samson scraped the honey out of the carcass. 'Would you like some, too?' he asked his parents when he returned. He didn't say where the honey had come from; a Nazirite may not touch a dead body. Nor may a Nazirite drink wine. Manoah and his wife were horrified; the drink was to flow abundantly at the wedding, for seven days, and Samson clearly didn't plan to sit there teetotal.

The great day dawned. The village elder performed the ceremony; Manoah and his wife understood little of it and Samson had eyes only for his bride. After that there was a procession to the bride's house. There was eating and drinking, laughing and dancing; there was no stopping the musicians, and no stopping the guests either. Manoah and his wife sat there somewhat lost; they knew no one there. Even Samson's ushers – around thirty in number – were strangers to them.

'I'll tell you a riddle,' exclaimed Samson cheerfully. 'If you guess it within seven days, I will give you thirty sets of underclothes and thirty festal garments. If you don't guess it, then you will give me thirty sets of underclothes and thirty festal garments.'

'All right,' they said, tell us.'

'*Out of the eater came something to eat, out of the strong one came something sweet.*'

The ushers had no idea. However, that wasn't a disaster, they still had time to solve the riddle. But would they ever work it out?

'Don't you know it yet?' taunted Samson after three days.

After seven days of pondering the men still hadn't guessed it. They couldn't think of losing, they'd pledged their clothes and their underclothes; if they didn't solve it they would be standing there in nothing but their shirts. This was no longer a joke; it was bitter earnest. They took the bride aside. 'You must get Samson to tell you the secret, otherwise we'll set your father's house on fire with you inside. Surely you didn't ask us to the wedding to let us lose our clothes?'

The bride couldn't withstand their threats. 'Samson, tell me the solution to the riddle, please, I'm so curious, I can't wait.'

'I haven't told it to anyone, not even to my parents.'

'But you can tell it to me, I'm your wife. Surely you've no secrets from your wife?'

'The seven days aren't up yet.'

The girl wept. 'Look, it's just as I thought, you don't love me. You hate me. If you really loved me…'

'Promise that you won't tell anyone else.'

She dried her tears. 'Aren't we husband and wife?'

The wedding feast came to an end. Once again the wedding songs were sung, once again the food went round, once again the drink flowed. The sun had almost set. 'You must surely know it by now,' exclaimed Samson, delighting in the failure of the uncircumcised.

The thirty ushers came forward, not looking as sad as on all the other days of the feast.

'Out of the eater came something to eat, out of the strong one came something sweet. What is that?'

'*What is sweeter than honey, what is stronger than a lion?*'

Samson went pale: his bride had cheated him. That could only be it. '*If you had not ploughed with my heifer you would not have guessed it!*' he exclaimed furiously.

The young men's answer was indeed a strange one. As a solution to the riddle they came out with a new riddle. What is sweeter than honey what is stronger than a lion? Isn't that love?

But love was no longer so sweet for Samson. He felt cheated, and resolved in his turn to steal from other Philistines the garments that he owed them. Samson was a judge with a very distinctive view of justice and righteousness.

He went down to Ashkelon.

So after Timnah you can go down even further. In Ashkelon Samson killed thirty Philistines, took the clothes from their bodies and gave them to the men who had solved the riddle. He said good-bye to his wife and returned to his parents' house.

20

WITH AN ASS'S JAWBONE

JUDGES 15

Once home, Samson's anger slowly cooled, and he wanted to go back to his wife. Certainly she'd cheated him, but how could the dear girl do otherwise, with death staring her in the face? Perhaps she wanted him just as much as he wanted her. Those were the days of the wheat harvest, and there was a festival in Timnah. There was nothing Samson wanted more than to be with her. Leading a kid on a rope he knocked on her door. Her father opened it.

'I've come to see my wife.'

'Your wife? I'm sorry, Samson, but she's no longer your wife, I've married her off to one of your ushers.'

'You've given my wife to someone else, to one of those lads who threatened her with death?'

'But didn't you yourself say that you hated her?'

That's chutzpah, for Samson hadn't said that; those were the words of the man's own daughter. 'You hate me,' she said sobbing, when Samson wouldn't give up his secret.

Samson was beside himself with anger, whereupon his father-in-law who was no longer his father-in-law thought that – given Samson's immeasurable strength – it would be advisable to become his father-in-law again quickly: 'Samson, you know that she has a younger sister, prettier than she is. Take her!'

However, Samson was furious. Now that his passion couldn't flare up, his anger did. 'This time I shall be blameless towards the Philistines when I avenge their evil.'

Did he then feel guilty for killing those thirty men, that this time he felt exonerated from the start? Samson caught three hundred foxes, a *tour de force* even for him, took torches, tied the foxes together two by two, and drove the whole mass into the standing corn; the farmland was soon ablaze, and the fire also took hold of the vineyards and olive orchards.

The Philistines exclaimed, 'Who has done this?'

'Samson has done this, the son-in-law of the Timnite, who took his wife away from him and gave her to another.'

The Philistines, fearing even more disaster if they didn't give Samson satisfaction, went to Timnah and set the house on fire; father and daughter perished in the flames. What the bride had wanted to avoid with her cheating had now taken place.

But rather than calming Samson's anger, the Philistines aroused it all the more. 'You did that. I shall not rest until I have avenged myself on it.' Samson went to battle and broke their spines one by one. After that he went down to the cave of Etam.

Now the Philistines were again out for vengeance. They set out to join battle against Judah, in Lehi.

'Why are you going out against us?'

'To bind Samson, to do to him what he did to us.'

The men of Judah went down to the cave of Etam. 'Samson, don't *you* know that the Philistines rule over us? Why are you doing this to us?'

'As they did to me, so I have done to them.'

'Samson, we've come to bind you and to hand you over to the Philistines.'

'Swear that you won't kill me.'

'We will only bind you and give you to the Philistines. We shall not kill you.'

Brotherly! They bound Samson with two new ropes and took him with them from the cave. So Samson came to Lehi. The Philistines were waiting for him and cried out against him with their battle cry. Then the spirit of the Lord seized Samson. The ropes which were around his arms were like threads of flax burning in the fire, they melted away from his hands. And look, there was a fresh ass's jawbone. Samson stretched out his hand, took that jawbone and slew all his attackers one by one, a thousand men. Triumphantly Samson exclaimed:

With the jawbone of an ass,
ass, ass,
with the jawbone of an ass,
I slew a thousand men.

After that he threw the jawbone away. From then on the place was called Lehi. *Jawbone.*

Not long afterwards Samson was seized with a fierce thirst. 'Lord,' he cried in despair, 'you have given this great liberation into the hand of your servant, and now I am dying of thirst. Soon I shall fall into the hands of the uncircumcised.'

What has happened to Samson? Not long ago he was celebrating his heroic deeds, boasting and bragging – 'with the jawbone of an ass I slew a thousand men' – but it's as if he now wanted to put this boast right: 'Lord, *you* have given this liberation into my hand.' The undeterred hero who afflicted the land of the Philistines is no more; he's a pitiful piece of humanity, longing for water, creeping away under a bush to get some shade. And he does what we haven't seen him do before: he prays. 'O God, how is this possible? Yesterday I slew a whole army and today I'm dying of thirst?'

Our Samson is like the Greek hero Heracles, but Israel knows no Heracles. Samson too, like any other mortal, is dependent on God's grace, Only the Lord can restore his strength.

God split open the chasm of the Ass's Jawbone, water streamed out and Samson drank. His spirit returned and he came to life again.

Since then this spring has been called the Spring of the one who calls.

21

DEATH BETWEEN THE PILLARS

JUDGES 16

How Samson thirsted for water has remained an unknown story, but he was famed far and wide for his thirst for women. So he ventured into the red-light district of Gaza. The Philistines, so long on the lookout for public enemy number one, saw his enormous figure go to a woman and laid an ambush by the side of the city gate. 'As soon as it's light we'll seize him; Gaza will become his grave.'

At midnight Samson got up.

'Where are you going, my love? Surely you're not going away?'

'Yes, I'm going away.'

'Where will you go? The gate is shut. Lie down again, Samson, remain here until daybreak.'

'No, I must go.'

Samson slipped out to the city gate, seized the enormous doors and took them off their hinges, bolts and all – no guard dared to come near him. He loaded the doors on his back and carried them up the hill which lies opposite Hebron.

Even in the dead of night the sun child is invincible. But why does the storyteller make our mighty man carry the doors all the way to Hebron? Is it in order to honour father Abraham, who made a covenant with his God in Hebron and also lies buried there? Is it in order to bring a greeting in advance to David who will be anointed king in Hebron, the great David, who finally conquered the Philistines after Samson had made a beginning of it?

The adventure in Hebron has turned out well, but it's to be feared that Samson's weakness for women will prove fatal for him. At the brook Sorek he had found a new love, Delilah was her name. *Woman with the hair that hangs down.* It was whispered that Samson could regularly be found with this Philistine woman, and it wasn't long before the five city rulers of the Philistines went to Delilah. 'This is a nice home you have here, with a view of the brook. Is it true that you receive Samson here? Of course, you can, but on the other hand you must understand that... we'd like to make you a proposal: if you... of course it's not without risk, and from our side we certainly want... we had thought: eleven hundred silver pieces. What do you think of that?'

'Do you love me, Delilah?' Samson asked that night.

'You're my great treasure,' said Delilah truthfully. 'And you're so strong. Where does all that strength come from and with what must you be bound to constrain you?'

Listen, Samson, listen carefully. This woman is disconcertingly honest; she says precisely what her plan is.

'If you bind me with seven damp bowstrings which have not yet been dried, then I shall become weak and be like any other man.'

The city rulers brought Delilah seven damp bowstrings, not yet dried, and they bound Samson with them while he was lying sleeping on her breast. The Philistines had hidden themselves.

'Samson, the Philistines are upon you!'

Samson sprang up out of his sleep and snapped the bowstrings, as a strand of flax breaks as soon as fire touches it. The source of his might remained a secret.

That evening Delilah dared a second attempt. 'You fooled me, Samson, you didn't tell me the truth. Tell me what you must be bound with.'

'If you bind me with new ropes, not yet used, then I shall become weak and be as any other man.'

Delilah took new ropes and bound him with them while he was lying asleep on her breast. The city rulers were again lying in ambush.

'Samson, the Philistines are upon you!'

Samson sprang up and broke the ropes as if they were thread.

'Now you've deceived me for the second time! Why don't you tell me truly what you must be bound with?'

'If you weave the seven locks of my hair with the web...'

That night *the woman with the hair that hangs down* zealously sat at the loom, while close by the great Samson had fallen into a deep sleep. When she had woven the seven locks into the web, she tightened the pin of the loom. 'Samson, the Philistines are upon you.'

Samson woke with a jolt and pulled out both the pin and the web.

'Will you still tell me, Samson, that you love me when you've now deceived me three times? Why is your strength so great? Tell me, tell me now!

What is there about our hero that he *still* doesn't see it? Does love make him blind? It's as if in his over-confidence he thinks that he's as invulnerable as the invincible sun which rises from the dead day by day. Does God still exist for this Nazirite or has he himself become God?

Delilah desires Samson, Samson desires Delilah. Except that it's another desire that drives her, and Samson, blind though seeing and deaf though hearing, doesn't grasp it. With his last words – '*weave my hair in the web*' – he has almost got to his secret. Delilah is warm and she knows it.

'*How can you keep saying that you love me when your heart isn't with me?*'

Samson doesn't feel that *her* heart is anywhere else, and he is so weary of her incessant attempts to make him give up his secret that he finally gives way, wearied to death. '*No razor has ever come upon my head; from my mother's womb I have been a Nazirite of God. If my hair were cut, my strength would depart and I would become as weak as anyone else.*'

Delilah knew that Samson had now told her everything and summoned the city rulers. 'Now you must come. He has told me all that is in his heart.'

The city rulers came, eleven hundred silver pieces in a bag, and they hid in the house.

Again Delilah played her game with love and with Samson, again she let him sleep on her breast. Then she gave a sign to a servant, who rapidly cut the seven locks from his head. Delilah felt Samson's strength flowing out of him. 'Samson, the Philistines are upon you!'

Samson awoke from his sleep and thought that this time too he would get away with it. He didn't know that God had departed from him. No razor had come upon his head from the day that he came out of his mother's womb. Now, in the bosom of his mistress, Samson has been robbed of his strength.

Not that the power was in his hair. That is the outward sign of an inner conviction. Samson is a Nazirite of God. He must love his Lord, not his hair. By losing sight of his Lord he has lost his power and his hair.

The Philistines seized him, put out his eyes and made him go down to

Gaza. They fettered him with two bronze chains and made him grind grain in the prison. The Philistines had come upon him.

The exiles in Babylon are moved, for who is this story about? Of course it's about Samson, but the exiles are listening and above all reading their own history into it: the bitter fate suffered by their last king, Zedekiah. Nebuchadnezzar had Zedekiah's sons killed before his eyes, and that was the last thing that their king saw on earth; they put his eyes out, fettered him with two bronze chains, and carried him off to Babylon.* End of story. Or is it?

And the hair on Samson's head began to grow, as soon as it had been cut off.
    Nothing very striking about that, you might say. What else does the hair on one's head do but grow again when it's been cut off? But again, this isn't about hair, but about what grows from within. There is the dulling routine of the treadmill in which Samson does his rounds, day in, day out, but at the same time a secret has remained in his heart, a power which grows. When he could still see, he was blind to the Nazirate to which he had been called; now that he is blind, he sees that. 'O God, you do not leave unfinished what you have begun. You will not leave unfinished what you began with me when I was still in my mother's womb. I have been unfaithful to you, blinded by desire. I was famous for my strength. In essence I was weak. I pray you, do not forsake me.'
    There is still a germ of strength in Samson. He is a grain of wheat which will bear fruit.

It's festival time in the land of the Philistines. The city rulers and the people assemble for the great sacrificial feast in honour of Dagon, the god of grain. What could make the festal joy even greater, if not for Samson, their tamed bear, now to appear? 'Call Samson, Dagon's own miller, let Samson entertain us!'
    They get the blind Hebrew out of prison; a boy leads him by the hand. Malicious pleasure in Gaza, the people shout with joy and cheer at the sight of the helpless giant. The temple is full of festal pilgrims and three thousand people are standing on the roof. They are highly amused. Look, there goes Samson, once a mighty man, now with hollow eye-sockets, dependent on a small boy.

'Let me go for a minute,' said Samson to the boy, 'let me touch the pillars on which the temple rests so that I can lean on them.'

Then Samson cried to the Lord, 'Lord, remember me. Make me strong again, just this once, so that I can have vengeance on these Philistines, one vengeance for my two eyes.'

Again a Nazirite had arisen in Israel. He was ready to give his life and asked God for strength. God heard his prayer.

Samson grasped the two central pillars on which the temple rested. He pushed against one pillar with his right hand and against the other with his left. 'Let me die with the Philistines!' Once again he gathered his tremendous strength, the pillars gave way and with a thunderous noise the temple collapsed, on top of the city rulers and all the people who were gathered there. Samson died with the Philistines; the dead which he killed at his death were more in number than those which he killed in his life-time. What did the angel say to Samson's mother even before he was born? *'A Nazirite of God shall he be, from his mother's womb until the day of his death.'*

Samson's brothers and the whole of his father's house went down to Gaza. They took Samson with them, and bore him up to bury him in his birthplace, in the tomb of Manoah his father. Samson had been judge in Israel for twenty years.

That's the story the exiles tell by the rivers of Babylon, with visible pleasure. The children think it an exciting story and their parents draw strength from it.

22

NO KING IN THOSE DAYS

JUDGES 17 AND 18

Did another judge then arise in Israel?

No, we've had that now, that's over. Now we hear a new refrain: *Everyone did what was good in his eyes, there was still no king in those days.*

For years the judges in Israel have judged. They brought enlightenment, but they didn't bring light. Every now and then they stood in the breach for an oppressed people, but they couldn't bring unity to the tribes and make them live in peace with one another.

What does a land look like which knows no judge and in which no prophet has yet arisen to anoint a king? It's a land where life isn't good: it lacks reverence and love for the Eternal One and it lacks reverence and love for human beings. The first commandment is trampled underfoot, and so too is the second, which is like it. Two stories will illustrate this.

There was a man from the hill country of Ephraim. Micayahu.

Micayahu. His name means *Who is like God?* That sounds reverent, but it's a bit of chutzpah, for Micayahu is totally remote from God, and indeed the narrator usually calls him Micah; he thinks it better to omit the divine name Yahu.

In an unguarded moment Micah had stolen eleven hundred silver pieces from his mother – the same amount that Delilah received for betraying Samson – and then he heard her pronounce a curse on the thief. Afraid that the curse would take effect, he repented of his misdeed and returned the silver pieces. Mother doesn't know how soon she has to turn the curse into a blessing: if only she can do something nice, something pious with that money. 'I dedicate this silver to the Lord.'

Micah takes two hundred of the eleven hundred silver pieces – you mustn't overdo such an offering – and has the silversmith make a divine image from them.

A divine image? Even Micah's mother is somewhat bewildered.

The silversmith makes a fine image; the accursed silver is laundered by religion, the Lord be praised. Micah gives it a place of honour in his house, and for one reason or another in people's eyes it's such a special image that they come to see it from far and wide. The house with the silver image becomes a place of pilgrimage, and in such a place of course a servant of God is needed, so Micah consecrated one of his sons priest.

There in the hill-country of Ephraim they've begun to say things differently. Things are going badly for faith, but they're going well with religion; the silver pieces stream in, the image fills a great need. *In those days there was no king in Israel. Everyone did what was good in his eyes.*

Now in Bethlehem in Judah there was a young man, a Levite. He lived as a sojourner.

However, the young man doesn't feel at home and sets out to seek his fortune. So he landed in the hill-country of Ephraim, near the house of Micayahu who is called Micah.

'Where do you come from?'

'I'm a Levite, sir, I come from Bethlehem in Judah.'

'A Levite? In that case you're welcome in my service. I'll give you ten silver pieces a year and clothes and food and lodging. Be to me a father and a priest.'

A wandering son of Levi is promoted to be father, the priest of a pseudo-sanctuary in Ephraim. Yes, religion is flowering in Israel, and Micah's relic shop has got official status. 'Now I know that the Lord will do me good, for a Levite has become my priest,' says Micah with delight. *In those days there was no king in the land.*

It happened that the tribe of Dan went in search of an inheritance, *for they did not yet have one.*

Nonsense, the Danites had long had a share of the land, but they didn't keep to the agreements they had made and in so doing broke the covenant with their brothers. It's as if we find ourselves back at the beginning of the book of Joshua, when the tribes of Israel still had to take possession of the land. And that's precisely what the story-teller has in mind, for he wants the history of all Israel to be repeated once again with the tribe of Dan. In this way he can tell the story of God, who gives the land, and of Israel, which takes the land, once again, but now differently.

Joshua had once sent out two men as spies: you need two or three men for a trustworthy testimony. In search of an inheritance the Danites send out five spies; the five represent all Israel.* Their task is the same: *'Go and view the land.'*

They go through the hill-country of Ephraim and land up at Micah's fake temple, where the Levite greets them. To judge from his accent he too, like them, comes from the south. 'What are you doing here?'

'I'm a Levite who was living as a sojourner in Bethlehem. I went out into the world and settled down here.'

'So you're a priest. That's good. Then you can be so good as to ask God if there is a blessing on the way that we're going.'

'Go in peace, the Lord is well pleased with the way that you are going.'

Precisely what the five spies want to hear. But is the Lord in fact so pleased with the way that they're going?

The spies go on, northwards, to Laish. There they see with their own eyes how the people live: *quiet and tranquil.* No tyrant rules the roost; they're far from the Sidonians and have nothing to do with anyone. Who wouldn't want to live there?

When the spies get home they give an excited account. 'We mustn't hesitate but must immediately go up against that people; they live there, quiet and tranquil, there's no lack of anything and there are no Sidonians to be seen anywhere around. What more could you want?'

Hardly have the spies spoken when the Danites prepare to depart, six hundred men, girded with weapons.

They go through the hill-country of Ephraim. 'A little further on is the temple of one Micah,' the spies report, 'and believe it or not, there they have a silver divine image.'

The Danites believe it. They also believe that it can't be a bad thing to take such an image with them on their way.

'What are you doing now?' the Levite protests. 'That image belongs to Micah, my master.'

'Yes, and now it's ours. Quiet! And one more thing: you can stay here or you can also go with us and be to us a father and a priest. Which would you prefer, to be priest in the house of one man or priest of a whole tribe, a family of Israel?'

The young man makes the best of a bad job. 'I will go with you,' he says, and takes the silver image outside with his own hands. Micah's chaplain becomes cardinal of Dan.

The Danites pursue their way, with those who are slow and the animals in front of them, the fighting men in the rear as protection. Look, Micah is already trotting up.

'What's the matter with you, fellow? You look so pale.'

'You steal the god that I made and my priest and you ask what's the matter with me? *What have I left?*'

Micah doesn't speak about the God who made *him*; he speaks about the god whom *he* has made. He has lost his self-made god, and he's lost his self-made priest. Micah is nowhere. 'What have I left?'

The men of Dan warn Micah to keep his mouth shut if he doesn't want to be silenced for ever. 'Push off!' Then they travel on to Laish, to the people that live there, quiet and tranquil; they hew it to pieces and set the city on fire. *There was no deliverer, the land was far from Sidon, no one could do anything to Dan.*

So Dan is no different from the pagans; Israel is behaving just like the *goyim*. This is no *entry* as in the time of Joshua, this is a *raid*. Is this the land that God has given, and does God want to take possession of it in this way? Is it surprising that God finally takes the land back from such a people and lets them be led away into captivity?

The sons of Dan set up the graven image. Jonathan the son of Gershom, the son of Moses, and his sons were priests to the land of the Danites until the day of the captivity of the land.

So the pseudo-priest was called *Jonathan*; we haven't heard his name before. He lived in Bethlehem as a *sojourner*. And Gershom is his father, no less than Gershom, son of the great Moses who was born abroad and therefore was given the name *Sojourner*.* How quickly and how deeply Israel has sunk! 'You shall love the Lord your God with all your heart and with all your soul and with all your strength.' The first and great commandment that the Eternal One gave to Moses is trampled under foot within two generations.

The people prostrated themselves before the graven image that Micah had made all the days that the house of God was in Shiloh.

The house of God in Shiloh? Does God live there? Could something good perhaps come out of Shiloh?

23

THE INFAMOUS DEED AT GIBEAH

JUDGES 19, 20 AND 21

So Israel soon forgot the first commandment. And what about the second commandment, now that the judges no longer judge and Samuel has yet to be born?

It happened in those days – there was no king in Israel – that a man, a Levite, lived as a guest in the hill-country of Ephraim.

A concubine from Bethlehem had left him and had returned to her parents' house. That was four months ago, and the man decided to go to Bethlehem *to speak to her heart and make her return.*

Whether the Levite did speak to the heart of his concubine the story doesn't tell. Probably he spoke more to the heart of her father, who proved a good host: they ate and drank to their heart's content for days on end. Early in the morning of the fifth day the Levite arose with his wife and servant and his pair of asses to return to the hill-country of Ephraim.

But his host wouldn't let him go yet. 'Come, there's more to eat and drink, it's a long time until evening.' And in the evening, when they were at last about to go: 'It's evening already; remain here overnight, then we can have something to eat and drink before you leave in the morning.'

'No, I really must go now.'

They went. But if you leave so late you don't get far, and it was almost dark when they got to the city of Jebus, the later Jerusalem. 'Let's stop here and spend the night with the Jebusites,' the servant suggested. But the Levite wouldn't hear of it. *'I am not staying in a foreign city where they are not of the sons of Israel; we will travel on to Gibeah.'*

The sun had already set when they got to Gibeah, the city of the Benjaminites. But none of the sons of Israel in the city square offered them hospitality. 'We would have done better to spend the night with the Jebusites,' the servant thought.

It was already late when an old man came in from the fields, a man from the hill-country of Ephraim, who was living as a sojourner in Gibeah. He saw the Levite sitting in the square and said to him, 'Where are you going? Where do you come from?'

'We're on a journey from Bethlehem in Judah to the hill-country of Ephraim. No one has offered us hospitality here, though I've brought straw and fodder for the asses and bread and wine for myself, the woman and the servant.'

An old man, a sojourner in Gibeah. As if you must be old and from elsewhere still to know how to behave. 'Peace be with you. Let me look after you, I don't want you to spend the night in the square.' He took them to his house, mixed fodder for the asses and sat down to table with his guests.

Suddenly they were rudely disturbed; the men from the city banged on the door, barbarians who were prepared to trample on the great good of hospitality. 'Let that fellow who is with you come out, we want to have intercourse with him.'

Sodom and Gomorrah in Gibeah.

'No, my brothers, do him no evil, I don't want to start any folly. Look, I will give you my daughter, who is still a virgin, and the Levite's woman; do to them what is good in your eyes, but do this man no harm.'

Israel cannot sink deeper. A cowardly father barters his own child, a frightened man his wife. Each one does what is good in his eyes; the service of men is already as dishonoured as the service of God.

We hear no more about the old man's daughter, but the Levite took his woman and sent her out. The men of the city raped her. Only when day dawned did they send her back. With her last strength the woman tottered back to the house, and there she collapsed at the entrance.

Early in the morning the Levite opened the door of the house to go his way, and there lay his woman, her hands on the threshold. 'Get up,' he said, 'let's be going.' The woman didn't reply.

The man put her on his ass, tied her tightly and took her to his house in the hill-country of Ephraim. There he took a knife, cut her body into twelve pieces and sent her round the whole territory of Israel. 'See what the men of Benjamin have done to me.'

The woman seems like lady Israel: violated, raped, torn apart by disputes between brothers.

Everyone who received the gruesome packet was horrified. *'Such a thing has never happened, such a thing has never been seen from the day when the children of Israel came up from the land of Egypt until today. Let us discuss that and speak.'*

Israel came together as one man: from Dan to Beersheba the people went up to Gibeah and demanded that the Benjaminites should hand over the perpetrators. 'We want to kill them, to exterminate the evil from Israel.' But the sons of Benjamin wouldn't listen to their brothers, the sons of Israel.

The dispute flared up, and only after many had fallen on both sides were the Benjaminites defeated and put to death: the men, the women, the children, the animals. Only a few hundred people escaped. The tribes deliberated among themselves and swore never to give one of their daughters to these Benjaminites in marriage.

But when the first anger had subsided and the wounds had healed somewhat, there slowly came a desire for reconciliation: without Benjamin Israel is no longer Israel, and without women no life perpetuates itself. How can thinned-out Benjamin be helped to have womenfolk without breaking the oath that had been sworn?

Let Jabesh provide women! The Jabeshites hadn't joined in the deliberation among the tribes, so they were good for plunder now: all the inhabitants of the city were murdered apart from four hundred virgins; the girls were given to Benjamin. And because four hundred was rather on the low side, the men of Benjamin were also given permission to hunt for virgins among the daughters of Shiloh.

Of Shiloh? There the barren Hannah prayed for a child in the house of God, and there Samuel, the son who was born to her, received his call. He was the one who was to anoint Saul king, a descendant of the tribe of Benjamin.

So this appalling history, this nadir in Israel's existence, ends not without the prospect of better times. Certainly the people of God seems to have lost its calling and cannot in any way be distinguished from the pagans – murder and killing, rape and abduction of virgins are the order of the day, as in the world of the *goyim* – but unless the signs deceive, that isn't the end of the story.

24

THE BIRTH OF SAMUEL

I SAMUEL 1; 2.1-11

It's high time for a king to arise. He will have to be a special king, a king by the grace of God. Therefore first a prophet must appear. No one in Israel can become king of his own accord; a man of God has to anoint you king. In Israel prophecy comes before kingship.

And it happened: a man from the hill-country of Ephraim, Elkanah was his name. He had two wives, Hannah and Peninnah. Peninnah had children but Hannah did not. The Lord had closed her womb.

Another barren woman in Israel. In Hannah, Sarah once again stands before us, the barren matriarch from whom Israel was born. In her the mother of Samson also appears, the barren woman to whom God showed his grace when the people had taken possession of the promised land. Now once again we are told of a key moment in the history of the people; it has to be that God will once again show his grace to barren Israel. Without the Eternal One they are nowhere; the name of the man from the hill-country of Ephraim says it all. *Elkanah: God brings forth.*

Every year Elkanah went with Hannah and Peninnah and her children to the temple in Shiloh, there to offer the fruits of the land and to celebrate the holy meal. And every year Hannah became more conscious that she was another year older and that she still had not borne fruit. At table Elkanah shared out the food, a portion for everyone and a double portion for Hannah, because he loved her so much. Peninnah saw how much her husband loved her rival and was full of jealousy. She mercilessly mocked Hannah's childlessness, and day in, day out she rubbed salt in the wound by flaunting her own brood. Elkanah might love Hannah more, but at least *she* had children. Hannah was near to despair and couldn't get a bite down her throat. She wept.

'Why are you weeping?' asked Elkanah. 'Why aren't you eating?' 'Why aren't you drinking? Why are you so sad?'

Doesn't Elkanah know why Hannah is weeping? Can't he see her powerless longing and doesn't he too hope that the two of them will have a child? It's as if Hannah isn't allowed to be sorrowful: 'Am I not worth more to you than ten sons?'

What answer must Hannah give him now? Must she join Elkanah in his self-accusation, begin to mother him, say that of course she loves him more than ten sons? Must she beg for a bit of understanding?

Hannah said nothing. She and Elkanah shared their love, but they couldn't share their sorrow. Hannah got up. She didn't want to lose herself any longer in her sorrow; she gathered her remaining strength and went to the temple. Hannah is her name. *God is gracious.* Then let God make his name true. She went into the temple. Eli the priest was sitting on a chair by the doorpost. He saw her going by. What was the matter with that woman?

Hannah prayed. She shrieked it out, she cried to heaven. 'Lord God, do look down on your handmaid, give me a child.'

Hannah believes in miracles. Those who don't believe in miracles have a meagre faith. Then God becomes a heavenly Elkanah who gives you bandages for the bleeding but doesn't really help. A God who says, 'You won't get what you want, but after all, don't you have me?' But God isn't like that. Surely God is gracious?

'Lord God, if you give me a son, then I will give him to you all the days of his life; a razor shall not come upon his head.'

Hannah believes in miracles. The priest of the Lord believes that she's drunk: 'Are you going to keep behaving like a drunkard here? Go and sleep it off."

Eli knows just as little about Hannah's desperation as Elkanah. This woman drunk? Not a bite, not a drop down her throat! 'Sir, I'm deeply unhappy, I'm pouring out my heart before the face of the Lord.'

Eli sees his mistake. 'Go in peace. You have opened your heart to God, may God open your womb. May the Eternal One hear your prayer.' Hannah went her way. She ate and drank, for hope brings life. The next day she returned home with the others.

Elkanah had intercourse with Hannah, and the Lord thought of her. And it happened at the turning of the days that Hannah became pregnant.

The days took a turn, the days of the pilgrimage had come to an end, and also the days of Hannah's solitude. She returned to life.

And Hannah bore a son and she called his name Samuel, for, she said, I asked him from the Lord.

It's as if the narrator knows no Hebrew. For that isn't what Samuel means at all. Samuel means *The Lord has heard. I asked him from the Lord* in Hebrew is *Saul*. So the narrator is playing with language. Samuel, the prophet child, hasn't yet been born and the name of the king whom he is to anoint is already resounding in the distance. The moment that Samuel appears on stage, we already hear that Saul is coming.

Hannah asked Samuel from the Lord, and he shall be for the Lord. As soon as she had weaned him, she took him with a three-year-old bull, a measure of meal and a jar of wine. And she brought him, still a young boy, into the Lord's house at Shiloh. She said to Eli: *'With your permission, sir, as truly as your soul lives, sir, I am the woman who stood here by you to pray to God. I prayed for this boy and the Eternal One has granted me the wish that I wished from him. See, I have dedicated him to the Eternal One; all the days of his life may he be "a Saul", the one asked for from the Eternal One.'*
   And Samuel bowed before the Lord.

Then Hannah sang her song:

> *My heart is joyful in you, O Lord,*
> *my horn lifts itself up for you.*
> *my mouth opens itself wide against my enemies,*
> *indeed I rejoice over your liberation.*

Centuries later the evangelist Luke would tell of another woman in Israel who might bear a prophet through the grace of God, Mary of Nazareth. She too has a song of praise put in her mouth, the *Magnificat*.

> *My soul magnifies the Lord,*
> *And my spirit has rejoiced in God my saviour,*
> *For he has looked upon the low estate of his handmaid.**

It is a song which is the spitting image of the song that Hannah sang. As if the two of them were mother and daughter. And popular piety could think of no better name for Mary's mother than Anne, the Greek for Hannah.

25

THE CALL OF SAMUEL

I SAMUEL 2.11-26; 3

Just as Hannah in former days dreaded the annual pilgrimage to the temple of Shiloh, now she looked forward to it. There her Samuel was growing up; he was serving before the face of the Lord, wearing a linen coat. Every year Hannah made a new coat for him and took it with her. A sign of her care, and without knowing it, in her motherly love at the same time she depicted the love of God.

Before she returned home, Eli blessed her. 'May the Lord give you descendants to take the place of the boy whom you have given to the Lord.'

And the Lord looked upon Hannah, so that she became pregnant and bore three more sons and two daughters.

The word of the Lord was rare in those days, visions were not frequent.

Had *God* become so silent or were there no longer *people* to hear the word of God? Had the Eternal One ceased to appear, or was there no one left with eyes to see the revelations of the Eternal One?

Probably the latter, for it was a mess in the house of the Lord. Hophni and Phinehas, Eli's priestly sons, desecrated the holy of holies, and the aged Eli wasn't up to averting the evil; it raged on unpunished. Priests have to put themselves in the service of God and the people, so that the holy covenant between these two can be confessed and celebrated. Hophni and Phinehas, however, weren't afraid of doing a bit of trade with the sacrificial meat given by the believers. And they also lay with the temple prostitutes, just like the pagans, to divinize the fertility and the potency.

The Eternal One could no longer look at this and sent a man of God to Eli. 'Thus says the Lord, "Did I not reveal myself to the house of your father Aaron when you were oppressed in Egypt? From all the tribes of Israel I chose Aaron as priest to go up to my altar and make incense rise.

Why do you despise the holy sacrifice? Why do you honour your sons more than me, why do you do yourselves proud with the best of every sacrifice that my people offers?"'

The Aaronite priesthood will remain, but that doesn't apply to the house of Eli. The day will come, says the man of God, when there will no longer be any old men in the house of Eli. Hophni and Phineas will die in the prime of life; there is no future for godless priests in the holy land. But for Israel: 'I shall raise up a faithful priest, I shall build him a lasting house so that at all times he shall walk before the face of my anointed.'

The man of God disappeared.

When will this faithful priest appear? Who will feel called?

It was night, Eli was asleep. Those were dark times in Israel; everything that offered support and certainty in this life had collapsed, and God was absent from the very place where you might hope for him to be present, in his holy temple. The ark was certainly there, the sign of God's presence, but it no longer gave any inspiration. There was indeed talk about God, but God himself no longer spoke. And Samuel, what did little Samuel do there? He lay tossing in his bed; his heart was restless.

Eli slept. His eyes had grown weak and he could no longer see well. *But the lamp of God had not yet gone out.*

This is the lamp of God which burns in the temple from evening to morning. It's also the little flame of Eli's life which still burns. He was old and almost blind, but God's lamp still flickered in his innermost depths.

Samuel couldn't get to sleep. He had prepared everything for the night, lit the lamp, shut the temple doors, said good night to Eli.

'Samuel!'

Samuel got up and went to Eli. 'Here I am. Did you call me?'

'No, I didn't call you. Go back and lie down.'

Samuel went back and lay down. Again he heard his name called, again he got up and went to Eli. 'Here I am. Surely you called me?'

'No, my boy, I didn't call you. Go back, lie down again.'

Samuel didn't know that the Lord was calling him, *he did not yet know God*, no light had yet dawned on him, the word of God had not yet been revealed to him.

Didn't he yet know God? He's the son of mother Hannah; his name means *The Lord has heard*, and he's a priestly servant in the temple where the ark of the Lord dwells. And he still doesn't know the Lord?

Yes, but Samuel didn't really know why he had this name, he wasn't yet on a familiar footing with God. He indeed knew of God's existence, but it still meant little in his own existence. Samuel didn't yet know himself called by name.

'Samuel!'

For the third time he heard the voice in the night; Samuel didn't yet hear that it was the Eternal One who was calling. For the third time he thought that it was Eli. Vocation has to mature. 'Eli, here I am, surely you called me?'

Then it was this old blind man who once again shed his light before it was quenched for ever. 'God is after you, my boy. Go, lie down again, and when he calls you, say, "Speak, Lord, for your servant hears."'

Don't think that *I* have called you. I'm not God. I can't decide for you who you are before God. God must tell you that himself.

It slowly began to dawn on Samuel. He lay down again in his place. Again the Lord appeared to him and called as before, 'Samuel, Samuel.'

'Speak, Lord, for your servant hears.'

'Samuel, anyone who hears what I am going to do in Israel will not believe his ears. I will inflict on Eli's house what I have sworn, because of the behaviour of his sons for which he has not rebuked them.'

Samuel lay there until daybreak. Then he opened the doors of the house of the Lord; it was as if he was opening the doors for God himself. What must he say to Eli when he asked him about his vision in the night?

'Samuel, my son.'

My son? Eli had never called him that before. Does the old man sense that Samuel has been called to take the place of his sons?

'Here I am.'

'What is the word that the Eternal One has spoken to you?'

The roles are reversed. Now the young Samuel must be the mediator between God and Eli. 'Do not conceal any word from me.'

Samuel told him all, without concealing anything.

'It is the Lord,' said Eli. 'Let him do what is good in his eyes.'

Samuel grew up, and the Lord was with him, and did not let any of his words fall to the ground. And all Israel, from Dan to Beersheba, came to know that the Lord had entrusted to Samuel the office of prophet.

26

THE FATE OF THE ARK

I SAMUEL 4, 5 AND 6

A child weeps in the night. An orphan, Ichabod is his name. *The glory of God has departed*. Why does the child bear this name? How has he become an orphan?

The story comes from the time when the Israelites sat orphaned as exiles, prisoners by the rivers of Babylon. The glory of Israel has departed, Jerusalem is destroyed, the temple lies in ruins. How could this have happened? Prophets saw the hand of God in it: punishment for sin because the people didn't want to listen to God. A people weeps in the night. Who will comfort it?

Listen, someone is telling a story.

'Long ago our people went to battle against the Philistines. That was at Ebenezer, *Stone of help*, a holy place, which became terror for us and not help. We were defeated before the Philistines. *Before* the Philistines, not *by* the Philistines. Well, yes, of course by the Philistines, but essentially they were really only instruments in God's hands. We snapped our fingers at the Ten Words, given to us for life; the priests' sons Hophni and Phinehas cared nothing for God and his commandments, and instead of firmly opposing their idolatrous practices, father Eli let them perpetrate them. Then things went as was only to be expected.

Our people organized a second campaign. "This time let's take the ark with us and go out to battle against the Philistines again. God will be with us."

We took with us the ark, the holy chest with the Ten Words engraved on two stones, as a mascot. God with us! Hophni and Phinehas gave our soldiers every assistance when they came to Shiloh to ask for the ark; the sons of Eli carried the ark to our camp with their own hands and all Israel let out a shout of joy, so that the earth shook. The Philistines also trembled. "Their God is in the camp! Woe is us, such a thing has not happened to us yesterday or the day before yesterday. Woe is us! Who will save us from the power of these gods? They are the same gods who once smote the Egyptians with plagues in the wilderness."

Granted, this was Philistine talk, about "gods", and their archaeological knowledge was also defective on one or two points, but the pagans had more sense of God's liberating salvation than our people in those days. And they weren't cowards, for after they'd admonished one another, they went out to battle and Israel was put to the sword. The ark was captured, Hophni and Phinehas were killed.

A man from the tribe of Benjamin escaped from the battle and rushed to Shiloh, his garments torn and earth on his head as a sign of penitence. Eli sat on his chair by the temple at the side of the road, in tense expectation. His heart trembled; he was fearful about the ark of God. When the Benjaminites had reached the city and had reported the news, a loud cry of mourning arose from Shiloh's streets; the blind Eli heard it.

"What has happened, my son?"

"Israel has taken flight, my Lord, we have suffered a great defeat. Hophni and Phinehas your sons are dead, the ark of God is taken."

When Eli heard that the ark of God had fallen into the hands of the Philistines he fell from his chair. He broke his neck and died.

His daughter-in-law, the wife of Phinehas, heavily pregnant, heard the disastrous news and, overcome by her woes, brought a son into the world. She herself died. The midwife tried to restore her to life. "Fear not, you have borne a son." But she wouldn't let herself be comforted. "Ichabod shall be his name," she said. *The glory of God has departed.* For the ark had gone and her father-in-law had gone and her husband had gone. Then she yielded up the spirit. A child wept in the night. An orphan child.

In triumph the Philistines took the sacred ark away with them.'

The story-teller by the rivers of Babylon paused, as if he wanted to increase the tension in his story still further. His audience knew all too well what he was talking about. This wasn't just a story, this was their story. Not long ago they themselves had been exiles and all the temple treasures had been stolen. Had God's glory now disappeared from Israel for ever, or would it return again one day? How were things going with the ark? What would happen?

'In triumph the Philistine took their war trophy with them, and when they arrived in Ashdod they put it in their temple before the image of their god Dagon.

His name means *grain*. He's a god of bread. "Dagon make me greater. Make us strong, make us powerful."

Our people had taken the ark into battle with the same prayer in their hearts, and so although it's forbidden us, we had again made an image of God to compel victory. Whereas this ark is simply a protection for the ten words which call on us to live not only by bread but from every word that goes forth from the mouth of God.*

The Philistines thought that they had imprisoned our God in Dagon's temple, and all Ashdod celebrated. But what happened the next day? Dagon hadn't been able to stand up to our God overnight: the god of the Philistines lay stretched out before the ark, with his face to the ground, as if in worship before the throne of the Eternal One.

The Philistines became afraid; they very carefully set their fallen god back on his feet again. But the next morning Dagon proved once again to have fallen on the ground, now in bits and pieces, with no head and no hands.

With our God it's like mother Hannah's song: the humiliated are lifted up, and those who have sat in high places he casts down. Both Israel and the Philistines had thought too early that all was up with our God.

The people of Ashdod had a hard time; their divine image lay in smithereens, and then in addition they were tormented by a plague of boils. They couldn't get rid of that ark quickly enough. But where to? They took the ark to Gath, and there very soon afterwards the same plague broke out. Up to Ekron, but there too they preferred the ark out of the way. And when once again a plague of mice came to try them, the five city rulers of the Philistines resolved to send the ark back to Israel.

"But it can't be done just like that," one of them exclaimed. "We can't send that ark back without an expiatory offering to Israel's God. Let's send five golden boils as expiatory offerings and five golden mice, according to the number of our five cities. Then let's prepare a new cart with two milch cows, who have never yet had a yoke laid on them. Let's attach these cows to the cart; we'll keep the calves in the stall."

So the Philistines were in two minds. They were finally ready to bow to our God, and at the same time they wanted to put the power of our God to the test. If the cows wanted to get out from under the oppressive yoke, and made their way straight back to their calves, then our God had shown himself powerless and the plague must be a coincidence. If the cows went in the direction of Canaan, then Israel's God had revealed himself to be a powerful God, and it was better for them to be rid of the ark.

The ark was put on the cart, along with a chest of golden boils and mice, bizarre jewellery of Philistine making to assuage God's anger. Gee up!

And gee-up it was! Against the call of nature the cows immediately took the road to Beth-shemesh, in the direction of Israel. No carter showed the way, and they didn't divert either to the left or to the right. That strange God of Israel went his way completely contrary to nature; the God of the Ten Words showed the way to the promised land.

The people of Beth-shemesh were busy harvesting the wheat in the valley. They looked up, and look, with loud lowing the ark returned to Israel, to the field of a certain Joshua.'

That was the end of the story. The story-teller wanted to finish with a mention of the name of Joshua. In so doing he reminded the exiles in Babylon of the great Joshua who had crossed the Jordan with the ark to go to live with the Torah in the land. In the story the glory of God returned to Israel, and by God's grace the people might make a new beginning. Will God also be gracious to the captives and send them back home?

Once back in the land they will again by filled with more reverence for the Eternal One than the inhabitants of Beth-shemesh, when the ark stayed in their midst. With a terrible lack of awe they made it into a tourist attraction. So they were no better than the uncircumcised Philistines, indeed they were worse; it was *their* ark, *their* God. Again there was killing. Only when they came to their senses there in Beth-shemesh and put the ark under the care of a man of God on a holy hill did peace return.

27

WE WANT A KING

I SAMUEL 7 AND 8

The glory of the Eternal One has returned to Israel. May God grant that now Israel also returns to the Eternal One. *'If with all your heart you want to return to the Eternal One,'* said Samuel, *'then put away the strange gods from your midst, turn your heart to the Lord and serve him alone. Then he will save you from the power of the Philistines.'*

These stories – to make the point once again – aren't about two neighbouring peoples at loggerheads with one another. The Philistines stand for all the 'uncircumcised', both Israelites and pagans, who hold the God of the Torah in contempt. The wars that are waged in these stories are battles for true humanity; they depict a spiritual struggle. That struggle must begin close to home; Israel must first deal with idolatry in its own circles, arrogance and the unbridled greed that poisons its own thought and action.

And the children of Israel rejected the Baals and Ashtaroth from their midst; they served the Lord, him alone.

Samuel said, 'Gather all the people in Mizpah.'

The people gathered in Mizpah and did penance. *'Samuel, cry for us to the Lord our God, that he may free us from the power of the Philistines.'*

Samuel took a sucking lamb and offered it to the Lord. And Samuel cried for the people to the Lord, and the Lord answered him.

The lamb, still drinking milk, stands for little vulnerable Israel, which even now can still barely stand on its own feet.

Samuel called and God heard. Even while the prophet was offering the sacrifice, the Philistines attacked, but the Lord sent thunder and lightning through the sky, so that they fled in confusion. They never attacked Israel again.

Samuel was judge over Israel all the days of his life. Year by year he made a circuit through the cities of the land. After that he returned to

Ramah; there was his house, there he judged Israel and there he built an altar to the Lord.

And it happened that when Samuel had grown old, he appointed his sons as judges over Israel; his firstborn son was called Joel and the second Abijah.

They have nice names: *The Lord is my God* and *God is my Father*, but they aren't nice sons. Just as the sons of Eli embody the degeneration of the priesthood, so Samuel's sons are a blot on the reputation of the judges. They too believe more in the idol of money than in the God of the Torah. They're only after profit: they take bribes and pervert justice. Must such sons judge Israel when Samuel is no more?

The elders of the land gathered. *'Look, Samuel, you have grown old, and your sons do not walk in your ways. Appoint a king over us to judge us, a king like all the other peoples have.'*

Samuel did not approve of these words; he was offended by the harsh judgment that Israel's elders passed on him. Had he failed so miserably as leader of the people and as father? 'Do you hear that, Lord, what they're asking of me?'

'Don't let it affect you, Samuel; they have not rejected *you* but *me*. They do not want *me* to be king over them. Really that's been the case since the day I brought them up out of Egypt. They went to serve other gods; they forsook me and now they're also forsaking you. Nevertheless, Samuel, listen to their voice.'

Samuel was horrified. The Eternal One was on his side, but he wanted the prophet to listen to Israel's desires. The Eternal One even wanted him to stand beside the elders of the people in this hour by telling them about the rights and duties of a king. *'Tell them the rights of the king who will be king over them.'*

Samuel spoke to the people: 'These will be the rights of the king who shall be king over you: he will take your sons, he will make them do service with his wagons and horses, and they will have to run before his chariots. They will have to plough his fields, harvest his harvest, make his wagons and his weapons. He will take your daughters to prepare perfumes, to cook and to bake. He will take your fields, your vineyards and olive groves and give them to his servants. He will take tithes of your corn and wine and give them to his courtiers. Your servants, your serving maids, the best of your young men and your asses he will take to work for him. He will take tithes of your sheep and you will even be slaves. The day will come when you complain about the king whom you have chosen for youselves, but the Lord will not answer you in that day.'

Was this what Samuel had to say from the Eternal One? Or did he want to spare the people a disappointment by depicting the monarchy in such negative terms? Or perhaps himself? A king who knows only rights and not obligations, a king who doesn't give but only *takes;* the people will certainly be afraid of such a king.

However, the people refused to listen to Samuel. 'We want a king; we want to be like the other peoples. Our king will judge us, he will go before us to battle.'

Is it only a dream of unworldly prophets: a land, a people that is different, because the Eternal One is its king?

Samuel heard the words of the people and brought them to the Lord. And the Lord said to Samuel: 'Listen to their voice and make them a king.'

Then Samuel said to the men of Israel, 'Go, each to his city.'

Is he, Israel's insulted judge, the seer who sees things so differently from the Eternal One, the right figure to give the people a king? Samuel needs time. Perhaps he hopes that delay will mean abandonment. 'Let everyone return to his city.'

28

A KING FROM BEHIND THE BAGGAGE

1 SAMUEL 9 AND 10

And it happened, a man from the house of Benjamin – his name was Kish, an able-bodied hero – he had a son. Saul was his name, a youth who stood head and shoulders above the people.

One day Kish's asses had disappeared and Saul was sent out with a servant in search of the animals.

Saul went to the hill-country of Ephraim, but didn't find the asses. He went through the land of Shalishah – not an ass in sight. He went through the land of Shaalim – no trace of them. Saul went through the land of Benjamin and didn't find the asses there either. At long last, when they got to the land of Zuph, he said to his servant: 'Come on, let's return home, otherwise my father will be more worried about us than about those asses.'

However, Saul's servant didn't want to give up: 'There's said to be a seer in the neighbourhood, a man of God, highly respected. Everything that he foretells happens. Let's look for him. Who knows, he can show us the way that we must take.'

One might expect this servant to say, 'Who knows, the man of God may know where the asses are.' But he doesn't say that. It's as if this servant knows deep down that this quest isn't about whether Saul gets on the track of the asses but rather whether he finds his destiny, the way that he must take.

Saul said, 'We have nothing to give the man of God as a gift. Our bread is finished, what can we take for the *profit* of this man?'

Those who heard the old story must have grinned. They know all along that this unknown man of God is the *prophet* Samuel; with a word-play in the Hebrew which works just as well in English, the story-teller is alluding to this.

'Look what I have in my hand, sir, a quarter of a silver shekel. I can give this to the seer and he will show us the way.'

'That's good, then. Let's go.'

Saul and his servant went to the city on the hill where the man of God was. While they were going up, they met girls who were going to draw water. 'Do you happen to know where the seer is?'

'Listen,' said one of the girls, and in their excitement they all talked at the same time. 'He's ahead of you. You must be quick; the seer has just arrived in the city. Today there is a sacrificial meal for all the people. If you're quick you will catch him before he goes up to the high place for the meal. The people won't eat before he's there. First the seer must pronounce the blessing, and only then do those who've been invited eat. If you go up, you'll certainly find him.'

The men made their way up, and the moment that they reached the gate of the city, Samuel came out to meet them.

Now the day before, the Eternal One had made it known to Samuel that in the city on the hill he would meet the man whom he had to anoint king, someone from the house of Benjamin. 'Anoint him ruler over my people, he is the one who will free them from the power of the Philistines, for I have been concerned for my people, I have heard their cry for help.'

Samuel saw Saul approaching the gate of the city, and at that moment the Lord indicated to the prophet, 'This is the man of whom I spoke, he it is who will lead my people.'

Samuel went up to Saul: 'Can you tell me, sir, where the house of the seer is?'

'I am the seer. Go before me from the high place to sit with me at the sacred meal. Tomorrow morning you can go off again. Your asses are fine, you needn't worry about them any longer. A quite different matter is, who is the man that the whole people wants. Shall *you* not be Israel's king?'

'*I? I am a Benjaminite, son of one of the smallest tribes of the people. And isn't my family the least of all the families of Benjamin? Why do you speak this word to me?*'

Saul may be large in stature, but inside he feels small.

Samuel took Saul up to the high place and put him at the head of the table. Samuel said to the cook, 'Now bring the piece of meat that I gave you, that I told you to put on one side.'

The cook took the right rear leg, the best part of the animal, and gave it to Saul. The other guests were very surprised.

So that day Saul ate with Samuel, God's seer. After that they went down to the city, and Samuel spoke with Saul on the roof of a house under the wide starry sky, while people were sleeping.

Early in the morning they arose. 'I shall escort you out,' said Samuel. At the edge of the city he stopped. 'Send your servant ahead of us. But you are to remain with me so that I may tell you the word of God.'

Samuel took a jar with oil, poured it over Saul's head and kissed him. 'Thus the Lord appoints you ruler over his inheritance.'

Saul bowed his head meekly. He hadn't been looking for the kingdom; he'd only been looking for his father's asses. What he'd been looking for he didn't find, and what he hadn't been looking for he did find. The seeker proved to be the sought; it is the Eternal One himself who calls him to the kingship.

'Soon, when you've gone away from here, you will meet two men by Rachel's tomb, in the land of Benjamin. They will tell you that the asses are all right but that your father is very worried about you. Then, when you get to the tree of Tabor, you will meet three men on the way to the house of the Lord in Bethel. One of them will be carrying three kids, another three loaves, and the third a jar of wine. They will give you two loaves which you are to accept from them. Finally, you will get to the hill of God, where the posts of the Philistines are. It will happen that when you've arrived there a group of prophets will meet you, coming down from the high place, playing on lute and drum and flute and lyre. They will be prophesying in an ecstasy. Then the spirit of the Lord will also come upon you and make you another person.'

Another person. Saul will no longer be so much the son of Kish and in his father's service; from now on he will be the son of Samuel and closely related to the prophets of Israel.

And it happened that when Saul turned away to depart from Samuel, God gave him another heart.

Everything happened precisely as the seer had foretold. Two men greeted him by Rachel's tomb, three men by the tree of Tabor. And when he reached the hill of God, lo and behold, a host of prophets came to meet Saul, and the spirit of the Lord seized him; he was in an ecstasy and prophesied with the prophets. The people who knew him from before were amazed. 'What has happened to the son of Kish? *Is Saul also among the prophets?*'

Saul went on. On the way his uncle met him. 'Where have you been?'

'We were looking for father's asses, and when we didn't find them we went to Samuel.'

'And what did Samuel tell you?'

'He told us that they had been found.'

Saul didn't mention that Samuel had talked to him about the kingship all night long and had anointed him king. Really he wasn't yet a king. You become a king by acting royally. Soon Saul will be called upon to do that. Then it will prove whether he has indeed become another person.

Samuel summoned the people in Mizpah. 'Thus says the Lord, the God of Israel: I brought you up out of Egypt, I delivered you from the hands of the Egyptians and from the hands of all the people who oppressed you. But now you reject me, the God who freed you from all distress and pain. Give us a king, you cried.'

The prophet wants once again to impress on the Israelites that their call for a king can only look like a sign of mistrust. At the same time the Eternal One shows himself ready to accede to their request. The Lord also sees the people's longing for a king as a cry of distress and pain from which he wants to free them. They can get their king.

Samuel made the twelve tribes of Israel approach and cast the lot. The lot fell upon Benjamin, Israel's smallest tribe. Samuel made the families of Benjamin approach and cast the lot. The lot fell on the family of Matri. And in the family of Matri the lot fell upon Saul, the son of Kish. *But when they looked for him, he was nowhere to be found.* Saul had gone missing.

In the first act the seeker proved to be the sought; in the second act the one who is sought is lost. There is always a search. Saul didn't seek the kingship; he had to be sought. It was finally God himself who had to show where he was: the son of Kish was hiding among the baggage.

So we are told of one special development after another. It began with the barren Hannah producing new life. After that, at a time of spiritual barrenness, the little Samuel heard his name called. And Saul, an unknown farmer's son from the smallest of the twelve tribes, is chosen to be Israel's first king.

The shy Saul was scared to death of this; they had to get him from among the baggage. You couldn't tell from the outside that he was so afraid inside; he stood head and shoulders among the people. 'See whom the Lord has chosen. There is no one like him among all the people.'

The people shouted for joy, 'Long live the king.'

After that, Samuel, the prophet, spoke. He told them about the rights and duties of the kingship and wrote all this down in a document. He put the document next to the ark, before the face of the Lord.

Saul returned home, accompanied by able-bodied men who felt called to do so. There were also those who expected nothing good from his kingship: 'Will Saul liberate us?' They didn't deign to look at him and gave him no presents. Saul kept silent.

29

SAMUEL BIDS FAREWELL

I SAMUEL 11 AND 12

Suddenly the hostile army of king Nahash was standing before the gates of the city of Jabesh. King *Snake*. The villain crops up just as unexpectedly as the snake in paradise. Now is the time for Israel's anointed to appear; now he has to join battle and shatter the head of this monster. Now Saul has to prove himself a king.

The men of Jabesh were overcome with fear, 'King Nahash, if you will make a covenant with us, then we shall serve you.'

'All right,' said king Nahash, 'on condition that I put out your right eyes, to the shame of all Israel.'

Without a right eye no marksman will be able to attack king Nahash; the humiliation done to Jabesh will be an insult to the whole people. What is their answer to be? Will the brothers come to the aid of their brother in need?

'Give us another seven days respite, your majesty, and then do what is good in your eyes.'

Nahash is evidently so certain of his cause that he grants them the postponement that they ask for. Meanwhile the men of Jabesh were not as feeble as they might seem; they immediately sent messengers to the man who had been anointed king by Samuel. The inhabitants of Gibeah, the region where Saul lived, heard their report with horror and lamented over it.

'Why are you lamenting so?' asked Saul, returning from the field where he had been ploughing with his oxen. *When Saul heard the message from the men of Jabesh, he was seized by the spirit of God and burst out in fierce anger.* He took the team of oxen which had just been pulling his plough, cut the animals in pieces and sent the parts to all the regions of the land: *'Whoever does not go out behind Saul and Samuel, this shall happen to his cattle.'*

98

From the bloody, stinking bits of meat the children of Israel can see what is going to happen if the paralysis isn't shaken off and brotherhood takes no tangible form. Saul wants to make the loose tribes into a unit; the people have to rally behind their leader without any divisions. A torn body is no longer a body. Does Israel realize that?

That Saul kills the oxen says a great deal: they belong to the life that he is now leaving. Another field awaits him; from now on as king he will care for the whole land and for all those who live in it.

Fear and trembling before the Lord seized them and they went out as one man. The men of Saul said to the messengers from Jabesh: 'Say to the people of Jabesh, "Tomorrow, when the sun is high in the heaven, your liberation will come."'

The men of Jabesh heard the news and rejoiced exceedingly. They said to king Nahash, 'Tomorrow we will hand ourselves over to you, then do with us what is good in your eyes.'

And that day it happened that king *Snake* suffered a devastating defeat even before the sun was high in the heavens. *The survivors were driven out, so that no two of them were left together.*

King Saul had proved to be a true king with a heart for his people, a ruler who helps those who have no helper, who shatters the oppressor in order to liberate the oppressed.*

And the people who had turned away from king Saul – 'Will he liberate us?' – and so despised him that they didn't even give him any gifts, should the liberators now chop off their heads?

'No, you mustn't do that,' said Saul, who wanted no day of vengeance. *'No man shall be killed on this day, for on this day the Lord has brought liberation to Israel.'*

So Saul wisely doesn't heighten the internal division further; he doesn't go too far; he gives God alone the glory and, unlike king Nahash, grants his opponents light in their eyes.

'Come,' said Saul to the people, 'let us go to Gilgal and there renew the kingship.'

They went to Gilgal and made Saul king, before the face of the Lord. They offered peace offerings, and Saul and all the men of Israel rejoiced exceedingly.

Now the moment had come for Samuel to take his farewell as Israel's leader. 'From now on your king will go before you. I have become old and grey and I have no sons who can follow me. I shall no longer go at your head.'

This farewell was obviously painful to Israel's last judge. Has he failed, that the people desired a king? At least let the people bear witness that he was a good judge!

'Bear witness to me before the Lord and his anointed. Whose ox did I take, whose ass did I take, whom did I put under pressure, whom did I treat dishonourably, or by whom did I allow myself to be bribed so as to turn a blind eye? Tell me, and it shall be restored to you.'

They said, 'You have put us under no pressure, you have not treated us dishonourably, nor accepted anything from anyone.'

Samuel said, 'Today the Lord is witness and his anointed is witness that you have found nothing wrong in me.'

'Yes, witness!'

Then Samuel spoke his words of farewell. He reminded the people of the great men whom the Lord had given them; time and again the Lord sent a liberator. Granted, it was sad that the people had rewarded this trust with the request for a king. 'Look, there now stands your anointed, the king whom you wanted. The Lord has given you this king. If you fear the Lord and serve him, if you listen to his voice and do not rebel, you and your king will find the Lord our God at your side. But if you do not listen to his voice and rebel, then you will find the Lord God against you.'

Once again the old Samuel preaches a thunderous sermon. That is to say, *he* preaches the sermon and the Eternal One provides the thunder to reinforce his words. It made a deep impression on the people. 'Pray for us, Samuel, to the Lord your God; do not let us die. We should never have asked for a king.'

But although Israel has sinned, God's blessing will bind together people and ruler. God's yes exceeds his no. 'Do not fear, serve the Lord with all your heart. He will not cast out his people for the sake of his name, he will make you his people. And as for me, I would sin against God if I stopped praying for you. Rather, I want to show you the good and right way.'

Israel's last judge will be Israel's first prophet. Israel has a king, just like the other peoples. But in Israel, in contrast to the peoples, near Israel's kings there will be always prophets to remind the man on the throne of the Torah and of the kingship of God.

30

A STAR WHICH RISES AND FADES

I SAMUEL 13 AND 14

A star has risen in Israel, shining brightly in the heavens. But it's a star which fades quickly. That 'other heart' that Saul got didn't last long.

Again battle had to be joined against the Philistines. The people had already set their hope on the new king; their king would go before them. But Saul did nothing; Saul waited for Samuel, who had promised that he would come to offer the burnt offering within seven days before they were to join battle.* Saul waited in vain. Where was the prophet? When after seven days he still hadn't appeared, the muttering warriors began to depart. Saul felt compelled to take things into his own hands.

'Bring me the burnt offering.'

They brought it, and Saul offered the burnt offering. The fire was still smouldering when Samuel appeared.

'What have you done, Saul?'

'The warriors were deserting me and you didn't appear within the agreed time. I was afraid that the enemy would attack before I had asked for the Lord's favour, so I undertook to offer the burnt offering myself.'

Samuel flared up in anger. 'You have acted foolishly.'

Why foolishly? Saul was under pressure; his men were complaining, and Samuel hadn't kept his promise. Is the prophet right to be angry?

Not if this was a story from the human world. But it's a story from the kingdom of God. In that kingdom it isn't fear but trust that reigns, and whoever is king goes before his people in that trust. A liberator of Israel ultimately puts his trust more in God his Lord than in his army. Didn't Gideon win the victory with a handful of men?

Samuel couldn't see in Saul the shining example of what a king in Israel had to be. 'You have acted foolishly. If you had trusted in God, he would have confirmed your kingdom for ever. Now it will not endure; the

Eternal One has chosen another, a man who shall be Israel's new leader after his heart.'

Samuel went away.

Together with his son Jonathan, Saul was camping with his men in Gibeah. The Midianites put up their tents in Michmash. The enemy was armed to the teeth, and on Israel's side only Saul and Jonathan had a sword and a spear. *There was no smith to be found in Israel.* The Philistines had the monopoly in working with iron and were careful not to give up their knowledge and thus the secret of forging. *On the day of battle neither sword nor spear were found in all the people that was with Saul and Jonathan.*

It may be therefore be regarded as a miracle that Israel emerged victorious from the battle with such an iron opponent. Though that was more thanks to Jonathan than to Saul. With the same courage and faith as Gideon in former days he saw a chance to cause so much confusion in the enemy camp that the Philistines were put to flight. The Israelites regained their self-confidence; they emerged from their hiding places and joined in the pursuit.

Now without Jonathan knowing it, in his fear Saul had sworn a senseless oath: *'Cursed be the man who takes food before the evening, until I have taken vengeance on the enemy.'* Again Saul wants to regulate God.

None of his warriors took any food, not even when they found honey in an open field in the wood. However, Jonathan, who was dead tired, dipped his staff in the honeycomb and ate some of the sweetmeat. He did this quite openly.

'Your father,' said a soldier, 'has made the people swear: cursed be the man who takes food today. That is why the people are so exhausted.'

'My father will cause disaster to this land one day. If everyone had been able to eat freely from the booty, how great the defeat of the Philistines would have been!'

Night falls. Should they pursue the Philistines further? Saul didn't want them to stop. But a priest asked himself whether the king's motives were pure. 'Let us approach God.'

The oracle was consulted. God was silent. Why? Had someone incurred guilt, that the Lord kept silence? Saul made the leaders approach. 'Who amongst us has incurred guilt? *Even if it was Jonathan, my own son, he shall surely die.'*

Why does Saul have to think of Jonathan at this particular moment? Was that right? Saul, *the one asked for*, was no longer wanted. He had recently been told that by the prophet. Did Saul have to fear that he would have to hand the kingship over to Jonathan, to the son who had become much more popular among the people through his heroic action. 'Even if it was Jonathan.' It sounded noble, but was it?

'Who has incurred guilt?'

The people were silent. Everyone understood what was up; no one spoke a word. The lot was cast, and the lot fell upon Jonathan. 'What have you done, Jonathan, my son?'

'With the point of the staff which was in my hand I took a little honey, father. I am prepared to die.'

'So be it, Jonathan, you shall die.'

If frightened men are consistent, you'd better get out of the way.

Then the people intervened: 'Must Jonathan die, who has won such a great victory today? Far from it! As the Eternal One lives, who has fought side by side with Jonathan, not a hair of his head shall be harmed.'

The children of Israel so wanted a king, but they already had to protect him from such a fatal lapse. They had a purer feeling for the Eternal One than their anointed.

31

THE REJECTION OF SAUL

I SAMUEL 15

*Samuel said to Saul: 'The Lord has sent me to anoint you king over Israel.
Now listen to the word of the Lord. Thus says the Lord: I have seen what
Amalek did to Israel when he barred the way to the people that came out of
Egypt. Now, go and annihilate Amalek, put all his possessions under the ban,
do not spare him. Kill the men and women, the children and the infants, the
sheep and the oxen, the camels and the asses.'*

The Lord God isn't quoted as speaking like this every day! Why this
devastating judgment and this divine order to exterminate Amalek?

In the stories of scripture the Amalekites stand for the arch-enemy of
Israel's liberation. Amalek is degenerate man, who wants to maintain his
domination with relentless cruelty. In the past Amalek fell unexpectedly
on the rear of the people that went up out of Egypt, where the weakest
were to be found, the old, the mothers with children.* Humanity stands
or falls with the fight against Amalek, the monster of the Old Testament,*
the incarnate enemy of freedom and peace. He keeps rising from the dead.
When in the years of the occupation the Jews were deported, the words
'Remember what Amalek did to you' were chalked on a wall in Amsterdam.
They are words from Holy Scripture: *Remember what Amalek did to you,
on the way, when you were going out of Egypt, how he fell upon you on the
way and cut off all the weak in your rearguard, when you were weary and
exhausted, and how he did not fear God. Once you have arrived in the
promised land you shall wipe out the memory of Amalek under heaven. Do
not forget it.*

Saul knows what he has to do: it's up to him as king of the promised land
to wipe out the memory of Amalek from under heaven.

The killing of innocent citizens, including children and infants, together
with their defenceless beasts, is nothing by comparison with the violence

of the Amalekites. Does the God of the story-teller use the same weapons as corrupt Amalek?

There's an important difference. Saul's task is to exterminate evil root and branch without deriving any profit from it. And it's here that he fails. Saul defeats the Amalekites, puts the men, women, children and infants to death, along with the weak and sick cattle, but contrary to God's commandment he spares the life of Amalek's king Agag, along with the best part of the sheep and cattle.

The story of the battle between Saul and Amalek can also be read as the account of an inner conflict within Saul. He has to exterminate the evil in himself; here half measures are of the evil one. And Samuel has already told him bluntly what is evil in the eyes of the Lord: it is his own lack of trust in God. When it comes to the point, Saul is afraid: afraid of the kingship, afraid of the Philistines, afraid of his people. He should be able to overcome his fear by turning to God and listening his voice, but Saul is too self-centred and listens only with half an ear. He exterminates Amalek, but he spares king Agag, the instigator of the evil, just as he also didn't overcome his fear, the source of the evil.

Then the word of the Lord came to Samuel: 'I regret that I made Saul king. He has turned away from me and has not listened to my words.' This word affected Samuel deeply and he cried out to the Lord the whole night.

Is it because of Saul that Samuel lies awake so angrily this night? Is it because of the people? Does he see it as a personal defeat, now that the kingship in Israel for which he bears a share of the responsibility has immediately ended in failure? And how are things to go on from here?

The next morning Samuel makes an early start to tell Saul God's devastating judgment. Saul, unaware of any evil, has erected a monument to commemorate his victory. He greets Samuel cheerfully: 'Be blessed of the Lord, whose word I have kept.'

'Whose word I have kept? Then what is that bleating of sheep and goats that sounds in my ears and the lowing of cows that I hear?'

'The people have saved the best of the animals to sacrifice to the Lord your God, all the rest we smote with the ban.'

'Be silent, I shall make known to you what the Lord has told me this night.'

'Speak.'

'Have you not, although small in your eyes, become head of all the tribes of Israel? Has not the Lord anointed you king? And did not the Lord send you out to exterminate the evil people of Amalek? Why did you not listen to the voice of the Eternal One? Why did you throw yourselves on the booty and did you do what is evil in the eyes of the Lord?'

'I did indeed listen to the voice of the Lord. The whole of Amalek, except for Agag, I smote with the ban. But the people took the best of the animals to slaughter them before the Lord your God.'

'Which do you think that the Lord has greater pleasure in, burnt offerings or listening to his voice? Because in your stubbornness you have rejected the word of the Lord, the Lord has rejected you as king.'

'I have sinned. I have disobeyed the command of the Lord. I feared the people and listened to their voice. If you will nevertheless forgive me my sins, return with me, I will bow before the Lord.'

Saul's plea was in vain. 'I shall not return with you. You shall no longer be king over Israel.'

Harsh words from the prophet. He turned away and wanted to go. Saul grasped the hem of his garment. Samuel has to remain. God has to remain. 'Do not leave me alone!' The garment tore. Samuel said: 'On this day the Lord has torn the kingship over Israel from you, he has given it to your neighbour, better than you. The Eternal One speaks no lies and knows no repentance. He is not a human being that he should repent.'

Then doesn't Samuel have any compassion on Saul, whom he himself anointed king? Doesn't he see how the uncertain ruler needs his support?

'Samuel, I have sinned, but leave me my honour with the elders of the people. Return with me, that I may prostrate myself before the Lord your God.'

Then Samuel allowed himself to be persuaded and returned with Saul. And Saul bowed low before the Lord.

What Saul failed to do, Samuel then immediately carried out: 'Bring me Agag, the king of Amalek.'

Not suspecting that death awaited him, the reprieved Agag appeared before Samuel. Agag was confronted with a shattering riddle song, but the victim only realized how shattering it was with the last word:

As women   were made childless by   your sword
so among women   shall be made childless   your mother.

Agag's mother would suffer the same fate as the many women whom her son had made unhappy. *Samuel cut Agag to pieces before the face of the Lord.*

Samuel returned to Ramah, to his house; Saul went back to Gibeah to take his place on the throne that had already been denied him. They never saw each other again.

32

HEAVEN HAS CHOSEN THE
LITTLE ONE

I SAMUEL 16.1-13

God said to Samuel, 'How long will you continue to grieve over Saul? I have rejected him: he is not king over Israel. Fill your horn with oil and go. I am sending you to Jesse, the Bethlehemite, for among his sons I have seen a king.'

Saul's kingship has failed. Saul was already afraid that this would happen, and so was God. Samuel mourns. He mourns for the people that no longer wanted to have God as king but desired an earthly king, and he mourns for Saul, the anointed who failed. God shouldn't have begun with him. And he, God's prophet, certainly shouldn't have either.

Is he hearing things aright? Does God want to go through with it? Samuel is hearing things aright. God clearly doesn't want to give up the venture of a king over Israel. Among Jesse's sons the Eternal One has seen a new king. But why must he in particular, an old man, be the one to anoint the new king? If Saul hears of this, Samuel is no longer sure of his life.

God helps Samuel on the way. 'Take a calf with you and say to Jesse: I have come to make an offering to the Lord. Invite him to the sacrificial meal and I shall tell you what you must do.'

The Eternal One lays on a ritual for Samuel; a sacrificial meal will mark the transition in his personal life and in the life of his people. When Samuel has performed the ritual, the Lord will reveal to him what he must do. Then the seer will see whom he must anoint. 'Anoint for me the man that I tell you.'

Samuel has to go to Bethlehem, the place where in bygone days Benjamin was born is the field of Ephrathah. Matriarch Rachel, who gave birth to him, died there in childbirth. 'Son of my pain,' she said then. But father Jacob said, 'No, his name shall not be son of my pain, but son of my right hand, Benjamin.'

Bethlehem, the place where Ruth, the Moabite woman, went to pluck ears of corn in the field of Boaz and where she could hide under his wings and under the wings of Israel's God. Obed was to be their son, Jesse their grandson.

Samuel travels to Bethlehem with mixed feelings. The elders of the city come to meet him trembling; a prophet doesn't just appear. Is disaster to be expected? 'Does your coming mean peace for us?'

'Yes, peace!', say Samuel, keeping back his unease. 'I have come to offer a sacrifice to the Lord. I warmly invite you to the sacrificial meal, especially Jesse and his sons.'

Jesse appears, together with his seven sons; Eliab, Jesse's oldest, a giant figure, is the first to appear. Samuel is sure that he is the man whom the Eternal One foresaw as king.

But Samuel the seer hasn't seen things aright. What has his soul failed to see? Just as recently he had accused Saul of being too hasty, so now he is doing the same thing. Why not first have a relaxed meal, trusting that God would tell him what to do in his own time? Now he's being misled by his own eyes. 'Samuel, you mustn't go by his appearance or by his giant stature, for I have rejected him. What human beings see isn't important, Samuel. Human beings see what is before their eyes; the Lord looks at the heart.'

The prophet is looking with a human, all too human gaze. He sees a proud figure, Eliab, a man like Saul, and already his hand is reaching into the folds of his coat for the horn with oil to anoint Jesse's firstborn king. He's caught up in the old patterns; he's repeating himself. But God doesn't want history to repeat itself. God wants to disclose a new time. Then the prophet finally hears God's voice. 'Precisely what you think, Samuel, a man like Saul! But we mustn't have someone like that; you're sadly mistaken. Why don't you look at the heart of the person, at the concern of his whole being, the source on which he draws? Why do you see only what is before your eyes?' Samuel listens to God thinking.

Abinadab comes forward, Jesse's second son, but Samuel doesn't receive any sign from heaven. He too isn't God's chosen. Jesse presents Shammah, his third son, to Samuel. Nor is he the one. The fourth comes, the fifth, the sixth, and they aren't the one either. So it must be the seventh, 'Where is your seventh son?'

'Here is the seventh, sir.'

But it isn't the seventh son either. All Jesse's sons have been reviewed, but none of them proves to have been chosen. Samuel is counted out. Can no king after God's heart be found in Israel? It certainly seems as if the Eternal One has made a mistake. Samuel could have spared himself the visit to Bethlehem.

'Are those all your sons, Jesse?'

'Oh, sir, what shall I say? There is one more, but he's the *little one*, our Benjamin, who is tending the sheep in the field of Ephrathah. He's still wet behind the ears. It can't be him, he's the eighth.'

'Perhaps God looks in a different way from us, Jesse. Call the little one, will you?'

Jesse's little afterthought will soon be invited to the sacrificial meal, and until he is there it will not be started. People are waiting for *the little one*. No one can go any further until he is there, neither Samuel, nor the elders, nor Jesse and his seven sons, nor the story-teller. First the eighth one must come. He is the one for whom Israel and Israel's God are waiting

Eight. That's a divine number. Usually people don't count further than seven, for example seven days; that's our scheme. But God made a covenant with Abraham on the eighth day, a day that we really don't know; for us it's the first day again. The eighth day isn't on the calendar; that day isn't in time, that day is in eternity. It's a day which transcends the ordinary course of time. Therefore Aaron is consecrated priest on the eighth day, and therefore Israel's sons are circumcised on the eighth day. Eight is the number of the new beginning. On the eighth day a reality of a higher order enters the life which we know by nature. On the eighth day ordinary life becomes a life with God.

The little one enters the room. Will the Eternal One make a new beginning with him?

'Samuel, arise, anoint him, for this is the one.'

Samuel looks at him, Jesse's youngest, the shepherd boy with the catapult with which he keeps his flock together and drives off wild animals. The little one with his harp, on which he plays, keeping watch over his flock. Samuel took the horn with oil and anointed him in the midst of his brothers. This one will be important for them all.

'What is your name?'

'David, sir.'

And the spirit of the Lord fell on David, from that day on.

David will become king. But in his heart he must remain a shepherd, a guardian of God's flock: driving away wild beasts, protecting those who come to shelter under the shadow of his wings, large and small. He must also remain a minstrel, who plays God's songs for the people, songs of praise on which the Eternal One is enthroned.

33

LITTLE DAVID, PLAY ON YOUR HARP

I SAMUEL 16.14-23

God's spirit has departed from Saul and an evil spirit has seized him; the king has become a pitiful bit of humanity, a prey to fears.

The servants at court can't see why their king who was once so proud is now suffering so pitifully. 'Your majesty, won't you have something to eat? Something to drink? Why don't you go for a walk in the palace garden? It's a cool evening.'

Saul doesn't reply. He only stares into the distance with eyes which don't see anything. The king is sick. No one knows how sick. And there is no one who can help him.

Or perhaps there is someone? One of Saul's servants has heard in Bethlehem how well a son of Jesse can play on the harp. David is his name. When his hand touches the strings, it's as if the heavens open; God's peace descends.

'Sire, shall we ask someone to play for you on the harp? When the evil spirit comes upon you, he can conjure it away with his playing.'

'Do you know such a person? What is his name?'

'His name is David, the son of Jesse, the Bethlehemite. He is a brave hero, a man of war, well-spoken, fair of form, and God is with him.'

Saul despatches messengers to Jesse. 'Send me your son David, who is with the sheep.'

David, a shepherd in the field of Ephrathah, must come to the palace to become Saul's shepherd.

'David, take an ass's load of bread with you, a wineskin and a kid. Give them to Saul, whose servant you shall be.'

So David came to the court as a minstrel. And whenever the evil spirit came to torment Saul, David silently entered the room, put his hand to the strings and played his sweetest melodies. Then the mist departed from Saul's soul, the clouds in his brain disappeared, and the king could again see something of heaven, inspired by the music which welled up from the singing heart of Israel.

And Saul loved him and David became his armour-bearer. 'Stay with me, young man, stay with me always.'

In the next chapter we shall hear another story about David's first encounter with Saul; it doesn't take place in the palace, where David seeks to heal a depressed Saul with music, but in the open air, where he goes into battle for a wavering king and a wavering people against a giant, Goliath, the champion of the Philistines. The story-teller takes that story from an earlier tradition* which talks of an anonymous giant who *taunted* Israel and had his head cut off by a brother of David, and of another giant called *Goliath, who had a spear with a shaft like a weaver's beam,* who was slain by one Elhanan.

So Goliath is slain twice in the Bible. The prophetic story-teller clearly found the original story so significant that it had to be included in his testimony to true kingship in Israel. He boldly adds it to the stories of David. He wants to impress on Israel that it must resist tremendous paganism with shepherd-like means, and is that not precisely what David, the great David, did?

Reflecting on the past by the rivers of Babylon, the exiles depict in David the future of which they dream. All the piety and spiritual power, the courage and humility, wisdom and warmth, playfulness and self-control that they wish for themselves, they attribute to David. We can no longer reconstruct the historical nucleus of the story, what comes from the later invention of an admiring people and what is the proclamation of the story-teller. A people with many facets depicts a person with many facets: shepherd and bandit leader, king and priest, sinner and saint, statesman and poet. It's impossible to imagine all this in one person. But he isn't one person; he's the whole of a people which dwells in this king. This one person is the dream of a people which feels itself called to be a holy people, a people after God's heart.

34

DAVID AND GOLIATH

I SAMUEL 17

Israel is at war. The Israelites have camped on a slope on one side of the Valley of the Oaks, the Israelites on the slope opposite. Then a champion form the Philistine army came forward. *Goliath* was his name. He was six cubits and a span tall, and armed to the teeth. He had a bronze helmet on his head and he wore chain armour with a weight of five thousand shekels of bronze. He had greaves of bronze and on his shoulder he carried a bronze spear. The shaft of his lance was *like a weaver's beam* and the point of his lance was six hundred shekels of iron. A shield-bearer went in front of him.

That is what paganism looked like to Israel: gigantic, overwhelming, terrifying, invincible. Hear how it boasts and *taunts*: 'Who do you think you are to oppose us Philistines in battle? Are you servants of Saul? I know what we'll do. Choose a man to fight with me. If he wins, we shall be your servants. If I win, then you shall be our servant. I ask you, give me a man, for us to fight together.'

Day after day Goliath hurled his insults at Israel, for forty days, morning and evening, particularly when the Israelites were offering the morning and evening sacrifices. Could they draw a great deal of confidence from the ritual? The morale of the troops was shattered; Saul and his men were very afraid.

Among Saul's men of war were the three oldest sons of Jesse, Eliab, Abinadab and Shammah. From time to time David, the youngest of Jesse's eight sons, came to bring his brothers food and news from home. Afterwards he went back from the front to Bethlehem to tend his father's sheep.

'David.'

'Yes, father.'

'Go to your brothers in the Valley of the Oaks, will you? Take a bushel of roasted corn with you and ten loaves. And these ten milk cheeses for the king. Go and see how your brothers are doing and bring a pledge from them, a sign that they are still alive.'

Early in the morning David arose, loaded his goods and went to the Valley of the Oaks.

At the very moment he reached the camp, the army was going out. Israel and the Philistines were taking up positions, army against army. David hastened to the warriors. There he found his brothers. He asked how things were with them.

While he was speaking with them, Goliath again came out from the ranks of the Philistines to mock poor Israel. 'Give me a man...' At the sight of the giant, Israel's warriors took flight as one man.

David said, 'Who is this uncircumcised Philistine who comes to taunt the ranks of the living God?'

Contemptuous words said in innocent simplicity. But by now David is the only one in the Valley of the Oaks who is not paralysed with fear; he is ashamed of his people, who risk yielding to tyranny. Only David senses that here the heart of Israel's faith is touched and only he still speaks of the living God. 'What kind of a wretch is this who defies Israel and Israel's God? And what is the reward for the man who kills him?'

'The king will load the man who kills him with wealth. Moreover the king will give him his daughter, and his family will never have to pay taxes again.'

Eliab, Jesse's firstborn, heard all this. Surely little David won't...? He grudgingly asked David why he had really come, 'I know all too well how arrogant you are and how malicious.'

The oldest brother, called to be leader in accordance with the tradition, but passed over by Samuel, reacted irritably as soon as he began to suspect that David wanted to go out to battle against Goliath. Fear struck him, now that this late arrival was threatening to break through attitudes re-inforced by nature. 'You've come to see the battle.'

Why shouldn't David come to see the battle? Is Eliab ashamed now that David had seen *him* as he is: a fearful big brother, fleeing before the enemy?

'What wrong have I done you?' asked David, 'I only spoke a word.'

But of course David is a man who adds deeds to his words; Eliab had clearly sensed that. And while the voice of the Philistine was still ringing

out through the Valley of the Oaks – 'Give me a man! Give me a man!' –
David went to Saul's tent. 'I will be that man,' he said.

Saul and David, they stand in the opening of the tent. Saul is the king,
God's anointed, called to resist paganism to the face. But no inspiration
flows from him any longer. Is this the man who at the beginning of his
kingship, seized by the spirit of God, forced mighty Amalek to its knees
and liberated the city of Jabesh? The spirit of God has departed from him.

And David? The spirit of God fills him. He has ears to hear who it is
calling from the hill over there. He knows that here paganism is spreading
and taunting the people of God. And he also knows what Israel has to do
now. Saul and David stand facing each other: the king who should have
done it and the shepherd boy who does it. 'I will be that man.'

Saul can't believe his ears. What kind of boy is this? 'You're only a
youth, Goliath is a warrior, long practised in battle.'

'I am a shepherd, your majesty, who keeps his father's sheep. If a lion or
a bear comes to take a lamb from the flock, I rush up, strike him down and
rescue the lamb from his mouth. If he turns against me, I seize him by the
beard and kill him. Your servant has killed lions and bears, sire. So will it
also be with these uncircumcised Philistines who defy the ranks of the
living God. The Lord who saved me from lion and bear will also save me
from the claws of the Philistines.'

'Go, my boy,' said Saul. 'The Lord be with you.'

Saul put his own coat of mail on David, placed a bronze helmet on his
head and gave him a suit of armour. David girded himself with the king's
armour and tried to walk.

'I can't walk in this,' he said, 'I have never worn such a thing.'

David won't encounter the Philistine as a second Saul, as a warrior in
armour, as a miniature Goliath, but as himself, as a shepherd. He could
only see the giant as a beast that threatened God's flock, a lion, a bear, a
dog that had to be challenged. And he took his staff in his hand and looked
for five smooth stones from the river bed.

He was a *tsaddiq*, a righteous man, who had learned a new way of thinking from the five sacred books of Moses, in which power no longer stands
over against power and in which violence isn't overcome with violence. He
had to sort things out with these five stones. He put them in his shepherd's
bag and went up to Goliath, his sling in his hand. The Philistine almost
overlooked him and felt insulted: such a young man. 'Am I a dog, that you
come after me with a staff?,' he exclaimed, and he cursed David to his gods.

David said: 'You come to me with sword and spear and shield. I come to you with the name of the Lord, the God of the ranks of Israel, whom you have taunted. Today God will give you into my hand. I shall slay you. I shall cut off your head. The whole earth shall know who is Israel's God and that the Lord does not liberate by sword and lance. This is about that God, this is his battle.'

The Philistine came closer and look, David rushed up to him, put his hand in his bag, took out a stone, slung it, and hit the Philistine on the head. The stone penetrated deep into his forehead and Goliath fell to the ground, as if to worship David's God.

So David defeated the giant, with a stone as small as human faith.* He rushed up to the Philistine, seized his sword, drew it from its sheath and cut off his head. *Goliath's* sword. David wore no sword. The giant fell by his own sword.

The Philistines, seeing that their hero was dead, took flight. The men of Israel leaped up, uttered a battle cry and pursued them in the direction of Gath, to the gates of Ekron. Corpses lay all along the way.

When Saul saw David go to meet the Philistine, he said to Abner, the commander of his army: 'Whose son is that young man?'

'As truly as you live, your majesty, I do not know.'

'Ask whose son he is, that young man.'

Here the story-teller depicts Saul as being in ignorance. Israel's anointed is blind to the spirit of God which drives David, the young man with the five stones in his shepherd's bag.

David returned from the battle, the Philistine's head in his hand. Saul looked at him. 'Young man, whose son are you?'

'The son of your servant Jesse, sire, from Bethlehem.'

And David brought the head of the Philistine to Jerusalem, and his armour he put in his tent.

What's this? Surely Jerusalem doesn't belong to Israel? It will still be years and years before David conquers Mount Zion, to establish the capital of his kingdom there.* That's true, but the story-teller doesn't want to end his story without mentioning the name of Jerusalem. The name of the royal city must already resound in this first royal story. Where else would David have put that head? Where can it better silence paganism than in the city of peace of which Israel dreams? And where can the armour better be kept than in *his tent*, the tent of David's God?*

35

SAUL ISOLATED

I SAMUEL 18

And it happened that Jonathan's soul was joined with David's soul. Jonathan loved David as his own soul.

Jonathan would never forget the moment when he stood there in his father's tent, together with David, the shepherd boy from Bethlehem who all alone had broken through a world of fear and unbelief. Jonathan saw that by David's act the people of Israel had been raised as it were from the dead. There they stood, the three of them: Saul his father, a demoralized man; David, himself in a disarming way because he was so utterly of God; and he, Jonathan, the crown prince. But was this place indeed his? Jonathan had barely met David when he knew: this is the one.

Of course that was also Saul's thought: this is the one. But for Saul it represents a deadly threat, while for Jonathan it is new life. David and Jonathan are kindred spirits; they share each other's secret. Later, after Jonathan's death, David will sing of their love in a moving lament as a love *more wonderful than the love of women* – and in those days David knew quite a bit about the love of women.

That he can admire so passionately and so royally is the best thing about Jonathan. He seals their friendship with a powerful, sacramental gesture. He takes off his cloak and gives it to David. It isn't just a cloak; Jonathan parts with more than just a garment; he parts with the throne. Jonathan takes everything off: his armour, his sword, his bow and his girdle. Jonathan has recognized David as the anointed one. *'You shall become king over Israel, I shall be second to you.'** Any envy is alien to him. So Jonathan made a covenant with David, his friend.

David entered Saul's service as a warrior, and wherever he went his work prospered, so that Saul set him over the army. That was good in the eyes of the people and also good in the eyes of Saul's servants.

Once, when David returned from a victory over the Philistines, it happened that the women came out from all the cities of Israel to welcome their king with drums and triangles, singing and dancing: '*Saul has slain his thousands, David his ten thousands.*'

If only Saul could have heard the song with Jonathan's ears! If only just, like his son, he could have admired the young man from Bethlehem and experienced him as a gift from God! But in his fear and faint-heartedness he thought that the women were mocking him. Envy and suspicion poisoned his soul more and more.

The next day David again played on the harp, but Saul could no longer bear the lovely sounds and suddenly a spear flew through the room. 'I shall pin that David to the wall.' Saul, king of Israel, is like Goliath. David escapes the spear a second time.

Saul is consumed with jealousy, for God is with this David, the same God who has departed from him, from Saul. Saul makes David leader over thousands; he will continue to go out at the head of the warriors. But to Saul's secret sorrow he keeps returning intact; even the spear of the enemy cannot hit God's favourite.

Saul is obsessed with just one thought: how can he rid himself of David? What if he gave Merab, his oldest daughter, to David? After all, she was the reward that he had promised to the warrior in Israel who slew Goliath. He could appoint his son-in-law supreme commander of the army and then hope and pray that David would fall at the hand of the Philistines.

Does David smell a rat? Doesn't he fancy Merab? Or does he mean it when he tells Saul that he is of too lowly descent to be able to be the king's son-in-law? Saul sweeps away his hesitations. However, towards the time of the wedding Merab is married off to one Adriel. No one is as incalculable as the desperate Saul.

But there is another princess, Michal. 'Father, please may I marry David? I love him.'

The people love David, the women sing his praises with triangles and tambourines, the warriors see him as their leader, and nearer to home Jonathan loves him and now so does Michal. The only one who can cherish no affection for David is Saul himself. The clouds of approaching madness gather round his mind, suspicion of David which poisons every-thing, the theft of his happiness and of his glory, the man who has taken it all away from him: the heart of his people, the heart of his daughter, the friendship of his son. Soon the son of Jesse will even make himself master of the throne. A lonelier man than Saul cannot be found in Israel.

'Of course you may marry David, my child. I will send him news today.'

Saul sees another possibility of getting rid of David. He sends a messenger. He cannot himself tell David that he very much wants to give him his daughter in marriage; someone else must tell the lie.

'Does Saul see me as a son-in-law, Michal's husband? I've already told him that I'm poor and of lowly descent.'

'The king doesn't desire any dowry for his daughter befitting a rich and well-to-do man; the king requires a dowry befitting a brave hero: for a hundred foreskins of uncircumcised Philistines she is yours.'

Saul had thought that David would never survive that. David returns in triumph with two hundred foreskins. 'Saul asked for one hundred foreskins and David brought him two hundred,' sing the warriors in the pubs.

Thus everything that Saul undertakes in his despair brings David nearer to the crown. With every move on the chessboard, Saul makes his position worse. David's name and fame grow in the face of oppression.

36

WHEN DAVID HAD TO FLEE
BEFORE THE TYRANT SAUL

I SAMUEL 19

Again the Philistines attacked little Israel, and again David and his men were able to resist them. However, the greatest danger that threatens him doesn't lurk in the enemy but in Saul. The king now speaks openly with Jonathan and his servants about his plan to kill David.

Jonathan hastens to David. 'My father wants to kill you. Be on your guard, look for a hiding place and keep concealed there. I shall go out with my father into the field. There I shall talk with my father about you. I shall report the outcome to you.'

Three times Jonathan says *my father*. So Saul still remains his father. Jonathan doesn't want to let go of David, but he doesn't want to let go of his father either. He continues to treat him with respect, a failed messiah, a man who was once great but who is still his father. And David is his brother.

Jonathan must have been torn apart inside, and it testifies to great gifts of head and heart that he could endure this tension. Soon he will meet death with his father, fighting for a lost cause. Towards David he keeps the word that he spoke when they established their friendship: '*God shall be there between you and me, for ever.*'

Saul and Jonathan went out into the field. Jonathan said: 'Let not the king sin against his servant, David. Has he ever sinned against you? On the contrary, his deeds have only done you good. David risked his life and slew Goliath; he is an instrument of God. He allows the people to breathe in freedom; you have seen it and rejoiced in it. Why should you shed innocent blood and kill David without reason?'

Samuel listened to Jonathan's words and swore that he would not kill David. '*As God lives.*'

And he meant it, Saul really meant it. But just like the throne that was denied him, so too his heart tottered now that the spirit of God had departed from him.

However, Jonathan could report good news to David and David returned to the court. He was again before Saul's face, just like the day before and the day before that.

Again David went out to battle against the Philistines and again he was able to defeat the enemy. Again Saul could not see this victory as other than a defeat for himself, and a savage anger seized him. *Saul sat in his house with his spear in his hand, and David had a harp in his hand and played on the strings.*

Two of the Lord's anointed, and each has something in his hand. Then, suddenly, Saul's spear soars through the air and drives quivering into the wall; David barely manages to avoid it and flees to his house.

Saul immediately sent out soldiers to watch David's house and to kill him at dawn. Michal, *David's wife,* sensed trouble.

She is still divided inwardly, for isn't she also *Saul's daughter?* There are two men in Michal's life, and she loves both of them. But now she must choose: it's a matter of life and death. 'Flee, David, flee now, tomorrow it will be too late. Flee to the prophet Samuel, you will be safe with him.'

Michal lowered David down by a rope through the window; in the darkness of the night she saw him disappear.

'Now to gain time,' thought Michal. 'David has to have gone some distance before the soldiers notice that the bird has flown.' She took the *teraphim,* a divine image, put it in the bed, draped it with a net of goats' hair around the head, and covered it with a cloak.

An old heirloom, that *teraphim,* the divine image with which fertility can be sought. But you can also rescue someone in distress with it and thus serve the God of Israel.

Michal's action is far from being a magical action: at the moment when the newly-wed gives up her desire to be fertile in order to save her husband, she puts the *teraphim* in her bed in place of David. God grant that one day she shall again be able to share this bed with David.

'Open up!' The soldiers bang on the door. 'Open up, we must have David.'

'David? David's sick. Just look.'

In the semi-darkness the soldiers see David lying in bed motionless.

'He's being well looked after,' they say to each other. They return to the palace to tell Saul that his son-in-law has suddenly fallen sick.

Saul is furious. 'Then bring him here, bed and all.'

In a grotesque procession Saul's soldiers carry an empty bed through the streets of the city.

'Why have you deceived me?' exclaims Saul. 'Are you still my daughter?'

Saul has misjudged his daughter; her love for David is stronger than the ties of blood. She is more than her father's daughter, she is her husband's wife. In fear of her life she tells Saul that David had threatened to kill her. Saul asks no more questions. He would rather not know the truth.

*So David has to flee before the tyrant Saul,** and he seeks refuge in Ramah, with Samuel the prophet who anointed him and called him to be king.

Saul came to hear of this and he sent men to take David prisoner. The warriors arrived in Ramah and drew their swords, but to their amazement they met a crowd of dancing prophets, naked men with beards, all in a trance, with Samuel in their midst. And the prophets – they don't even see those soldiers; in a rapture they dance their dance and it isn't long before the seductive song also enwraps Saul's soldiers in ecstasy; they put down their swords and take off their clothes and dance with the prophets, so that they cannot carry out their wicked plan.

The tidings go all round the land, but Saul can't see the funny side of it; he sends a second squad to Ramah. This mission, too, comes under the spell of the prophets, and so too does like a third which Saul calls for. There's nothing for it: if he doesn't want to lose face again, the king himself will have to go to Ramah.

'Where are Samuel and David?' he asks the girls who come to draw water from the well.'

'They're in Ramah, sire.'

Then the spirit of the Lord again moved Saul. He too went to Ramah, he took off his clothes, the cloak of his majesty, he too was in an ecstasy and prophesied before the face of Samuel. David, too, must be there somewhere, hidden and anonymous, but he need fear no danger: the king who was recently filled with hatred is now utterly under the spell of prophecy. The people are amazed: '*Is Saul also among the prophets?*'

So there are two anointed among the prophets. David is there because he sought refuge with the prophet. Saul is there against his will; he was looking for something else.

37

DAVID AND JONATHAN

I SAMUEL 20

David fled from Ramah and sought refuge with Jonathan. 'What have I done, what is my offence, what is my sin against your father, that he seeks to kill me?'

'Far be that from you, David! You certainly shall not die. My father does nothing without telling me; why then should he keep this thing hidden from me? In no way!'

But David couldn't set his mind at rest. 'Your father knows all too well that you are fond of me. Therefore he keeps his plans hidden from you, so as not to cause you sorrow. But as truly as the Lord lives and as truly as you live, there is only one step between me and death.'

'What do you want me to do for you?'

'Tomorrow is the new moon, then I will be expected to sit at table in the palace. But I shall not go. I shall hide in the field, and also the day after. If your father misses me, then say, "David asked me if he might go to Bethlehem, the city of his birth. He wanted to celebrate the annual festival there with his family." If your father says, "That is good," then I know that I am safe. If he bursts out in anger, know then that he wants to carry out his evil plans and be close to me; we have made a covenant before God's face. But if you think that I acted wrongly, then put an end to my life here and now; I would rather that than that you should hand me over to your father.'

'Never! If I am convinced that my father intends evil, then I shall not keep it hidden from you.'

But how far can the son of Saul go in his love for David without having to fear for his own life? David didn't dare to ask Jonathan directly to tell him about Saul: 'If your father is unyielding, who will tell me?'

'Come on, David, let's go outside into the field. There no one can see us.'

They went outside, into the field.

'David, I swear to you by the Lord, the God of Israel, tomorrow or the next day about this time I shall ask my father what he thinks about you. If you need not fear any danger, I shall tell you. If he plans evil against you, I shall also tell you and you will be in a position to make your escape. *In peace you shall go, and God shall be with you, as he was with my father.*'

As he *was* with his father. For the spirit of God has departed from Saul; the spirit of God is now with David, and Jonathan knows and recognizes that. It's as if Jonathan already believes more in David's future than David himself.

Jonathan is essentially concerned with the kingship after God's heart. Jonathan doesn't love David so much because the young man from Bethlehem is so attractive and so handsome, but because he has revealed himself from God as the royal liberator of Israel. Jonathan knows that through David he is involved in this kingship. He doesn't want to be disloyal to Saul, but he will not abandon David, the anointed. Unlike Cain in the field, Jonathan is his brother's keeper. He could have gone the way of nature; he could have followed the law of blood and together with Saul could have killed David to secure the throne for himself. But what he does is in the line of Abraham, the father of believers: he dissociates himself from his father's house. Jonathan chooses. His name means *given by God*.

'*In peace you shall go and God shall be with you, as he was with my father.*'

Will David, once he has become king, in turn let Jonathan go in peace? A new dynasty often exterminates its predecessor. Surely David will not sin here? 'If I am still alive at that time, David, then be gracious to me in your turn, so that I do not die. Show me then God's loving-kindness, to me and my house.'

David swore it to him. And so they renewed their covenant.

'When it is new moon tomorrow, David, then keep hidden in the field, and also the next day. On the third day come to the stone of Azel and sit in its shadow. I shall shoot three arrows in that direction, as though I am aiming at something. I shall tell the boy who is with me to look for the arrows. If I say to the boy, "The arrows are nearby," then appear, for as the Lord lives, you are safe. But if I call to the boy, "The arrows are further away," then go, for then the Lord wants you to make your escape. The Lord keep us together, David, you and me, for ever.'

David hid in the field.

The new moon rose, the king was sitting at table. He sat where he always sat, by the wall, the wall to which he would have pinned David had the young man not leaped away in time. Jonathan too was sitting there. David's place remained empty. Saul saw this but kept silent. 'David must be unclean.' That can happen for once, can't it?

But not a second time. When the day after the new moon David's place again remained empty, Saul asked Jonathan: 'Why wasn't Jesse's son here yesterday and why isn't he here today?'

Jesse's son, says Saul. He wouldn't speak David's name.

'David urgently asked me if he might go to Bethlehem to celebrate the sacrifice there with his family. He said, let me escape to see my brothers.'

'Escape! Is Jonathan so torn that he's made a slip of the tongue, or does he want to indicate on whose side he stands? Saul immediately sees what's going on and breaks out in a fury. First Michal has been helpful to David in his flight, and now Jonathan has also helped David to escape. He looks high-born, prince Jonathan, but in Saul's eyes he's a degenerate son who denies his origin and puts his future at risk. 'As if I didn't already think that you've opted for this son of Jesse, to your shame and to the shame of the nakedness of your mother.'

Saul cannot say more crudely that Jonathan is destroying the dynasty. 'This much is certain, Jonathan, as long as Jesse's son is walking around on earth there is no longer a place for you, and the kingship will also pass by you!'

Saul gave orders to arrest David; the son of Jesse will not escape. 'He is a son of death.'

'Father, why do you seek David's life? What wrong has he done you?'

Saul was no longer open to reason. He seized his spear, his constant companion, and threw it at his son. So much has Jonathan become David's brother that he too must fear for his life.

Deeply shaken, Jonathan left the room. It was the second day of the new moon. That day he ate nothing, broken-hearted about David, from whom he must now part.

The next morning, when it was still early, he went out into the field to meet David; he took a small boy with him. 'Run, look for the arrow that I shoot.' The young boy ran and Jonathan shot an arrow beyond him. When the boy had reached roughly the place where the arrow had landed, Jonathan called, 'The arrow is further away. Quickly, go on. Don't stop.'

The boy picked up the arrow and came running quickly back. He knew nothing. Only David and Jonathan knew.

But did they have to say farewell like this, the sworn friends, without seeing each other just once more face to face?

'Go back to the city, my boy, and take my arrow and bow with you. Go on ahead.'

David appeared from the shadow of the stone of Azel and knelt three times before Jonathan. Saul may regard his son as a traitor; David continues to see him as the son of the anointed. He bowed to him. They kissed each other. They wept.

'Go in peace, David. Have we not sworn before God's face to be faithful to each other? May the Lord keep us together, you and me, your seed and my seed, for ever.'

So once again they swore to be faithful to each other. They felt that life might very well drive them apart unless a greater force held them together. 'May the Eternal One stand by us.'

David disappeared.

Jonathan returned to the city.

38

THE TRICKS OF A MESSIAH

I SAMUEL 21 AND 22

David has to flee before the tyrant Saul. The foxes have holes, the birds of
the air have nests, but this anointed, this messiah, has no rest. In solitude
he goes through the hill-country. Instead of going to Bethlehem, *the house
of bread,* he is on his way to another house where bread must be, the house
of God in Nob. Starving, he knocks on the door of the priest Ahimelech
on a sabbath; the priest comes to greet him trembling. What leads a man
like David to travel all alone to Nob? Does his coming mean disaster?
'Have you come alone, unaccompanied by anyone?'

'The king has given me a special task,' lies David. 'My mission is strictly
confidential, you'll understand. I've sent my men to a secret place. Have
you something to eat? Give me five loaves, or whatever is there.'

'I have no ordinary bread, but there is the sacred bread. Provided that
your men have abstained from women.'

'Yes, we have, we're engaged in a holy battle.'

It's the sabbath, the day on which the priests replace the twelve show-
bread in the temple with fresh bread. Only the priests may eat of that holy
bread, that is the Law of Moses. So won't the bread be desecrated in the
hand of David?

Necessity knows no law, Ahimelech must have thought. And we who
know what Ahimelech did not know, that it was the Lord's anointed who
had knocked on the door of the temple here, know that in giving these five
loaves Ahimelech is acting in the spirit of the Torah and is doing right by
the deepest concern of the five books of Moses. You must be able to play
with the holy things, otherwise they become rigid.

Ahimelech gave the hungry David the sacred bread. Thus the anointed
could complete his holy task, his secret mission, as he had claimed falsely
in speaking the truth.

However, one of Saul's servants witnessed this, a certain Doeg from

Edom, Saul's chief herdsman. Is he as well disposed to David as Ahimelech, and will he know to keep silent?

David said to Ahimelech: 'Have you any weapons here, a spear or a sword? I couldn't take anything with me, so urgent was the task that the king gave me.'

'The sword of Goliath is here, the Philistine whom you slew in the Valley of the Oaks. Look, here it is, wrapped in a cloth behind the ephod.'

So from behind the priestly garment appears the trophy which David had once carried in triumph. 'You may take it,' said Ahimelech, 'it is the only weapon that I possess.'

'There is nothing like it,' said David. 'I'm most indebted to you.'

Is this the same David who exclaimed in the Valley of the Oaks that the Lord doesn't liberate by spear and sword? Surely he isn't going to raise the sword against Saul?

David flees further, beyond the frontier of the land. He hopes to be safe on foreign soil, in Gath, in the land of the Philistines, where Achish is king. But David is soon recognized. *'Is that not David, the king of Israel?'* ask the servants of Achish in amazement.

They're making a mistake. David isn't yet the king of the land. At the same time these uncircumcised Philistines are prophesying, for what will David soon be, if not Israel's king?

'Isn't that David? Isn't he the one about whom the women over there were singing in a choral dance, *"Saul has slain his thousands, David his ten thousands?"*.'

David hears it and terror strikes his heart. Perhaps king Achish will want to kill him. Or will he want to take him – a skilled warrior – into his army and compel him to fight against Saul, God's anointed? David doesn't know which is worse.

'I'll act crazy,' David thinks, and as in a fit of insanity he scrabbles with his nails on the doorposts of the gate, while he lets his spittle drip into his beard: a pitiful, slobbering man, possessed by evil demons. What must the people of Gath think of him? 'Haven't I enough fools?' exclaims king Achish.

In the distance you can hear them laughing in Israel, for here Achish is really telling a precious joke. The king is right, indeed they have no lack of fools in the land of the Philistines. Fools enough there.

What will the people in Gath do with David? They do what people often do with fools: they throw him out. Go away! And of course that's precisely what David intended. David's isn't stupid.

But in the eyes of paganism Israel's messiah is a fool, and so it will remain from generation to generation.

The flight went on. David looked for a hiding place in the cave of Adullam. His father and mother and his brothers joined him; clearly their lives too were in danger. And not only they, but all kinds of people pursued by creditors or in other trouble, the bitter, beggars and adventurers, sought refuge with David. And David became their leader, a redeemer for all these outcast of the earth.

Saul meanwhile grew more and more alienated from people and from God. He sat in the high place of Gibeah, in the shadow of a tamarisk, spear in hand, armed men around him. 'Listen to me, you Benjaminites. Do you really think that this son of Jesse will give you fields and vineyards, wealth and prosperity? Will he appoint you chiefs over hundreds and thousands of men? Why are you all conspiring against me? Why has no one told me that my son has made a covenant with the son of Jesse? None of you is cares about me, no one has come to tell me that my son has stirred up my servant to take up the sword against me.'

There was silence. A sorry figure, a prince entangled in mistrust, sick of God, sick of himself, sick of his son and of David. A king in his stronghold, still surrounded by his men, but lonelier than anyone else in his kingdom. There was silence. Why does no one say anything? Is there no one who will speak up for him?

There is one. Doeg, the man from Edom, Saul's chief herdsman. 'Your majesty, I have seen the son of Jesse arriving in Nob, at the house of the priest Ahimelech. Ahimelech prayed to God for him; he gave him bread and in addition the sword of Goliath.'

Ahimelech is summoned and all the priests of Nob with him. 'Why are you conspiring against me? Why did you give bread and a sword to Jesse's son, and why did you pray to God for the man who is lying in wait for me?'

'None of your servants is as loyal as David, sire, your own son-in-law, a prominent member of your bodyguard, honoured throughout your house. That sabbath day was truly not the first time that I prayed for him. That he is lying in wait for you is news to me; it has never come to my ears.'

Ahimelech pleads in a dignified way for himself and his people, but Saul is no longer open to reason. He neglected to wipe out under heaven the memory of Amalek, godlessness incarnate, but he did away with the priest Ahimelech, a guardian of God's holy Torah. 'You must die, Ahimelech, you and your father's house and all the priests who are with you.'

The sentence is quickly passed but not quickly carried out, for who must execute it? *The servants of the king did not want to stretch out their hands to kill the priests of the Lord.*

Saul has become a stranger in his own land. Is there then not one servant to be found to stand by his side and carry out the sentence?

There is one. Doeg, the man from Edom. His name means *the cautious one*; he is cautious in carefully observing the rules, even at the cost of humanity. An order is an order, and Doeg kills the priests with his own hands, with the edge of his sword, eighty-five men. The numerical value of the Hebrew word for priests is eighty-five.

One priest, Abiathar, son of Ahimelech, managed to escape the massacre and fled to David, who had pity on him. 'It is my fault that your father died. Remain with me and do not fear. Here you are safe.'

39

A TEMPTATION IN THE WILDERNESS

I SAMUEL 24

David and his men went on further, into the hill-country of Engedi. He is a stranger in his own land, hiding in the inhospitable regions of the wilderness where the ibex are and where a person can only survive with great difficulty. For how long?

David's life is played out in the long period of waiting between the anointing and the coronation, between the promise and the fulfilment. But there is nothing that indicates that this promise will be fulfilled, for the months go by and Saul will not give in. He pursues David wherever he goes.

The king's spies have reported that David and his men are in Engedi, opposite the Ibex Rock, and Saul goes up with around three thousand men. Will a final battle now be fought between these two anointed, the rejected and the chosen? Where will they meet one another, at what place?

At 'a certain place', the place where even kings and emperors go on foot. David and his men have hidden at the back of a cave and at that precise place Saul appears, *to cover his feet,* as the King James Version puts it so tactfully. Rembrandt has drawn the scene with much humour: a guard discreetly looks the other way, Saul is squatting to relieve himself, holding the hem of his mantle back with one hand so as not to soil it; from the darkness of the cave David creeps closer with a knife in his hand.

This is a chance in a thousand, a gift from heaven. For of course this can't be chance, David's soldiers also immediately notice that: this must be divine providence. '*This is the day,*' they whisper, '*this is the day when the Lord God says to you: See, I give your enemy into your hands, do with him what is good in your eyes.*'

In the time of the judges, we are told, everyone did *what was good in his eyes, for there was no king in those days.* Now there is indeed such an anointed, there is David, king to be. What will he do?'

'David, this is your chance. God is well-disposed towards you.'

It sounds pious, but is it? A person cannot be careful enough about saying that God is on his side. *You shall not take the name of the Lord your God in vain.* 'God is smiling on you, David.' Those are pious words, but it is not for nothing that here the story-teller puts those words in the mouth of bandits.

Then aren't the bandits right? Doesn't everything suggest that at this point David should rapidly put an end to Saul's era? He has already been pursued so long by this maniac; is it now too bold to see the finger of God in this event? Isn't this *the* moment to remove for ever the king who has removed himself to answer nature's call? The murder of the eighty-five priests cries out for vengeance, and such an opportunity won't occur again. The king isn't exactly in a position to run off immediately. Surely Saul is the rejected one and David the chosen one? This must be a gentle hint from above to settle things below. Of course it's one or other: if David doesn't strike, Saul will, for Saul isn't wandering around with a botanical case, and attack is still the best form of defence.

Yes, if you're going to argue. Perhaps it was indeed a blessing that David had no time to argue. He had to take his decision in a flash, and in that flash he proved himself to be a man of God.

David crept up, knife in hand, and without a sound he cut off a piece of Saul's cloak. The men looked on in bewilderment. Why in God's name not strike?

Precisely for that reason, for God's name. *'May the Lord protect me from stretching out my hand against the Lord's anointed.'* Saying this, David held his men back and was able to prevent them doing evil to Saul.

Saul got up, left the cave and went his way. Some moments later David also left the cave and called out to him: 'Your majesty!'

Saul looked round. David knelt down and bowed before his ruler. 'Why do you believe what people say: Look out for David, he means evil against you? Today you see with your own eyes that the Lord gave you into my hand. They said that I should kill you, but I have spared you. I will not lay hands on God's anointed. *Look, my father, see a piece of your cloak in my hand.* I only cut off the skirt of your coat, I did not kill you. So be convinced that I mean no evil or rebellion against you, and that I have done no wrong to you. However, you seek my life, you the king of Israel. Who are you really pursuing? A dead dog. A single flea, no more. May the Eternal One be our judge and judge between you and me. May he decide my cause.'

'Look, my father.' David can't kill Saul; he is the father of Jonathan, his friend, his brother, he is the Lord's anointed. By calling Saul father, David is also appealing to him to behave like a father.

At the same time, however, what David does isn't so innocent. He has not just taken a piece of material; he has cut off the hem of Saul's royal cloak, and this can only remind Saul of the painful incident that time with the old prophet Samuel: *'So shall the kingdom be torn from you.'*

By sparing Saul, David is lengthening the difficult way to his destiny. That's messianic, not of this world, so David's companions understand nothing of this. But Israel later called David a man after God's heart. A man who for years and years looks to the kingship and who, when it lies before him, can say, 'I will not steal it.'

Saul wept.

He wept for God and for David. He wept because his life was a failure and could only end in defeat. He dreamed of being a father to his children and being remembered as a good and righteous ruler, but he has failed as ruler and as father. Saul wept.

'Is that your voice, my son David?'

'Let it be again with us as it was before, David, that I am a father to you and you are a son to me. You are a righteous man, I am not. You did me good, whereas I have done you evil. Today the Eternal One gave me into your hand but you did not kill me. May the Lord reward you, David, for the good that you showed me. See, I know very well that you will rule as king over Israel and that your kingdom will endure. Then be gracious to me, me and my house.'

David promised him that.

40

NABAL AND ABIGAIL

I SAMUEL 25

The prophet Samuel has died.

All Israel gathered and mourned over him and buried him in his house in Ramah.

All Israel. Except for David, for despite all the fine promises Saul renewed his crusade against him and it was better for David not to show himself in the inhabited world. *David went down to the wilderness of Paran.*

How did Samuel die? Did David meet him once more before he died, and did Samuel say something, a word of comfort for the anointed who now had to go on alone? Not that they saw much of each other, but the mere thought that Samuel was there did David good. What did Samuel's death do to him?

David went down to Paran. Is David 'down', now that Samuel is no longer there? Then one may hope that the Eternal One will send someone on his way to stop this descent.

David sets up his tents in Paran, in the hill-country where shepherds pasture the three thousand sheep and a thousand goats of a rich shepherd ruler. David and his men plunge into being shepherds of these shepherds; as a kind of ranger David protects them against all kinds of riff-raff that are going about. But at the moment when our story takes place, we don't find those shepherds in the hills; they've driven their flocks together and have gone down into the valley; the sheep have to be shorn. Then the annual sheep-shearing festival will be celebrated; no shepherd will miss that.

And David, where is David? There is no place for him in the inn of happiness. Scraps of music come to him in the hill-country; over there in the valley will be the girls, there will be drinking and dancing. And they've every reason to feast abundantly; there will be a surplus of wool and mutton. The great sheep farmer would prefer to forget that the size of the harvest is due to David's protection. David and his men aren't invited. *He was called Nabal, and his wife was called Abigail. The woman was of good understanding and beautiful, the man was churlish and ill-behaved. He was a real Calebite.*

David has proved to be a protector of Nabal and has made a powerful contribution to the tranquillity and prosperity in this territory, and an appropriate reward is justified in every way. He sends ten servants to receive this. It's the festival, and they hope that Nabal will be in a good mood. 'Ask him in my name about his prosperity. Say: *Peace be with you. Peace be with your family. Peace be with all your sheep.* Don't be put off by that man, see that you return with a good reward.'

The men go to Nabal. 'Peace be with you, peace be with your family, peace be with all your flocks, from David, the son of Jesse, whose servants we are. Your shepherds were with us in the hill country. We did not hinder them in any way; on the contrary, we protected them and their possessions against robbers. Not a single lamb was lost, you can investigate yourself. Now, Lord Nabal, let us share in the joy and give us what your heart inspires you.'

'David, who may that be? I have never heard of a son of Jesse. Nowadays there are so many servants running away from their masters. Must I share *my* bread and *my* water and *my* cattle with a fellow I do not know at all?'

You can hear him saying this. Words of a rich capitalist of around three thousand years ago, but the mentality is that of all times and all places.

David's servants return with empty hands. '"David, who is David?" that skinflint said; he refused to give us anything.'

David went pale. Formerly he hadn't been so quick to take offence, but now everything was different. Samuel is dead, the man of God who had witnessed his call and had anointed him king. For David the great loneliness has begun and there's no longer anyone behind him. For David it's as if a bit of Samuel has died with him; he's no longer himself. 'David, who is David?' Good question. Nabal's words strike deep into his heart. He will show this man who he is!

Nabal. His name means *fool.* Mr Fool. In Israel this means that you're away from God. *The fool says in his heart, there is no God.** A fool is someone who cares neither for God nor for his commandments. Everything turns on *his* bread, *his* water, *his* sacrificial animals. He says that these days servants run away from their masters, but he too is a runaway servant: 'Peace be with you.' However, Nabal will know no peace and refuses to share the good gifts from God that he has received.

No peace? Then the sword. *'Let every man gird on his sword!'* Then every man girded on his sword. David too girded on his sword.

David went up. 'The Calebite has recompensed me good with evil. They are dogs, *pissers against the wall;* I shall teach them a lesson, not one of them shall live to tell the tale.'

What did the young David once say to Goliath: *'You come up against me with the sword, but I come up against you in the name of the Lord of hosts.'* Now it seems as if he's lost sight of the Lord of hosts. And the language of the Lords' anointed could be more subtle. Is David threatening to become like Saul, a man who is guided by anger and feelings of revenge?

One of Nabal's servants rushes to Abigail. What he doesn't dare to say to Nabal he tells Nabal's wife. 'The men of David were good to us, they were like a wall around us, all the days and all the nights that we were pasturing the sheep there. And your husband is insulting them. Now they're on their way to wreak bloody vengeance. You alone, Abigail, can bring salvation; it's impossible to talk to your husband.'

Abigail, *father's joy.* So she's the opposite of the foolish Nabal, who is so full of himself and who only causes the Father sorrow. Abigail acts quickly. She takes two hundred loaves, two jars of wine, five prepared sheep, five measures of roasted grain, a hundred clusters of raisins and two hundred bunches of figs, and travels to meet David. David and his men are to get their reward for what they had done. *She said nothing to Nabal.*

No, we'd already understood that clearly, this isn't a very happy couple. Mr Foolish and Lady Wisdom, they don't go together easily. By now we also understand that the story-teller is telling us not so much a history as a parable.

Abigail, seated on her ass, went down through a gully and look, David and his men were coming down towards her. She rapidly sprang off her ass, prostrated herself before David, bowed to the earth and said: 'On *me* rests the guilt, on *me.* Let your handmaid speak before your ears, listen to the words of your handmaid. Pay no heed to Nabal, that unreasonable man. His name says it all: he is a fool.'

By throwing herself at David's feet, Abigail has stopped his angry progress. With wisdom, tact and grace she then reminds him of his descent and his destiny. *'May the Lord preserve you from blood-guilt, may no evil be found in you; you will soon be king of Israel!'*

Samuel is dead, but that doesn't mean that prophecy is also dead in

Israel. Thank God, *Father's joy* is there, Abigail, the woman who sees that David is being tempted and who protects him from falling, a woman who believes in him and reminds him of his vocation. And a vocation never comes out of thin air; a vocation is always mediated through human beings. However, the one who is called himself experiences it as a gift from heaven. That is also precisely what David replies to Abigail in a threefold blessing: *'Blessed be the Lord, the God of Israel, who sent you on my way this day; blessed is your wisdom, and blessed are you who protected me from blood-guilt. Go hence in peace.'*

Thank God for the *blessed* Abigail. The *sword* remains in the sheath and so this story can end in *peace*.

Not, however, completely in peace, for things turn out badly for Nabal. When Abigail returned home, Nabal was holding a drinking bout *like the drinking bout of a king;* the man was blind drunk. Abigail said nothing to him. Only the next morning did she tell him what had happened. Nabal was frightened to death. No, that isn't completely true; Nabal had a heart attack, *his heart died within him, he became like a stone.* Nabal lived another ten days, then it was all up with him. *The Lord struck him so that he died.*

Not long after that David married Abigail. She is to take Michal's place, for father Saul has taken Michal from David and given her to one Palti. Abigail becomes David's wife. A piece of luck. Who better can a king have beside him than a wise queen, a prophetess, who is beautiful into the bargain? So after Samuel's death the inner bond between kingship and prophecy in Israel is maintained.

41

THE WOMAN OF ENDOR

I SAMUEL 28

Does king Saul also have an Abigail, now that Samuel is no longer there?

The lonely Saul no longer has anything or anyone; he cannot expect any salvation from anyone in the realm of the living. What if he were to turn to the realm of the dead? Shall he seek refuge with a woman who can cause the spirits of the dead to appear?

But that's forbidden in Israel. So at one time Saul zealously ordered all soothsaying and occult arts to be banished. Was he also moved by the temptation – then already, deep in his heart – to trust not only in the God of Israel but also in astrology and other pagan practices?

But now Saul is at the end of his strength and also probably at the end of his kingship and his life, for the Philistines have massed their armies and are preparing to inflict a devastating defeat on Israel. Moreover Saul is afraid that David and his men have joined the enemy camp. In his despair he calls on God. *But the Lord did not answer him, either in his dreams or in oracles or through the prophets.*

Is God silent because Saul will not listen? David can listen and therefore hears everything. He hears from Abigail what will happen *if he does not turn* from his disastrous way. He listens to the voice of God. Saul will not hear of a conversion; he has no ears to hear nor eyes to see, and therefore his dreams don't reveal anything to him. The oracles of the priests bring no help, nor does the good advice of his wise men. *The Lord did not answer him.* Saul begs and prays, but the Eternal One keeps silent, and then Saul can't understand this telling silence.

At the end of his tether, Saul wants to consult a necromancer, a member of the dark guild that he once sought to exterminate root and branch. 'Find me a woman who can conjure up the spirits of the dead.'

'There is such a woman in Endor, sire.'

Saul disguises himself, and accompanied by two of his servants he knocks at the door of the woman of Endor at dead of night. 'I want you to prophesy to me through the spirit of a dead man, to make the man whose name I shall give you come up from the realm of the dead.'

'Sire, surely you know that that is forbidden? Has not king Saul exterminated all the necromancers in the land? Why are you laying a trap for me? Do you desire my death?'

The nocturnal visitor swears to the woman by the God of Israel that she will never be blamed for anything. He says it with as much assurance as if he were Saul himself and as if he knows of Israel's God.

'Who do you want me to bring up for you, sire?'

'Bring up Samuel to me.'

Why does Saul want the spirit of Samuel to appear to him? Does he hope that where the prophets of the day have left him in the lurch, the man of God from of old will free him of his fear and will recant this prophecy of disaster? Does Saul want Samuel to give him posthumously the comfort that he withheld from him in his life? Will Saul still let himself be told something by the prophet? Or does he want to compel the God of Israel to speak by making his servant rise from the grave? 'Let Samuel come.'

In the spirit the woman of Endor sees Samuel looming up from the darkness of the realm of the dead, and as soon as she sees the prophet, she also sees who it is who has come to her like a thief in the night: Saul himself! She cries out in dismay, 'Why have you deceived me? You are Saul!'

'Do not fear, rather tell me what you see.'

'I see a man... I see an old man... he's coming closer... he's wrapped in a cloak.'

Saul understands that it's Samuel and prostrates himself with his face to the ground. Samuel doesn't seem happy with this reunion. 'Why have you disturbed my rest?'

'I am in distress. The Philistines are going into battle against me and God has departed from me. He no longer gives an answer either through dreams or through the mouth of the prophets. I beseech you, tell me what I must do.'

However, the dead Samuel is as relentless as he was in his lifetime. Saul mustn't think that he can drive a wedge between God and his servant. Nor has God forgotten that Saul at one time neglected to put an end to Amalek and thus exterminate the memory of Amalek for ever. God is now making short shrift of him. Instead of making the anointed of the Lord God visible on earth, Saul has obscured the sight of the Eternal One. No wonder that God has departed from him. Why then does he go to ask questions of Samuel? *'The Lord has done as he said through my mouth. He has torn the kingship from your hand and he has given it to your companion, to David. The Lord will give you and Israel with you into the hand of the Philistines. Tomorrow you and your sons shall be with me.'*

How cold it is this night! Is there then no one who has any compassion on Saul? Must we imagine Israel's God to be as relentless as the spirit of Samuel? Is there nowhere a minstrel of God who can play something for this wretched man on the harp of faith? Indeed, who is speaking here? God? Samuel? Has this seer read in the king's eyes what is haunting him in his soul? Saul hasn't heard anything new this night in Endor.

'Tomorrow you and your sons shall be with me.'

Saul fell full length to the earth, terrified by Samuel's words. There was no more strength in him; he had eaten no bread all that day nor in the night.

Then this woman of Endor had pity on her fallen ruler. 'I have listened to *you*, now listen to *me*: let your servant give you a bite of bread, so that you regain your strength. You cannot go from here like that.'

Saul refused, but the woman and Saul's two companions insisted, and finally he agreed. He revived and lay down to rest.

The woman gave him more than a bite of bread. She hastened to kill the fatted calf for this lost son of Israel. She also took flour and kneaded it and made unleavened bread of it. Saul's last supper. Tomorrow he will go out to battle with his sons, and none of them will see the evening.

In this hour, in which God is silent and Samuel speaks only of defeat, it is the woman of Endor who has compassion on her tormented king before he disappears into the darkness of the night, to meet the Philistines.

42

AGAINST AMALEK

I SAMUEL 29 AND 30

In order to escape Saul's grasp David had again sought refuge in the land of the Philistines, with Achish, king of Gath. Fortunately this time he doesn't have to behave as a *meshuggah* to get away again,* he's even acquired a position: he may remain as a minor ruler in Ziklag, from where he undertakes forays against tribes which threaten his own Judah from there. So he makes the close acquaintance of Philistine war-making, knowledge which will later prove useful to him; as a well-behaved warrior he always gives the booty to Achish, making the king believe that he has been fighting against his own Judah. Achish indicates that from now on David shall be a Philistine with the Philistines. Hasn't he made his name *stinking* in his own land?*

But when the Philistines gather in Aphek to go out from there against Israel, the leaders of the army are mistrustful. Who will guarantee that David and his men won't suddenly go over to the enemy? 'What are those Hebrews doing here?'

'Waging war with us,' says Achish, thus putting David in an awkward position. 'This man has been here all the time, I have never heard anything suspicious about him.'

'David, sire? Didn't the women of Israel sing the song about him that Saul slew his thousands and David his ten thousands? And you want to go out to battle against Saul with this David? Far be that from you!'

Achish summons David. 'I know that you are an honourable man, and if it were up to me you could happily come with us. However, the city rulers have insuperable objections to that. I fear that I have to ask you to remain in Ziklag.'

'What then have I done?' says David, offended, carefully hiding his relief that he will not have to fight against Saul. 'Have you something to say against me?'

Again Achish describes David's services, the story-teller can't make too much of them. 'You are a good man in my eyes, an angel of God.'

Just think, an angel of God in the king's eyes!. Those are the eyes that David has thrown sand in. But it's as if God is protecting his anointed. The irony of this story is that David is protected from treachery by the arch-enemy of his people.

David and his men return to Ziklag, but to their dismay they find only the smoking ruins of what once was Ziklag. During their absence Amalek has attacked the city, carried off women and children as prisoners, and set the city on fire. David's two wives, Ahinoam and Abigail, have also been carried off. David and the warriors who accompanied him raise their voices and weep until they can weep no more. Amalek, always Amalek! And always the defenceless, the women and children, are their prey. Why *did* Saul neglect to wipe out for ever the memory of these monsters under heaven?

David is near to despair, and is even more upset when the people vent their wrath and sorrow on him and even want to stone him. *David was in great distress*, just as at the same moment Saul was in great distress when he sought his salvation with the woman in Endor. To whom shall David turn? Does he too seek help in the realm of the dead?

'Lord, shall I pursue this gang? Shall I catch them up?'

'Pursue them, David, you will surely catch them up and free the prisoners.'

So David strengthened himself in the Lord his God.

With the six hundred men who were with him, David set off in pursuit, until he came to the brook Besor. There two hundred men had been left behind with the baggage, too worn out to go on, too weary and too exhausted by the brute force of the enemy and the loss of their loved ones and their city. David continued the pursuit with four hundred men.

On the way they found an Egyptian, more dead than alive, who had clearly been abandoned by the Amalekites in the wilderness. That is what Amalekites do with a sick slave, they leave him like old rubbish, to die by the wayside. The men brought the youth to David and, of course, out of self-interest gave him bread and water, a bunch of figs and a few raisins; the youth hadn't eaten or drunk for three days and nights. And look, the spirit of life returned in him.

'Whose property are you and where do you come from?'

'I am a young man from Egypt, sir, servant of an Amalekite. My master left me here because I fell sick three days ago. We made an attack on the land of the south, where we burned Ziklag to the ground.'

'Are you ready to show us the way to this gang?'

'That I will do, if you swear to me by God that you will not kill me and that you will not hand me over to my master.'

The young man showed David and his men the way, and look, there lay the Amalekites, spread out in the field: they were eating and drinking and feasting, enjoying the booty that had fallen to them in the land of the south. David didn't hesitate for a moment; he struck immediately and massacred them from the dawn to the evening of the following day. None of them escaped, apart from four hundred men who had fled on their camels. David rescued all that the Amalekites had plundered; his two wives were unharmed. They missed absolutely nothing, neither sons nor daughters nor any share of the booty; David took everything back.

So David completed the work that initially Saul had been commissioned to do. Where Saul failed, he succeeded. And isn't the anointed of God who resists Amalek to the face *the* man to be king over Israel?

The warriors returned to the brook Besor, where they had left behind the two hundred men who were too weary to go on fighting.

'How is it with you?' asked David.

You would expect that first, those who had been left behind would ask the warriors how things had gone with them. But David reversed the roles. Wasn't he himself once someone who didn't count, an afterthought who was left behind while his big brothers went out fighting? 'How is it with you?'

The men who had accompanied David smelt trouble. That is, the bad ones among them, the villains. Surely David wouldn't also let those who had been left behind share in the booty? 'They didn't go with us, so they needn't receive anything. Who plucked the chestnuts out of the fire? Give them back their wives and children, but leave it at that!'

'You shall not do this, my brothers,' said David. 'You shall not act like this with what the Lord has given us, for he has preserved us and given into our power the gang that fell on us. The share of those who remained with the baggage shall be the same as the share of those who went to battle. We shall share fairly.'

So speaks an anointed of God. He doesn't stand up only for the strong, but equally for the weak. He secures justice for those who are weary and oppressed. And in order constantly to protect the weak against the strong, David has his words set down in a law. *So it has been from that day on: David made a regulation, a rule for Israel, to the present day.*

In the kingdom of Amalek the strong rule over the weak. In the kingdom of God the workers at the eleventh hour receive the same recompense as the workers from the first hour.*

43

HOW ARE THE HEROES FALLEN

I SAMUEL 31; II SAMUEL 1

While David was fighting and conquering Amalek, Saul went up against the Philistines. Saul, the man who should have wiped out the memory of Amalek from under heaven and have freed Israel from the hand of the Philistines. He lost.

The Philistines overtook Saul and his sons and they slew Saul's sons, Jonathan, Abinadab and Malcishua. Saul too was in trouble; the archers kept shooting at him. Fatally wounded, he asked his armour-bearer, 'Draw your sword and run me through with it, so that these uncircumcised ones do not have the satisfaction of killing me.' But even Saul's last wish was not to be fulfilled; his armour-bearer was afraid to lift his hand against the anointed. Then Saul himself took his sword and fell on it. The armour-bearer, seeing that Saul was dead, wanted to die with him and also fell on his sword. *So on that day Saul died, his three sons, his armour-bearer and all his men.*

When the Philistines came to plunder the bodies the following morning they found Saul and his sons, lying on the hills of Gilboa. They cut Saul's head off, plundered his armour and sent messengers to report the victory in the temples of their gods and to the people. They put Saul's armour in the temple of Astarte, and hung his body on the city wall of Beth-shean.

The inhabitants of Jabesh in Gilead heard what the Philistines had done to Saul and were utterly dismayed. Once Saul had been their benefactor. When their city had fallen into the hands of Nahash, king *Snake,* and no one else had cared for them, Saul had come to liberate them. When Saul's star was rising, he risked his life for them. Now that his star was quenched, they were to risk their lives for him. Saul may have fallen, but he had fallen while he was trying to defend his people as king, and he deserved an honourable grave.

In the darkness the men of Jabesh left their city and went to Beth-shean.

They travelled all night, right through the enemy lines. The body of the man whom they knew as a true king would not hang in shame; the uncircumcised and the vultures would be kept away from Saul. While the Philistines were celebrating their victory drunk in the city, the men of Jabesh took the dead bodies of Saul and his sons secretly from the wall and bore them to their city.

There, contrary to Israel's custom, they burned the bodies. Let holy fire cleanse them from the unclean, polluting hand of paganism. They buried their bones under the tamarisk, Jabesh's holy tree. Saul didn't perish without a name. He may have been a failed messiah, but he was a messiah.

> *Deep in my heart the madness burns unceasing;*
> *In royal mantle wrapped I lie there, shy.*
> *But in the silence of my inner chamber,*
> *I strike myself upon the face and cry.*
>
> *When I am dead, my enemies approach.*
> *They mock me, naked, laughing at the sight!*
> *Come then and save me from the wall of scandal,*
> *you men of Jabesh, come then through the night.*
>
> *Then let me perish in a scarlet flame,*
> *which purging cleanses me of shame gone by.*
> *My blazing colour lights the distant air,*
> *a purple cloak my image in the sky.**

Meanwhile David had returned from his mission against Amalek in Ziklag. A man from Saul's army came up to him with garments torn and earth on his head as a sign of mourning. 'Where have you come from?'

'From the army of Israel, sire. I escaped.'

'What happened? Tell me.'

'The people were driven to flight, sire, many of our men died. Saul and Jonathan his son also died.'

'How do you know that Saul is dead, and Jonathan, his son?'

'By chance I was on the hills of Gilboa, sire. Saul leant tottering on his spear, chariots and riders pressed him hard. He looked up, saw me standing there and called to me. "Who are you?," he asked. I said, "I am an Amalekite." "Come up to me," he said, "and kill me, a dizziness has seized me." Then I went up to him and killed him. Once fallen he would not have survived the battle. Then I took the crown that was on his head and I also took his armlet. See, I have brought them for you, my lord.'

David rent his garments and so did all those who were with him. They fasted and wept until evening, for Saul and Jonathan his son, and for the people of Israel, fallen by the sword.

It was as if only then did it dawn on David just who had brought him the bad news about Saul and Jonathan: an Amalekite, who in true Amalekite style thought that he would delight David with the news that his sworn enemy was dead. David understood that it wasn't this foreigner who had given Saul the *coup de grâce*. This must be a plunderer, who had found the king's body before the Philistines and who now hoped for a big reward. 'Weren't you afraid to raise your hand against God's anointed?'

David gave orders for the man to be killed.

Then David sang his lament over Saul and over Jonathan. *How are the heroes fallen.* Of course government had to go on, important decisions had to be taken, the army had to be re-formed, a divided land had to be united. David still had a long way to go before he could call himself king of Israel, but first there had to be mourning. Sorrow that isn't past begins to haunt the soul of a person and the soul of a people.

How are the mighty fallen. David goes before the people in his lament; lamenting he expresses their pain, then they all join in.

> *Your glory, O Israel,*
> *has been pierced through on your heights.*
> *How are the heroes fallen!*

Heroes, in the plural. For not only is Jonathan a hero for David; Saul too is an adornment for Israel. So David sang for the bold fighter that Saul also was, Israel's first king. And he sang for Jonathan, his friend.

> *I am distressed for you, my brother Jonathan,*
> *I loved you so,*
> *your love was more wonderful to me*
> *than the love of women.*

> *How are the heroes fallen,*
> *and the weapons of war perished.*

44

IN HEBRON

II SAMUEL 2, 3 AND 4

Saul is dead, but that doesn't mean that David is yet king. The kingship may have been given to him by God, but he still has to attain it. And he will attain it only if he remains in constant conversation with the good Giver.

Saul is dead. *After this David asked the Lord: 'Shall I go up to one of the cities of Judah?'*

The Lord replied, 'Go up.'

'Where shall I go?'

'To Hebron.'

In Hebron the patriarchs Abraham, Isaac and Jacob lie buried. There, in the heart of Judah, the first nomads of the faith had found their last resting place. Now in Hebron David is anointed king over the house of Judah. He will live there seven years before he is called to be king over all the kingdom.

The first report that reached David after his arrival in Hebron was that the men of Jabesh had buried the remains of Saul. David sent messengers to them: *'Blessed are you by the Lord, who did this deed of loving-kindness to your lord, to Saul, to whom you have given a grave.'*

Words of tact and gratitude. The men of Jabesh are of the Lord, full of blessing. David would also like to be king of such men, so devoted to their leader. *'May the Lord show loving-kindness and faithfulness to you.'* Saul can no longer do that, but perhaps David can. *'I too want to do good to you, in the same way that you did.'* The Lord goes before, David follows.

'But now, let your hands be strong, be brave. For although Saul, your lord, is dead, I too am anointed to be king over the house of Judah.'

David knows his place: first the Lord, then Saul, finally also him. His first word as king in Hebron bears witness to reverence for the Eternal One and for the anointed one who has gone before him.

However, the seven years that David spent in Hebron do not form an impressive beginning to his kingship; it's as if he is more ruled than ruler. Joab and Abner do the work: Abner, army commander and uncrowned king of Israel, the northern kingdom; and Joab in the southern kingdom, commander of David's forces. Joab is devoted to his king, although he snaps his soldier's fingers at the king's motives.

If Saul had to bear many years of David's presence, David has to live and reign for years in Saul's shadow. So the two anointed remain inseparable. They are voice and counter-voice, the rejected and the chosen, and in the meantime neither the good of the one nor the evil of the other is concealed. Good deeds are reported of Saul, and David's misdeeds aren't concealed. Together the two depict in light and darkness what messianic life is and what it isn't.

And what do their commanders Joab and Abner depict? A man's world of intrigues and violence, of sex and deception. To offer a bird's-eye view: Ishbosheth, a weak son of Saul, is crowned king over the northern kingdom by Abner, the one who really has the power. Abner fights against Joab, the general of Judah, the southern kingdom, and kills Joab's brother Asahel, a young man as light-footed as a wild gazelle, although he tried to avoid this. On the home front, king Ishbosheth and Abner disagree over Rizpah, formerly a concubine of Saul, who has now been transferred to Ishbosheth's harem. But Abner desires her and bluntly appropriates the king's wife. The powerless Ishbosheth protests weakly, but Abner overwhelms him with a charge of gross ingratitude: '*Am I a dog's head of Judah? I show steadfast love to the house of your father Saul, I have seen to it that you did not fall into the hands of David, and you accuse me of a fault with a woman?*'

Perhaps with the abduction of Rizpah Abner also sought an excuse to rid himself of Ishbosheth. Sensing that with so many enemies around there will be a future for the twelve tribes only if Israel makes a covenant with Judah, he indicates to David that he is ready to ensure that the north chooses David's side.

'That's fine,' says David. 'But there's no point in your coming to me unless Michal, Saul's daughter, is with you.' David also lets Ishbosheth know that he wants Michal back, '*whom I won as bride with one hundred Philistine foreskins*'.

Michal, the king's daughter, is pushed to and fro by men like a pawn in a political chess game. Saul gave her to David as wife for suspicious motives, and for equally suspicious motives he later took her away from David to give her in marriage to a certain Palti. Is it out of love that David now wants Michal's return? Or is he standing on his rights and is he concerned only to strengthen his position by binding the daughter of Israel's first king to him once more? At all events, a son born to them would unite the dynasty of Saul with that of David. It's impossible to think of a better heir to the throne.

Abner shows David his good faith by taking Michal away from her husband. Poor Palti must look on helplessly as his wife is carried off before his eyes. Desperately he follows her, weeping, begging them to let her go. Then Abner has had enough, and snarls to him that he must go back the way he came.

Ishbosheth is the great loser. Without Abner he's nowhere. Rizpah has been taken from him; he has to let his sister Michal go; he's just lost both his land and his crown to David.

Abner travels with Michal and with his men to Hebron, where David arranges a meal for them. Abner swears loyalty to David. 'I shall assemble the elders of Israel to make a covenant with you and so that you become king over all the land.'

'Go in peace,' says David.

Abner goes, but not in peace, for barely has he reached the well of Sirah when messengers from the palace in Hebron come to ask him to return.

Joab is behind this. David knows nothing of it. Returning from a campaign, Joab has found out that Abner has come over to their side. Immediately he indicates to David that he shouldn't trust him: 'What have you done? Surely you know Abner? Why have you let him go? He has only come to Judah to mislead you and to spy on everything here.'

Is Joab afraid that Abner will soon be the strong man in the united kingdom? David will certainly reward Abner when the northern kingdom has fallen into his hands without a blow.

Abner, thinking only that David wants to meet him again, returns with the messengers to Hebron. Joab is waiting for him at the gate; he asks him to come aside for a confidential discussion. Some discussion! In a recess, Joab stabs Abner in the stomach with a sword, so that he dies. To justify his action he explains to the palace that he has to avenge the death of his brother Asahel, the young man as light-footed as a wild gazelle.

David is shocked; the murder of Abner puts the fragile unity of the land in danger. Must he now in his turn take vengeance on Joab and shed his blood? He preferred to castigate him with words and cursed him with a curse so that the blood of Abner would not continue to cry from the ground: '*Joab, may there always be someone in your house who has a discharge or is leprous, someone who holds a spindle or perishes by the sword, or who suffers hunger.*'

We don't yet recognize David the poet…

Abner had a state funeral; David couldn't show the people more clearly how much he regretted his death. 'Tear your clothes,' he ordered Joab and his soldiers, 'put on mourning garments and go before Abner lamenting.' He himself went behind the bier. He wept at the tomb of Abner in Hebron and all the people wept. Then David gave the fallen warrior the last honours with a lament.

> *Must Abner die like a godless fool?*
> *Your hands were not bound,*
> *your feet were not chained in fetters,*
> *you have fallen as a man falls through an evildoer.*

'You must eat something,' said David's servants when he came home. But David wouldn't. 'Do you not know that on this day a ruler has fallen in Israel, a noble man? I may be anointed king, but I am still too weak and cannot cope with these hard men.'

David has no grip on Joab and continues to fear him; till his dying day he will not be reconciled with Joab. Certainly he made short shrift of the two Benjaminites who had cowardly murdered king Ishbosheth, a member of their own tribe into the bargain, in his sleep. They came to him in Hebron with Isbosheth's head in their hands. 'This day the Eternal One has avenged our lord the king on Saul and his offspring.'

The murderers don't know the Eternal One well, and they don't know David well either. They expect a reward, and meet with death. David is filled with abhorrence, just as formerly he was with the Amalekite who had claimed to have released Saul from his sufferings. David deals with them as it is fitting for the Lord's anointed to deal with Amalek and all who are like Amalek: he wipes out their remembrance from under heaven. As a deterrent their bodies are hanged by the pool of the city. Ishbosheth's head is solemnly laid in Abner's tomb. The one who was David's opponent during his lifetime may now rest in honour, ironically, in the ground of Hebron, the city where the throne of David stands.

45

THE TOPS OF THE MULBERRY TREES RUSTLED

II SAMUEL 5

Saul, Jonathan, Abner, Ishbosheth, all have fallen. Who will be the new ruler over Saul's territory? Shortly before his sudden death Abner had advised the elders of the northern kingdom to stop the civil war and to seek their salvation with David, once Saul's best commander.

Thereupon all the tribes from Saul's territory came to David at Hebron and said: 'We are your own flesh and blood. We want to belong to you, with all the fibres of our being. In former times, when Saul was still our king, you were the one who led Israel out to war and brought it back safely. The Lord has called you to pasture his people and to be ruler of Israel.' And they made a covenant and anointed David king over all Israel.

It began with a shepherd boy tending the sheep. Now he is a shepherd king, a man who knows that he has been called by God to tend his people. *David was thirty years old when he became king, and he reigned for forty years, in Hebron seven years over Judah and in Jerusalem thirty-three years over all Israel and Judah.*

Jerusalem, *the city of David*. No city of the north could ever be capital of the land, far less a city of the south. Therefore David's eye fell on the stronghold of Zion, in a neutral position between the two kingdoms, high on a hill, literally and figuratively exalted above tribal interests, in the heart of the land at a crossing of ways. There was only one difficulty: from time immemorial the Jebusites had occupied it, a people which felt safe in this steep impregnable stronghold. 'Do not think that you will enter here; the blind and the lame will drive you out.' But David's men were able to creep through the watercourse which links Jerusalem with the spring of Gihon, outside the walls, and take the city by surprise.

154

And David established himself in the stronghold and called it City of David, and he built fortifications round about. He became a mighty man and the Lord of hosts was with him.

That may be seen, for example, from the fact that messengers from Hiram, king of Tyre, announced themselves to David. Hardly is Jerusalem the city of David when the *goyim*, the peoples, stand at the gate. They have brought with them cedar wood from Lebanon; they come to help to build David's house, just as soon they will also join in building the house of God. That David has become a mighty man is also illustrated by the wives whom he acquires in this new spring and by the sons whom they will bear to him, eleven in number. A twelfth is to be expected. Then the numbers of the house of Israel will be complete.

Israel, no longer divided by mutual disputes, now forms an ever greater threat to the Philistines. Before David's power increases even more, they get ready to fight against Israel.

'Shall I go up?' David asks his God, 'Will you give them into my hand?'

'Go up,' said God, 'I give them into your hand.'

David went up and won the battle. He took with him from the battlefield the idols which the Philistines had brought with them to support them in the battle.

Again the Philistines made an attack, and again David took counsel with his God, now through a tree oracle. 'Shall I go up?'

'Do not do so,' said God. 'But rather make an encircling movement and attack where the mulberry trees are standing. *As soon as you hear the sound of marching through the tops of the mulberry trees, hasten, for then the Lord has gone out before you to smite the army of the Philistines.*'

The tops of the mulberry trees which rustle because the Lord of hosts is marching through them? Do you mean the wind, David?'

'Yes, I also mean that,' David will say, 'the wind of God.'

A poet of our time also had a similar experience. He believed that we are surrounded by *good powers*. This poet was called Dietrich Bonhoeffer. He was a German theologian who was imprisoned because he was involved in a plot to kill the Amalekite Hitler, the man who wanted to silence the people of the star of David because he had to silence his own conscience. He believed that the conscience was a Jewish invention.

Not long before his execution Bonhoeffer testified to his faith in one of his letters.

By kindly powers surrounded, peaceful and true,
wonderfully protected with consolation dear,
safely I dwell with you this whole day through,
*and surely into another year.**

He had heard the wind rustling in the tops of the mulberry trees; the spirit of God inspired this song in him.

The wind also blew at night through the strings of David's harp when he lay asleep.* Then he got up and wrote the song which had come blowing from on high. '*The Lord is my shepherd,*' he sang then.

46

A SHABBY KING

II SAMUEL 6

The city of David rises on Mount Zion; Jerusalem will be the beating heart of Israel. But not only David will dwell there; Jerusalem will also be the city of God: not only the political but also the religious heart of the land. How is this notion to be given form?

What has happened to the ark, Israel's holy chest containing the Ten Words of the God who liberates and shows the way? Years ago the Israelites went out to battle against the Philistines with this ark as a secret weapon, but God didn't approve of their using his name in vain and, as we are told, around thirty thousand men died. Thereupon the Philistines carried off the ark in triumph and put the trophy in their temple as a showpiece. But strangely enough, then this ark did immediately begin to work again: the God of the Philistines fell spontaneously to the ground from his pedestal, in worship of Israel's God. They put the dangerous thing with the utmost care on a cart, behind a couple of oxen who promptly went lowing towards Israel. Of course the joy was great; the Israelites saw it as a sign of forgiveness and reconciliation. They chopped the cart to pieces, lit a bonfire, sacrificed the oxen and held a banquet. But for one reason or another they didn't put the ark in a sanctuary, but left it with a priest somewhere on a hill.

What if David now brought back this ark and gave it a place of honour in Jerualem?

He takes around thirty thousand men on foot to bring the ark in triumph into the city.

Lift up your heads, O gates,
and be lifted up, O ancient doors,
*that the King of glory may come in!**

Wait a moment, David, which king does this song celebrate? Are you singing about God or secretly about yourself? Aren't you using the holy God to the greater glory of your kingship? Certainly it *isn't* your kingship, nor is it your city, any more than the earth is yours. The earth is the Lord's.

Thirty thousand men? That doesn't sound good; it's the number of men that perished in battle at that time. Is David going to hold something like a parade? And why all those musicians with instruments of cypress wood, with harps and lutes, with trumpets and bells and cymbals? David's royal military band.

And something else: why is the shrine put on a cart? They got that from the Philistines. However, it is written in God's holy Torah that the Lord doesn't want to be carried around on a cart pulled by oxen in such a pagan way, but to be carried in human hands. You can't put the stone tables of the Torah, a sign of God's presence, on a cart for the sake of convenience; you must keep on lifting them yourselves. Anyone who wants to serve the Eternal One must put his shoulders to the task. The story of liberating salvation and binding law must be carried close to the body.

David seems to forget this, and when that happens, misfortune strikes. The king goes before the ark in his royal garments, proud as a peacock. A long cherished wish is being fulfilled, it's the crown of the work of years. And then, when they are passing Nahlon's threshing floor, something goes wrong. The oxen stumble, the wagon totters, the ark begins to move, one Uzzah reaches out, grabs the ark, and is struck dead.

God is angry; he refuses to join in this masquerade. God doesn't want that cart. The poor Uzzah is of course full of good intentions; he wants to prevent the ark from falling, but this story tells how David mustn't try to harness God to his wagon. Uzzah must pay for his 'grab' with death.

David too is angry. Why must God thwart him like this? What does it mean? Does it mean anything?

Then David sees that he has taken a way that leads to a dead end. What must the king in heaven make of a king on earth who wants to make an entry with the ark rather than the ark making an entry with him? 'How can I accommodate God at the centre of my power?' was the question with which he began. David begins to sense that the question must be turned round: 'How will the ark of the Lord come *to me*?' As long as he doesn't have the answer to this question, it's better for the ark not to go to Jerusalem.

Temporary shelter is found at the house of a certain Obed-edom from Gath. A smart address. *Obed* means servant. The man will be a servant of strange gods, for if there is one name for paganism, it's *Edom*. And this man also comes from *Gath*, where Goliath is. So he's a real pagan, the Gathite Obed-edom, perhaps so that the ark does less damage to his house.

Less damage? The ark brings only salvation and blessing! *The ark of the Lord remained for three months in Obed-edom's house and God blessed him and all those who lived there.*

In the Bible we must always imagine such a blessing in a very earthly way. The harvest was abundant, well-formed twins were born and grandmother was cured of a chronic illness, something like that. Twelve weeks of blessing.

It is reported to David: '*The Lord has blessed the house of Obed-edom and all that he possesses, because of the ark of God.*' David understood that the curse had departed. Through God's grace he may now bring the sacred Torah into Jerusalem. He will go no longer as an enthroned king but as a lowly priest.

In divine rapture David dances before the ark, but now clad in a linen cloth, an undergarment like the priests wear. He has cast aside all outward signs of his dignity; David dances his dance almost naked. The ark is now carried, the Torah high on the shoulders and God in the heart. When those carrying the ark had taken six steps, they halted. David offered an ox and a calf. So they didn't just walk; their way was a prayer. They walked with God, they counted their paces, six in number, as a believer counts six days before, on the seventh day, the day of God, he takes rest in order to reflect, to offer sacrifice, to pray and again to know that this earth is God's.

The ark is brought into Jerusalem with rejoicing and to the sound of the trumpet. The holy words of God found their destination in the heart of the land and in the heart of the people. What Moses dreamed of, a kingdom of righteousness and justice, is to take form in the city of David. Utterly wrapped up in his dance, the king goes at the head of the procession. Michal. *Saul's daughter*, saw the scene from her window. She stood there unmoved. Her eyes were cold.

Why is she called Saul's daughter here? Isn't she rather David's wife? No, she isn't. Not any more. Once she had loved David and dreamed of an exalted throne. When he was in danger she helped him to escape through a window and put a doll in her bed. After years of separation – father Saul had given her away to one Palti – David had had her brought back. Did he desire her as a wife, or was it wise from a political point of view to ally Saul's daughter to him? Michal looks down in contempt on David from her window, this man of hers who in rapture is exposing himself to his people. She cannot see a king in this David. *And she despised him in her heart.*

David brought the ark to the tent which he had erected, and after making a sacrifice David blessed the people, the men and the women.

This blessing too is very earthly: everyone gets a loaf, a portion of meat and a cake of raisins. Blessing is sharing. After that the people goes its way, each one to his home.

David too went home, now he too wants to bless his house. Translated into earthly language, he wants to go to bed with Michal and have a child by her. If God wills, Michal will be in a blessed state: what would be finer than for David to father his twelfth son on this holy day?

Michal will have none of it. *Saul's daughter*, as she is called elsewhere, comes to meet David and heaps reproaches on him. 'A fine king,' she sneers, '*uncovering himself before the eyes of his servants' maids, as one of the vulgar fellows shamelessly uncovers himself.*'

That David has *uncovered* himself also means in Hebrew that he has *revealed* himself. Thus Michal is saying precisely what David has done. By going clad not in regal garments but in a priestly shirt, David has revealed himself as Israel's true king. It is a kingship that is alien to Michal, *Saul's daughter*.

David said: '*It was before the Lord, who chose me above your father, and above his house, to appoint me as ruler over Israel – and I shall dance before the Lord. I will make myself yet smaller than this, and I will be lowly in my eyes, shabby; and by the maids of whom you have spoken I shall be held in honour.*'

David will be *shabby*, a leader who no longer seeks his own honour and who precisely for that reason is worshipped by his people. 'Shabbily shall I dance before the Lord.'

Michal can't understand these messianic words. She can only look down on David from on high; no psalm will ring out from her window. Michal has no eye for God's glory; in her eyes *David's* honour has been damaged and with it also her honour. Insulted, she shuts herself up to David. Michal can't lose herself; she's barren, a woman with a life which will not let itself be blessed. And there indeed her story ends: *And Michal, the daughter of Saul, had no child until the day of her death.*

The house of Saul dies in Michal. No son will be born from her to unite the kingship of Saul and David. Michal will not be the mother of Israel's new king.

47

I SHALL BUILD YOU A HOUSE

II SAMUEL 7

He had wandered around for years, hiding in caves and clefts in the rock, his life unsafe. His existence was utterly sheer unrest, a time of expectation and of doubt.

> *Tossed to and fro unceasing,*
> *I know no rest at all.*
> *I wish I were a grape vine,*
> *I wish I had a wall.**

Now David finally has a wall. He has four walls, a fine house. He's settled down. But where does God live?

And it happened, when the king was sitting in his house – the Lord had given him rest from all his enemies round about – the king said to Nathan the prophet, 'See now, I dwell in a house of cedar, but the ark of the Lord dwells in a tent.'

It's time for a house to be built for God in Jerusalem; the prophet Nathan, too, must surely think that that's a good idea.

Suddenly the prophet appears on the scene. The story-teller thinks his arrival urgently needed. Now that a king is sitting on the throne who is powerful and is still extending his power, the voice of prophecy will be indispensable. For power corrupts, and Israel's king must be king by the grace of God. David understands that well, and therefore includes the man of God in his plan: 'I want to build a house for God.'

'Do what is in your heart; the Lord is with you.'

Nathan can hardly sleep that night. A house for God, that's new. God has never ever had a house. He has gone with his people through the wilderness. Ever since Israel can remember, the Eternal One has never lived other than in the tabernacle, that tent where the wind played through the canvas, the pegs were loose in the ground, for the next day the journey goes on. A house for God? Wouldn't you get a different God with a different house? God is like the wind which rustles through the mulberry trees; he comes and he goes, but you don't know where from or where to. He *is*, but he can't *dwell* with human beings, certainly not in the same street as the king. Isn't it a temptation to want to pin God down and to shut him up within the four walls of a temple?

Early in the morning Nathan reappeared at the palace: 'On further reflection I think it better for you to drop your plan.'

'What do you mean, on further reflection?'

'The Lord appeared to me last night.'

Had Nathan dreamed that God had appeared to him?

That could be. But Nathan also knows that God can reveal to a man in the night something that he doesn't see so clearly in the light of day. Job also knows that:

> God speaks repeatedly,
> but no one perceives it.
> In dreams, visions of the night,
> when deep sleep falls upon men,
> while they lie slumbering on their beds,
> then God wants to be heard,
> to turn this man away from a deed,
> to protect him from pride.*

'The Lord appeared to me last night: Go and say to my servant David, "Would you build me a house to dwell in? I have never dwelt in a house from the day that I brought the children of Israel out of Egypt until this day. I went with them in a tent. Have I ever said to one of the leaders of Israel, Why have you never built me a house of cedar wood?"'

David regrets the rejection by the prophet. At the same time he senses deep in his heart that the building of a temple was more *his* desire than God's. He so wanted certainty, a God as firm as a house.

'Has God said anything else to you?'

'Yes, sire. The Eternal One says not only that *you* should not build a house for *him*; he added that *he* will build a house for *you*.'

'A house for me?'

'For you, your majesty. God said: Say to David my servant, Thus says the Lord of hosts: I took you from behind the sheep to be leader over my people. I have been with you wherever you went. I have defeated all your enemies. I have made you a name, as great as the name of the great men of the earth. I have destined a place for my people Israel; I have planted it to dwell there so that it shall no longer be terrified and so that evildoers no longer oppress it. I have given you rest from all your enemies round about.'

'Truly,' said David, 'that is so. But what did God say about a house that he would build?'

'Say to David, said the Lord: I shall build you a house. When the days of your life are fulfilled and you have gone to rest with your fathers, then I shall raise up your son and I shall establish his kingship. It will be your son who shall build me a house and I shall establish his throne for ever. I shall be to him a father and he shall be to me a son. Whenever he does injustice I shall punish him. But my loving kindness shall not depart from him, as I made it depart form Saul. Your house shall endure and your kingdom for ever; your throne shall stand firm to eternity.'

What Nathan has uttered here is an unprecedented prophecy. It is as if God repented of having rejected Saul. God will never do that again. Although the sons of David will practise injustice and God will have to punish them for it, the last word will always be his loving kindness. He will not abandon what his hand has begun. There is a son in prospect, and the promise will continue to hold, for there is always a son in prospect. The prophet is referring to the coming of Solomon and to the house that this son of David will build for God, but far beyond that rises the promise of a throne that will last for ever. From this promise Israel's songs of the future are born, the visions of Nathan's sons, the messianic dreams of the prophets about a peaceful kingdom that knows no end.

Of course Nathan's night vision doesn't point to the figure of Jesus of Nazareth. But it's quite understandable that Jesus' followers should have referred to the image of the son of David to express how they had experienced the coming of this son of man as the grace of God. So synagogue and church share the dream of the messianic kingdom of peace and justice. It is the hope that gives them both life.

48

DAVID AND URIAH'S WIFE

II SAMUEL 11

The army of Israel has gone out to fight against the Ammonites; David's men have laid siege to the royal city of Rabbah. David doesn't think it necessary to be present. While his warriors are doing their hard duty out there under the leadership of Joab, David is walking at home on the roof of his palace in the cool of the evening. A king at the pinnacle of his power; a city, a land, a people, lies at his feet. Can he bear the burden? The higher you stand, the further you can fall.

In an adjacent garden David sees a woman bathing. How attractive she is!

'Who is that woman?'

'That's Bathsheba, sire, the daughter of Eliam, the wife of Uriah the Hittite. Her husband is at the front.'

The information from the king's servant is succinct, but David knows what he must do: he knows who she is and whose she is. Uriah's wife. And had David stopped looking, nothing more would have happened. David has the woman brought. It is at this moment that his life takes a turn and nothing will be the same again.

Uriah's wife appears at the palace, fragrant from her evening bath, and she shares a bed with David. Then she goes back home.

Not long afterwards she sends David a message: 'I'm pregnant.'

One deed prompts another: now Uriah the Hittite has to be brought home quickly from the front. The child that is soon to be born will have been fathered during this leave; anyone can calculate that exactly.

'Joab, send Uriah the Hittite to me, I must speak with him urgently.'

Joab sent Uriah to David.

'Thank you for coming, Uriah. How is the battle? How is it with the men? Will Rabbah fall soon?'

Uriah reports.

'Thank you, Uriah, for all that you've told me. I wish you a prosperous journey back. Don't forget to give my greetings to Joab. I don't need you here any longer, you'll be longing to see your wife after all these weeks. Farewell.'

Uriah went. But David wasn't reassured that he had gone home. Just suppose that this warrior, loyal to ruler and fatherland, wanted to observe the rule of war: you don't lie with a woman until the battle is over. Uriah may be a Hittite, not a son of the Torah, but what if his conscience nevertheless tells him that he must be loyal to the men who are besieging the city far from their loved ones?

David makes a sign to a servant: 'Go to Uriah's house and give him this gift.'

The servant returns. 'Uriah isn't at home, your majesty, he slept at the entrance to the palace with your staff. He didn't go home.'

The next day Uriah is again summoned by David. 'It was noble and conscientious of you, Uriah, to lie down to rest elsewhere. But you've come a long way. I will allow it if you should want to rest from the journey and the battle for a while under your own roof.'

'How could I, sire? The ark and Israel dwell in tents on the field of Ammon. How should I come to my house to eat and drink and sleep with my wife?'

Uriah knows his place. David doesn't. David isn't where he should be, with his men at the front. David is in his house. And he has Uriah's wife brought to that house, away from the place where *she* belongs, and shares a bed with the wife of the man who is risking his life for him in Rabbah.

'I give you leave to remain in Jerusalem today, Uriah. And return to me this evening, will you? I would like to hear more of how your life is going over there.'

The most savoury food is put in front of Uriah that night, and the drink flows abundantly. 'Drink some more, good fellow, they don't have such wine in Rabbah. Lehayim! To life! Life is short, Uriah, you must enjoy it where and when you can. Come here with your glass.'

Uriah could hardly stand when he took leave of his host – it was already dark. He left the palace and again lay down in his sleeping place among the servants of his lord. For he could hang on to one thought in his hazy brain: I'm not going home.

And now there's nothing for it, Uriah must disappear. David writes a letter to Joab: 'See to it that this man dies.'

'Have a good journey, Uriah. And be so good as to give this letter to general Joab, personally. See you soon!'

Joab returns to the battlefield with his death sentence in his bag.

Joab did what David asked him, and so Uriah died. Joab had put him in a dangerous position where he knew that Rabbah's best warriors would venture an attack as soon as some of Joab's men appeared just under the wall.

Joab sent a messenger to report the losses to his ruler. 'If the king bursts out in anger, if he censures you because we went too close to the walls of the city, then say: and your servant Uriah the Hittite is among the dead.'

A regiment may have perished through over-confidence; the Hittite is one of the fallen, and wasn't that what David was after?

Uriah's death is reported to David: David, the man after God's heart, who in earlier days wept over Saul and Jonathan, *How are the heroes fallen!* David doesn't weep. He can't allow himself that any more. David must go on, and he soothes the voice of his conscience by soothing Joab's conscience: 'Say to Joab: do not let this matter be evil in your eyes. Such things happen; the sword strikes now this one, and then that one. Say to Joab that he must continue the battle undiminished until Rabbah is laid waste. Inspire courage in him.'

Is this a man of God speaking? Or a villain? Or is David both?

When Uriah's wife heard that her husband was dead, she wept for him. As soon as the time of mourning was over, David took her into his house. She became his wife and bore him a son.

But the thing that David had done was evil in the eyes of the Lord.

Look, Nathan the prophet is approaching.

49
NATHAN'S PARABLE

II SAMUEL 12

'Your majesty, let me tell you what I heard,' said Nathan the prophet. 'There were two men in a city: one was rich, the other poor. The rich man had many sheep and cattle; the poor man had nothing but a little ewe lamb that he had bought and reared. It grew up with him, along with his children; it ate his bread, drank his milk and slept on his lap; it was like a daughter to him.

One day the rich man had a visitor. Because he thought it a shame to offer one of his own sheep or cattle to his guest, he took the poor man's ewe lamb and set it before the stranger. I though it good not to conceal all this from you, your majesty.'

David was furious. That something like this could happen in his kingdom! 'As truly as the Lord lives, the man who has done that deserves to die. He should recompense the ewe lamb fourfold because he knew no compassion.'

'You are that man,' said Nathan.

There was a long silence. David looked at himself in the mirror.

'Thus says the Lord, the God of Israel,' said Nathan, 'I anointed you king over Israel, I saved you from the hands of Saul, I put in your lap the house of your lord and the wives of your lord. I have given you the house of Israel, and if that is not enough, I will give you yet more. Why have you despised the word of the Lord and done what is evil in his eyes? You have killed Uriah the Hittite with the sword and taken his wife to be your wife. *Now, the sword shall never depart from your house, for eternity.*'

The punishment with the sword reflects David's crime with the sword. The sword shall not depart from his house. David has taken Uriah's wife, as the rich man took that ewe lamb. Kings take; Samuel had already warned about that when the people so urgently wanted a king: 'He will take your sons, he will take your daughters, your fields, your vineyards and your olive groves, corn, slaves, maidservants, sheep and cattle, all he will take.'*

The promise formerly made to David through the mouth of Nathan is not revoked, but from now on his life will be overshadowed by death. 'Thus says the Lord: see, I shall bring evil upon you, and it shall come upon you from your own house. Your wives shall I take from before your eyes and give them to your neighbour, and he shall lie with your wives in the broad light of day. You did it in secret, I shall do it in the sight of all Israel and in full daylight.'

'I have sinned against the Lord.' said David.

David and Nathan, two great men. Nathan is a great pastor. He loved David, he spoke the truth to him in love. Nathan knows how difficult it is for a fallen man to recognize his faults and to confess his guilt. How does one bring a man to acknowledge his guilt? And then not a guilt which paralyses but a guilt from which you can grow? With this sense of love Nathan found a story, a parable with which he could get to the heart of his king by a brief detour; a story which appeals to the goodness that there must also still be in this fallen ruler, the David of old, the shepherd boy. 'There was once a man... and that man took that ewe lamb...'

'A scandal before God and man,' said David.

'Yes,' said Nathan, 'you can say that.'

'I have sinned.'

Israel knows a penitential psalm which it has attributed to David, *when Nathan the prophet came to him, after he had gone in to Bathsheba.**

Have mercy on me, O God, according to your steadfast love,
according to your abundant mercy blot out my transgressions.
Wash me thoroughly from my iniquity
and cleanse me from my sin.
A broken and contrite heart, O God,
you will not despise.

Here lies David's greatness. He could have had Nathan killed, like Uriah; the one deed prompts the other. But David will not go further on this disastrous way. The king yields.

Nathan said to David: 'Your sins are forgiven you. You shall not die. The son who is born to you, he shall die.'

Nathan went home. And the Lord struck the child that Uriah's wife had borne to David. He became fatally ill. David withdrew into his bedroom and lay on the ground. He prayed for the little boy, he fasted, he wept. The elders of his house urged him to rise from the ground, but he refused. He didn't even want to eat with them.

And it happened, it was on the seventh day, that the child died. David's servants dared not tell him. 'When the child was still alive we spoke to him, but he wouldn't listen. How then can we tell him that the child is dead? He will commit another disaster.'

David saw his servants whispering with one another and understood that the end had come. 'Is the child dead?'

'It is dead, sire.'

The prophet had foretold that from then on the house of David would be overshadowed by death. At first sight this wretched story seems to be an act of revenge by the Lord God. It's better to read such a story as a parable, a parable which depicts what we also often see in reality: innocent children who are the victims of our actions, when the king of the land or the king and queen of the family, the father and the mother of the child, go off the rails. Evil propagates itself, sin strikes out around. Israel has already known this for a long time from bitter experience: the sins of the fathers are visited on the children, to the third and fourth generations.

'Is the child dead?'

'It is dead, sire.'

Then David arose from the ground, washed himself, anointed himself with oil, put on other garments, went to the house of God and knelt down. When he returned to the palace he asked for bread and ate.

'We don't understand you,' his servants said. 'While the child was still alive you fasted and wept. Now that it is dead you've risen and eaten.'

'As long as the child was still alive I fasted and wept. I thought, Perhaps the Eternal One will be gracious to me and keep the child alive. Now he is dead. Why should I still fast? Can I bring him back? I am going to him, he will not return to me.'

Initially David had imprisoned himself in his sorrow, and his servants were afraid of him. Now he returns to the light, enters the house of God who will not despise a broken and contrite heart, and returns to his own house. Cleansed and with fine clothes he wants to make a new beginning. There is a time to weep and there is a time to dry one's tears and begin to live again. David will have sorrow all his life. But sorrow will not have him.

And David comforted his wife Bathsheba.
    The story-teller no longer calls her *Uriah's wife*, for that is now a thing of the past. These two, David and Bathsheba, must go on together.
    David went in to her and lay with her and she bore a son and he called his name Solomon.
    A name which breathes peace, *shalom*. See, I make all things new. The sun of God's grace rises over them. Through the tears of guilt and penitence a new happiness is born. Therefore a thousand years later the evangelist Matthew cannot leave *Uriah's wife* out of the genealogy of Jesus, the king of the Jews whom he has born in the house of David.
    And the Lord loved Solomon, and he commanded Nathan the prophet to give him the name Jedidiah. Beloved of God.

David received a report from Joab: the besieged city of Rabbah had almost fallen. 'May I advise you to bring all the warriors together and take the city yourself, so that the conquest is not attributed to me but to you.'
    Joab does David the honour of the final capture of the city. David gathers his men. Rabbah is conquered by storm, the inhabitants are tortured and have to do forced labour in the brick kilns. So Joab helped David with his display of power to distract attention from what had been going on in his own house.

50

AMNON AND TAMAR

II SAMUEL 13

*And it happened that Absalom, son of David, had an attractive sister -Tamar
was her name – and Amnon, son of David, loved her.*

This story is about two sons of David, and again an attractive woman is
involved. We hold our breath over the outcome.

*Amnon loved Tamar and that made him ill, for his sister was a virgin and
he did not know how to approach her.*

Tamar, Amnon's half sister, was well guarded in the harem; he only saw
her at a distance and always in the presence of others. His secret longing
grew into a desire that couldn't be tamed. He was sick with it.

*Now Amnon had a nephew, Jonadab, son of Shimeah, David's brother,
who was very crafty in all things.*

An enthusiast who only makes the problem worse with his solutions.
'Why are you so downcast every morning? Tell me.'

'It's Tamar. I'm in love with Tamar, the full sister of my brother
Absalom.'

Jonadab knows what to do; we were already afraid of that. Why doesn't
Amnon make a virtue of necessity? 'If you're sick you must take to your
bed. Father David will certainly come on a sick visit. Then say, "Let my
sister Tamar come and give me bread to eat. Let her prepare it before my
eyes, so that I can see it. I will eat out of her hand."'

Jonadab has also clearly been in love once. Tamar mustn't just come
and bring the food; she must prepare it on the spot, *before Amnon's eyes.*
This woman is a delight to the eyes.

Amnon went to lie on his bed. His name means *the trustworthy one.*
He'is David's oldest son.

David came. 'Oh father, let Tamar, my sister, come and let her bake two
cakes before my eyes.'

Two cakes. To eat warm, as if they were *à deux.* That doesn't sound at all trustworthy, but David, otherwise acute enough, suspects nothing: 'I shall tell her to go to you.'

Tamar came, baked the cakes before Amnon's eyes and gave them to him. But Amnon didn't take the cakes; it was another hunger which he wanted to satisfy. He caught hold of her. 'Come and lie with me, my sister.'

'No, my brother! That sort of thing is not done in Israel. Do not commit this folly. Reflect. Where can I go if I have been robbed of my honour? And you will be known as a fool in the land. Why do you not go to the king and ask for my hand? He will not refuse you.'

That was possible in those days, a marriage between brother and half-sister; the law which forbids it is of a later date. Let Amnon marry her in the proper way. One moment of thoughtlessness will be disastrous for them both: Tamar will be shamed, no longer eligible for marriage and doomed to solitude, and Amnon, the crown prince, will be a godless fool in everyone's eyes, who has trampled on Israel's Torah.

Amnon wouldn't listen to Tamar. *He overpowered her, forced her and raped her. After that he hated her with a great hatred; the hatred with which he hated her was greater than the desire with which he had desired her.*

He loathed Tamar. 'Get up, go away.' It was as if, loathing himself, he wanted to undo the deed by showing his victim the door.

'To send me away like this is an even greater evil than the other that you did to me.'

Again Amnon wouldn't listen to Tamar's words. Having first lured her into the house, now he has a servant put her out on the street. In this way he once again humiliated Tamar in public. The door was bolted behind her, as if he wanted to banish her from his life for ever.

Tamar scattered ash on her head and tore the splendid garment that she might wear as a virgin princess. She was the victim of an act which cannot be covered by any garment. She put her hand on her head and went away wailing.

Where to? She fled to Absalom. 'Has Amnon violated you? My sister, be calm, he is your brother. Do not push this thing too far.'

Absalom seems to want to avoid a family scandal and doesn't want to make the matter public.

Tamar went to live in her brother Absalom's house, unloved, with still a long way to go. In the women's quarters she had been a happy virgin with sweet dreams; in Amnon's house she was humiliated and violated; in Absalom's house she lives in solitude.

King David heard what had happened and burst out in anger.

We don't hear that David also *did* something with this anger. Did he take Tamar's fate to heart? Did he put his arms round his wounded daughter? Or couldn't he do so? Did he blame Tamar for the rape – according to a well-tried recipe?

Meanwhile Absalom was out for vengeance. He patiently waited for the right moment, and after two years that moment seemed to have come: the sheep shearers' festival in Baal-hazor near Ephraim. Absalom invited all the princes. He said to his servants: 'When Amnon is merry with wine and I say "Kill him," kill him. Don't be afraid, I am the one who is giving you this order.'

And so it happened. Amnon grew merry with the wine, and before he knew it, he was dead. The other sons of the king leaped from the table and sought to escape on their mules.

Absalom had avenged his sister. The question arises whether he killed his brother, the crown prince, only to have his revenge for Tamar. Wasn't it at the same time a good opportunity to open up the way to the throne for himself?

David received the report that *all* his sons had been slaughtered by Absalom's hand. He sat down defeated. The sword would never depart from his house, but for the whole of his house to be smitten... Fortunately Jonadab could contradict the rumour. 'Only Amnon is dead; Absalom has fled.'

And David lamented over his son.

Which son? Amnon the murdered one, or Absalom the murderer? We don't hear that he lamented over Tamar, who lamented alone in Absalom's house. Her name isn't mentioned again.

No, that isn't true. When years later Absalom himself had a daughter, he gave her the name Tamar. Perhaps that was a comfort to Tamar.

51

THE WOMAN FROM TEKOA

II SAMUEL 14

After three years, David's suffering over Amnon's death was past, but his sorrow over Absalom, who remained in exile to avoid blood vengeance, would not pass. Joab, David's devoted general, saw how behind a wall of rancour and fury his king was tormented with sorrow over the son whom he had lost. It didn't wear off, but continued to devour him. Did it have to last down the years or could the impasse be broken through? But who could break through this wall in David to the father's love which lay behind it? Joab himself didn't succeed. Perhaps the woman from Tekoa can make an attempt to reconcile father and son. She's a wise woman, with a warm heart for God and for others. And brave into the bargain.

'Pretend to be mourning; do not anoint yourself with oil, behave as if you are someone who has long been mourning one dead. Go to the king and say to him these words.'

Joab put the words into her mouth.

Sunk in mourning and without having anointed herself, the woman from Tekoa entered the palace and bowed down before David. 'I hope that you can help me.'

'What can I do for you?'

'I am a widow, your majesty, my husband is dead. Your handmaid had two sons; they fought in the field and no one came between them. Then one struck the other dead. And now my family wants me to hand over the son who has remained to me in the land of the living. They are crying out for vengeance. They want to quench the glowing coal which still remains to me. The name of my husband will be wiped out; they are seeking his only offspring and want to kill him. He is a murderer, they keep crying. But he is also my son.' She looks imploringly at David.

'Woman, go home, I shall support your son. He can return to you without danger. If anyone wants to see blood and opposes this, just send him to me.'

'May I ask you, your majesty, to swear this oath before God?'

'As the Lord lives, I swear it to you,' said David. 'Not a hair of your son's head shall be harmed.'

And to think what a fine head of hair David's son Absalom has, the exile who has had to remain in hiding for three years now, if he's to escape blood vengeance.

David prepares to end the conversation, but the woman from Tekoa clearly has something else on her mind. 'May your handmaid be allowed to address one more word to you?'

'Speak freely.'

'Why, then, your majesty, do you cherish such thoughts against the people of God? According to the word that you yourself have just spoken you yourself are guilty as long as you do not allow the son whom you have banished to return. People have to die, they are like water that is spilt upon the earth and is not gathered up. However, God does not take life away, but looks for ways so that an outcast does not remain outcast by him.'

The king may not think of the people of God as David thinks about Absalom. People die, that's inevitable. Amnon is dead, that's the case. But Absalom is alive. Only he has no life, as long as blood vengeance rules. Israel's God is a father who looks for his lost son. Should David then do nothing? He can do no more for Amnon, but he can for Absalom. Surely there is still something like forgiveness and reconciliation in Israel?

'That is why I have come to you, your majesty; the way in which the people speak of you makes me so afraid. Your handmaid thought: the king will listen to me and certainly rescue his handmaid from the hand of the man who wants to see blood and seeks to destroy me and my son from God's inheritance. Your handmaid thought: the word of my king will give me rest, he is an angel of God, a man who can hear what is good and what is evil. May the Lord your God be with you.'

She is herself an angel of God, this anonymous prophetess, this mother in Israel. Just like Nathan, she has told a parable in order not to make David look into the depths of his guilt and show him his lack of courage. She isn't out to defeat him, she wants to win him over. She calls out the best in David. She brings to light the humanity that lies there, to be awakened in the darkness behind his fury and rancour. A child can be cast out for ever, of course that happens. But really that can't be. Not in Israel, the land of God. If the vicious circle is to be broken somewhere, then it is there. And isn't Israel's king called above all to show that to the world of the peoples? Now that the Lord's anointed risks forgetting his special calling, it is this woman who reminds him of it. She makes him small, but also again makes him great. She doesn't rob her king of his feeling of self-worth; on the contrary, she sets him high on the throne: 'You are an angel of God.'

And David *is* that also; he is *also* that. This king can indeed hear what is good and what evil. He can – strikingly for that time – even hear it from a woman.

David said, 'Do not hide from me, woman, what I shall ask you.'

'Let my lord the king speak.'

'Has Joab inspired you to this?'

'As truly as you live, your majesty, if you ask a question, no one can evade it. It is as you say. Joab has put these words into the mouth of your handmaid. Joab has done this to examine this matter again. You are an angel of God, I have said that already, for nothing of what happens on earth remains hidden from you.'

David instructed Joab to let Absalom return to his home. To Absalom's home, that is, for it was still too early for a meeting at David's palace.

Thus David had carried out his promise to the woman of Tekoa to the letter, but not in spirit. Was the bitterness too fierce, the wound not yet healed? Did David see it afterwards as a defeat that Joab and the woman taught him a lesson? For the moment David didn't want to see Absalom.

But Jerusalem saw Absalom, his proud hair waving in the wind. Whenever he had it cut – always at the end of the year, when the burden became to heavy for him – he weighed it, vain as he was. It weighed more than two kilos, by imperial weight. There was something of the Samson about him. He was a young god, but unable to persuade his father to have a reunion. For two years he waited for a report from the palace, but in vain. Shouldn't Joab once more play the role of mediator? He asked Joab to come to him, but Joab didn't. A second time he invited him, but again Joab didn't appear. Absalom was at his wits' end; only Joab could help. 'Look,' he said to his servants, 'Joab's field lies next to mine; the barley is in the field, set it on fire.'

The servants set the field on fire, just like Samson. Joab rushed to

Absalom's house. 'Why have your servants set my field on fire?' But fortunately Joab was wise enough to see Absalom's suffering rather than his deed. He understood how ardently Absalom longed to stop hovering between exile and sonship.

'Joab, be so good as to ask my father why he allowed me to come to Jerusalem. It was better for me to remain out there. I want to see him. If he doesn't want to see me because I'm guilty, let him say so. If he can't give me life, then why doesn't he bring me death?'

Joab hastened to David and told him Absalom's words. Then David summoned Absalom. Absalom came, bowed down before David with his face to the earth. The king kissed Absalom.

52

ABSALOM'S REVOLT

The reconciliation between David and Absalom is short lived. They had again come closer, those two, but it didn't remain like that; the gulf could not be bridged.

Absalom goes his own way, gets a chariot and horses, and has fifty men run before him: 'Clear the way, the king's son is coming.' He radiates power, this proud hero with his fiery eyes and waving hair; he is more a prince of the kind that the pagans desire. One day the prophet Zechariah will dream of a king who goes through the streets of Jerusalem on an ass.

From time to time Absalom makes the horses stop at the gate, the place where Israel's king pronounces judgment. Everyone who seeks justice comes there. 'You, sir, from what city are you? I can hear it already, you're in the right, there's no doubt about that, but you won't find a hearing with the king. Oh, if only I were judge in this land, everyone would come to me and justice would prevail.' *If someone bowed before him, Absalom held him firm and kissed him.*

Wasn't that what David and Absalom did when they were reconciled with each other: bowed and kissed? Appearances were deceptive. Appearances also threaten now: anyone who seeks justice in the gate falls into the hands of a man who is only out for power. What Absalom is doing there is low, but would he have gained so much faith and trust from the people had there not been a grain of truth in his lies? David continues to be pursued by the injustice done to the Hittite Uriah. And did David secure justice for Tamar, Absalom's violated sister? It's Absalom who taught the rapist manners.

Be this as it may, Absalom, the crown prince who wants to live grandly and win over the people, steals the favour of the people from his father and undermines his father's authority. Then he thinks that the moment has come to attempt to seize power. He packages his wicked plans in piety:

'Father, let me go to Hebron to fulfil a promise that I made when I was abroad. Lord, if through your grace I return to Jerusalem – I swore to the Eternal One – I shall serve you.'

Serve? Absalom wants to rule. But father David doesn't see it. 'Go in peace, my son.'

But not peace. War. Rebellion. Absalom has secured the powerful support of David's adviser Ahithophel and goes to Hebron, having first sent spies all over the land. 'As soon as you hear the sound of the trumpets, then proclaim that Absalom is king in Hebron.'

In Hebron, the age-old city in which Abraham lies buried, where David was crowned and Absalom was born, the city which finds it difficult to swallow the fact that David has made Jerusalem the capital of the land, Absalom has the trumpet blown and himself proclaimed king.

And so great is the number of those prepared to follow Absalom – so David is told – that David thinks it advisable to take refuge away from Jerusalem, *his* Jerusalem. Again he has to flee, now from his own son. The royal guard and the court go with him; he leaves behind ten concubines in the palace.

At the edge of the city David stops to see who has accompanied him on his hasty departure. Ittai, his general, has followed him, one of the *goyim*. David is moved by the loyalty of this foreigner, but he also thinks that he can't ask so much of him: he's been banished from his own land, why should he now wander around with David? 'Return, stay with the king, Ittai. You came to us yesterday, but surely not to go with us towards an unknown future. Return, Ittai, and may God's loving-kindness and faithfulness go with you.'

'As the Lord lives and as my lord the king lives, I will remain with you, wherever you go, to death or to life.'

David crosses the brook Kidron and goes in the direction of the wilderness. The people of the land weep. There goes their king; will he ever return?

Look, there too come the priests Zadok and Abiathar with their sons, the ark on their shoulders, for the ark belongs with the throne; where David goes, there goes the ark.

To the amazement of all who accompanied him, David says: 'Take the ark of God back to the city. If I find grace in God's eyes, it will bring me back and I shall see it again; if not – so be it. May the Eternal One do what is good in his eyes.'

David is experiencing one of the darkest hours of his life, but he doesn't claim before the Lord that he is right. He has learned that the fate of the ark may not be associated with the fate of the ruler. God isn't David's; David is God's.

But honesty also compels us to say that David would prefer to have the priests in Jerusalem; as his confidants they can do better service for him there than in the wilderness. 'Send me a report as soon as you return to the city; I will wait by the fords.'

David climbed the slope of the Mount of Olives barefoot. He lamented, his head bare. Those who were with him had also bared their heads and walked on, weeping.

David received a report that Ahithophel had chosen Absalom's side. 'Lord God,' he prayed, 'frustrate the counsel of Ahithophel.'

Look, his faithful counsellor Hushai came up to meet him, his clothes torn and with dust on his head, a sign of mourning. He wanted to join David, but David preferred his older friend and support to return to the palace, there to frustrate the counsel of Ahithophel. David was concerned for the command which he had just given to be obeyed. 'Tell Absalom that you were his father's servant and from now on want to be his servant. And do not think that you are alone there; the priests Zadok and Abiathar are also on our side.'

Hushai, David's closest ally, his friend in need, arrived in Jerusalem at the precise moment when Absalom entered the city.

David had reached Bahurim when a man appeared on the other side of a ravine, Shimei, an offshoot of the family of Saul. He threw stones at David, furious and raging. 'Go away, you man of blood! You who tainted the house of Saul with blood so that you yourself might be king. But God knows how to find you, and now Absalom will be king.'

Mention of David's blood guilt towards the house of Saul is a slander, but the rumour keeps cropping up. It's a curse which can't be allowed to go unpunished; words have power. Abishai, one of David's warriors whose brother was murdered by Abner, came forward. 'Just one jump over the ravine and I can chop his head off, that dead dog, who dares to taunt my king.'

'Leave him be. Let him curse me, Abishai. The Lord has said it to him.'

David is speaking as a believer and a politician. It wouldn't be sensible at this point to allow himself to be provoked and to earn the enmity of the family of Saul by killing Shimei. But David's refusal to have Shimei silenced is also the fruit of his pious heart. Shimei's curse comes from the Lord. 'My own son seeks my life, so how much more does this son of Benjamin despise me. Leave him be. Perhaps the Lord may see my misery and give me good in place of this curse.'

So they went on, while Shimei continued to taunt them and to throw stones and to fling dust. Utterly exhausted, David and his followers came to a place where they could rest.

53

ABSALOM'S DEATH

II SAMUEL 16, 17, 18 AND 19

Absalom goes up from Hebron to Jerusalem and takes possession of the palace, surrounded by his followers. Ahithophel is among them. Then Hushai, David's closest ally, also presents himself. Speaking with a double tongue he indicates that from now on he wants to belong to Absalom's camp. 'Long live the king,' he exclaims, 'long live the king.'

Nicely spoken, but which king does he mean, the father or the son? Absalom's suspicions are all too understandable. 'Do you call that being loyal to your closest friend? Why didn't you go with your closest friend?'

But that isn't Hushai's concern: by venturing as David's confidant into the lion's den, he is going with David. 'Whoever the Lord and the people of Israel has chosen, to him will I belong and with him will I remain.'

Again Hushai speaks in an ambiguous way, but if he wants to remove Absalom's mistrust he will have to be more frank with him. 'Isn't the man whom I want to serve his own son? As I have served your father, so I shall serve you.'

Hushai is accepted into Absalom's advisory council, but it is Ahithophel who is the first to give the young king advice: 'Go into the harem of your father which he left behind in the palace. Do that publicly.'

The counsel which Ahithophel gave in those days counted as much as a word of God, both with David and with Absalom.

The king's servants erected a tent on the roof of the palace – that roof had been a place of desire earlier – and Absalom went into his father's harem. All Israel saw it and knew: now the break is complete, there will no longer be any reconciliation between father and son. Once, general Abner had made himself master of Rizpah, concubine of Saul's son Ishbosheth, the king of the northern kingdom, and everyone had understood to whom power belonged. Now the people understands that again: Absalom is declaring David dead and taking possession of his father's wives, his most intimate possession. This is the same Absalom who killed Amnon because he violated Tamar, a woman who wasn't his.

Hadn't Nathan already prophesied this to David in days long gone by? *'Thus says the Lord: Your wives I shall take from before your eyes and give them to your neighbour, and he shall lie with your wives in the broad light of day, in the sight of all Israel.'* It is Absalom who, without knowing it, fulfils the prophecy with grotesque theatre on the palace roof.

Ahithophel has yet more advice: 'We must act quickly, your majesty, before David and his men are ready to fight again. Give me twelve thousand men, and I will set off in pursuit of him this very night. I shall attack David while he is weary and powerless. I shall terrify the warriors so that they flee. Only the king shall I kill; I shall spare his men and bring them back to you unharmed.'

Good advice on the part of Ahithophel. No doubt about that. The plan is simple, the chance of success great, and the people won't necessarily have their backs put up over Absalom. Indeed the plan can also command the approval of all Israel's elders. But what does Hushai think of it? Absalom also prizes his judgment.

'With your permission, sire, but it seems to me that this time Ahithophel's counsel is not good.'

Not good for David, let that be clear. Or better, let that not be clear. How to take in Absalom?

Hushai pours a flood of words over Absalom which make an impression. In military terms his argument is sheer nonsense, but it is packaged by Hushai in such an attractive way and presented so ardently that Absalom too falls for it. 'You know yourself, sire, that your father and his men are brave warriors; moreover they are as bitter as a she-bear who has been robbed of her young. Your father is an experienced general; he will not allow his people any rest this night. Without doubt he is hidden in one of the rocky clefts or in some other place. From there he can quickly rise up and inflict an annihilating defeat on you, and everyone will know that Absalom has suffered a defeat. The courage of even your bravest solider, with the heart of a lion, will sink in his shoes. Therefore my counsel is: gather all Israel around you, from Dan to Beersheba, a multitude as numerous as the sand by the sea. You yourself must also engage in the battle, your majesty, how could we go out without you? As soon as we have found David, we will fall on him, as dew which descends upon the earth. Of him and his men not one will survive. If he has ensconced himself in one city or another, then let all Israel set ropes around that city and then we will pull that city down, until not one stone is left standing on another.'

The demagogy goes down a treat with Absalom and the men of Israel: *'The counsel of Hushai is better than that of Ahithophel.'*

Whence that blindness? Is it a result of their fear, on which Hushai has played so well? For the story-teller, it is clear that God is behind it. 'Lord God, frustrate Ahithophel's counsel,' David had prayed on the Mount of Olives. That prayer is now heard.

There was only one man who saw through Hushai's deception, Ahithophel. He understood that Absalom's cause was lost, saddled his ass, went home, set his affairs in order and hanged himself. He was buried in the tomb of his father.

The story-teller speaks with some respect about this suicide. It's a well-considered death; it isn't the same as if he had come to a shameful end as one involved in high treason: Ahithophel finds a worthy grave.

Hushai had won valuable time for his king – a warrior knows that he wins plenty if he wins time* – and David could prepare thoroughly for an encounter.

The moment came when Absalom left Jerusalem to join battle with David. Hushai saw him go with pleasure: the rebel was going out to meet his downfall. David himself didn't engage in the battle; his men had besought him to keep away from the battlefield. 'You are worth ten thousand men to us.'

David stood beside the gate of the city where he was staying, and anxiously watched the departure of his men. Joab solemnly swore to save his son. *'Deal gently with the young man.'* David wants his throne back, but he doesn't want to lose his son. 'Do him no evil.' And all the people heard the king's orders to his commander about Absalom.

The battle flared up in the woods of Ephraim and Absalom's army suffered an annihilating defeat from David's servants: it was one great slaughter. *The wood devoured more people that day than those devoured by the sword.* It's difficult to escape in a wood.

David's men spied Absalom hastening away on his mule. Under a great oak tree, suddenly his waving hair got entangled in the branches, his mount shot from under him and Absalom was left hanging. He hung between heaven and earth by his hair which had once been his pride and glory.

This was reported to Joab. 'Why didn't you kill him immediately? I would have given you ten silver pieces.'

'Even if you gave me a thousand silver pieces, sire, I would not lay a finger on the king's son. With my own ears I heard how David besought you, "Deal gently with the young man."'

However, Joab didn't hesitate to put three darts into the heart of Absalom as he hung there defenceless.

Once Joab had interceded for Absalom and tried to reconcile father and son. Then he had to look on powerlessly as Absalom was able to undermine David's authority with impunity. Now Joab has no hesitation: Absalom must disappear; it's the only way to put an end to the political unrest and to an ongoing conflict between father and son. It's as David himself said when Uriah the Hittite was killed: 'The sword kills now this one, now that one.'

To avoid further bloodshed, Joab called off the battle; he too wanted to spare the warriors. Absalom was buried in a hastily dug pit in the wood.

The war was over, but not yet the story, for how were they to tell David? Who would report both the victory and the bad tidings to him? Ahimaaz, the quick-footed son of the priest Zadok, volunteered to go, but what if David immediately vented his wrath about the message on the messenger? Joab cared for Ahimaaz as if he were his own son. 'To be quite certain, it seems better for a black mercenary to bring the news.'

The messenger went off, but Ahimaaz continued to urge Joab to let him go too. Joab agreed: however quick he was, the priest's son certainly wouldn't reach David before the man from Ethiopia. Ahimaaz sped off, and within the shortest time was able to catch up the first runner and overtake him.

David sat at the doors of the city gate, between hope and fear, waiting expectantly for news from the front. A watchman above the gate peered into the distance. 'I see a man coming running, all alone.'

'If he's alone he certainly brings good news,' said David, allaying his fears.

The runner had already got a bit closer when the watchman saw a second runner. 'Look, there's another man hastening, he too is alone.'

'He too certainly brings good news.'

'To judge from his gait the first man is Ahimaaz, the son of Zadok.'

'He's a good fellow, he's certainly coming with good news.'

'Peace be to you,' exclaimed Ahimaaz to his king, and prostrated himself before him, face to the ground. 'Blessed be the Lord your God, who has delivered the rebels into our hands.'

'Is it well with the young man, with Absalom?'

'I do not know, sire. I saw a great crowd when Joab, your servant, sent me here. I do not know what it was.'

Then the mercenary came. 'My lord the king receives good news. Today the Lord has procured justice against all those who rebel against you.'

'Is it well with the young man, with Absalom?'

'May the enemies of my Lord the king and all who rise up against you fare as that young man.'

The man didn't say in so many words that Absalom was dead, but David knew well enough. Deeply distressed, he retreated into an upper room above the gate and wept. 'My son Absalom, my son, my son Absalom, oh that I had died in your place, Absalom, my son, my son.'

As king, David had been victorious; as father, he had suffered an irrevocable defeat.

Joab was told, 'The king is weeping and mourning for Absalom.' The warriors' flush of victory turned into consternation, the men came stealthily into the city as an army goes its way stealthily when it has fled shamefully from the battle. They heard David walking to and fro in the upper room above the gate; there seemed to be no end to his lament. 'My son Absalom, Absalom my son, my son.'

But Joab knew that this couldn't go on. The young man was dead, and a father's heart was breaking, but David had to see that he couldn't save both the crown *and* his son. Now it seems that he loves those who hate him and hates those who love him. Does it mean nothing to David that all those brave men have remained faithful to him and gone to battle at the risk of their own lives, while he has been able to stay safely in the city? 'Your majesty, would you have preferred Absalom still to be alive and us to be dead? Now then, get up, go outside and encourage your soldiers. For I swear to you, unless you go to them this very night, not one of them will remain with you. That evil will be greater than all the evil that has come upon you from your youth to this present day.'

David listened to Joab, got up, and sat in the gate. The rumour went around, 'Look, the king is sitting in the gate.' And all the men came.

David never forgave Joab for stabbing Absalom. And David never forgot the harshness with which Joab called him to order as king. David was embittered, like a she-bear which has been deprived of her young.

David went up, back to Jerusalem, back to the royal city. When he got to the Jordan, look, the foul-mouthed Shimei appeared there again, the man who had thrown stones at David when he had had to flee before Absalom. Abishai had wanted to kill Shimei, but David had not allowed him to. Wasn't it God himself who had inspired Shimei to curse like that?

Shimei, fearing for his life, fell at David's feet. 'I have sinned, sire, forgive me. See, I am the first to come to greet you.'

Abishai, full of mistrust, still wanted to settle the old score. 'I shall chop this villain's head off.'

'Do you say that today, Abishai? Shall anyone be put to death in Israel today? After all, today I am again king over Israel.'

54

RIZPAH

II SAMUEL 21.1-14

This is the story of Rizpah. It belongs earlier in the story of David, but the story-teller has put it here as a postscript, together with the two stories which follow.

Rizpah is a mother in Israel, a woman in opposition. Once she was one of Saul's wives. Life smiled on her, she was the beloved of the king and her children were royal children.

But that's a long time ago now. All that glittered wasn't gold. Saul was often a gloomy man, tormented with madness, and finally, seeing no way out, he had thrown himself on his sword. Rizpah is becoming older, her body is withering, but fortunately she still has her two sons, the joy of her old age – until the devastating news reaches her that both sons have been hanged as an expiatory offering by the Gibeonites, inhabitants of the mountain village of Gibeah.

In earlier days a non-aggression treaty had been concluded with the Gibeonites, but Saul seems to have violated that treaty. Now David is in power and famine has come upon the land. Is that just by chance, or is God behind it? David consults the oracle, and the priest reports to him that here the blood guilt of Saul is taking its revenge.

David summons the Gibeonites to him. 'Tell me how I can bring about reconciliation between you and me'

'It is not a matter of silver or gold, your majesty, far less is it our concern to kill anyone in Israel.'

'What do you want me to do?'

'You know who it was who wanted to destroy us and exterminate us. Give us seven of his sons that we may hang them before our temple in Gibeah, high on the mountain.'

'I will give them to you.'

Strange, in earlier stories David is cautious about laying hands on Saul and his family, but in this story he goes to work unscrupulously. Seven sons of Saul, the two sons of Rizpah and five grandsons, are handed over to the Gibeonites as an expiatory sacrifice.

The scholars call this 'primitive compensatory thinking', thus giving the impression that this kind of thinking is alien to us. As if we never pin the guilt of one person on another! And does David now do this simply because it's what the oracle has said, or does it also work out well for him? At any rate he kills two birds with one stone: he offers satisfaction to the rebellious Gibeonites and rids himself of a number of royal children, who are always a threat to any ruler.

Be this as it may, Saul called down a curse upon himself when he violated the treaty. Sons and grandsons must now pay for it; they will die the dead of the accursed; they will hang, and their bodies will not be entrusted to mother earth, but handed over to vultures and jackals. They are hanged above Gibeah's holy mountain, seven in number, and two of them were dear to the heart of Rizpah.

And suddenly she is there, at the foot of those seven stakes, in sackcloth and ashes. She spreads her mourning garments over the rock and will not go away; she endures the heat of the day and the cold of the night. Once she was the king's beloved, spending the night in a royal bed, but now that's a thing of the past, gone for good. This is another Rizpah, a crazy mother who, like one possessed, drives off the birds which want to settle on the corpses, and the wild beasts who steal up on the carrion. She never stops.

This is a battle with vultures, dogs and hyenas, but *in* them with the people who do not reverence life and do not allow the dead to rest in a grave, so that they are doomed to wander continually. Rizpah cries out against a world in which one curse is answered with another, a slight figure who continues against the odds to believe in the blessing. This is a fight with wolves and with people who are like wolves and with a merciless God who wants to see blood. That God cannot be her God. How can the *curse* ever be *God's* last word?

Rizpah is the *mater dolorosa* of the Old Testament, an Antigone in Israel. Once again she appears on the stage of history, on Mount Gibeah, and she keeps watch over the corpses.

She is talked about by those living in the neigbourhood, who see this slender women fighting her battle, hear her fighting her battle, over there. There is talk about it in the villages around, and news comes to the court of king David of how this woman has raised her voice day and night against the godforsaken cruelty of great lords, with the Lord on high supposedly on their side.

David hears of Rizpah, and David yields. He hears in her the conscience of Israel. The king bows, and the seven sons of Saul are buried. Together with the material remains of Saul and Jonathan, once lovingly laid in the earth by the men of Jabesh, they may continue to rest in the land of Benjamin. Heaven has been moved to tears, the rain falls, and the famine is over.

55

TWO STORIES TO END WITH

II SAMUEL 23 AND 24

David has grown old, weary of life. The story-teller will soon tell us about his death, but he has kept two stories from former times for now; they seem to him to form a suitable conclusion. These are two scenes which once again illustrate how easily a person goes off the rails, how difficult it is to become a king and yet remain a shepherd boy, and which also show how David regains the right path.

Together with his warriors David is wandering through Judah – at that time he was still a bandit leader. It's harvest time, high summer, and he ends up in the neighbourhood of Bethlehem. David is tired, and he's gasping for water; a cool drink from the spring in Bethlehem would do him good. Over there lies the village where he was born, the land in which he tended the flocks and played on his harp until Samuel summoned him to the kingship. If only he could taste once again the clear water from his childhood, the water with which he watered his flock! Bethlehem, he hasn't been there for years and now he is close by, but he can't get to it, since the Philistines have besieged it. *'Oh, if only someone would give me a drink from the well in Bethlehem which is by the gate!'*

Why speak this thought aloud? Doesn't David realize how much power he has? And that a king by the grace of God may never use this power to satisfy his own needs and longings?

Without his knowing it, three of his men risk their lives to bring David, their David, this drink. They creep straight through the enemy camp to the gate and draw water for David.

But when they get back to camp safe and sound David will not drink the water. They have risked their lives for him. He has prompted this sacrifice, but he may not accept it. *'Is this not the blood of men who have put their lives at risk?'* This sacrifice is not for him.

And David poured out the water before the Lord.

The author of the book of Samuel wants to tell us another story from earlier days.

God's anger has flared up against Israel – we can only guess at the reason – and in his anger he has David counting the people. And had David only seen this command as a temptation, the people would have been spared a disaster. Now there are going to be deaths.

An enigmatic story. What kind of a God is it who first prompts a man to sin and then punishes him because he sinned?

Centuries later the author of the book of Chronicles, who again turned these oral stories about kings into a book, felt challenged by this. And he made a discovery: *Satan prompted David to number Israel.** If the first story-teller had no difficulty in attributing this evil prompting to God, the second preferred to make Satan the mischief-maker.

Such a development in thought is food for theologians: the introduction of an evil Satan to shelter the good God. But the question is whether it gets us out of the problem, for God has then given this Satan more elbow room. Be that as it may, the narrator of *this* story here brings the Eternal One on the scene as the source of both good *and* evil. He knows of the light side of God – the Lord is gracious, and time and again has repented of the evil that he has done – but that is then immediately the Lord's dark side, for then surely God instigated that evil!

The Lord said to David, 'Very well, number Israel.'

It was Joab, David's army commander and advisor, who tried to make his king change his mind. Of course a king may count his subjects, but the king of *Israel* must be careful about doing this. Didn't the Eternal One promise Abraham that a great people would be born from him, as numberless as the grains of sand on the seashore and as the stars in the heaven? Does David want to count God's blessings? 'My advice to you, your majesty, is not to begin on it.'

Joab wants to persuade David to rely more on the promises of heaven than on earthly numbers. What has happened to the trust in God in which he once slew the giant? 'Reflect, your majesty.' But David persists, and so there is nothing for it but for Joab and his men to carry out the king's commands.

For months they go through the land, from Dan to Beersheba, from north to south, to count young and old.

And in the meantime David is having doubts. Has he followed the right course? Can the course his kingdom needs to take be captured in a figure?

David could have known. His own life story began with all too human calculations. Not only is this last David story about numbers, but so too is the first: Samuel, who is sent to Bethlehem to anoint one of Jesse's seven sons king. It was understandable that Samuel thought that the oldest son should be the elect, but he wasn't, nor was the second son, nor any of the seven. Then there proved to be an eighth, who initially wasn't counted, and *that* was the one: David. He could have known.

The measurements in the kingdom of God are different from those in the human kingdom. Jesus the son of David will later proclaim in a parable that in the kingdom of God one lost sheep counts more than the ninety-nine who are in the fold. And again later, a Jewish survivor of the concentration camps tells how in the kingdom of men, counting can lead to godless scenes: 'The guards counted their prey as a miser counts his gold, with sensual delight and excitement. The roll call was a sacred action to them, getting intoxicated to the extent of their power with an insatiable thirst.'*

It's night. David can't sleep. He regrets that he didn't listen to Joab and still went on counting. 'I'm a fool. I have sinned.'

The same night the Eternal One appears to the prophet Gad. 'Go to David and tell him: Thus says the Lord. I impose three punishments on you from which you can choose. Which would you like: seven years of famine, three months in flight from your enemy or three days of pestilence? Think and consider.'

'I am afraid. I would prefer to fall into the hands of the Lord, for his mercy is great, than into human hands.'

Flight again, delivered for three months to human whim? David immediately rejects this possibility. God will once again show mercy and cease to be angry, but one can't expect so much long-suffering from human beings. Rather than protect his people from disaster, David protects himself. God has to choose between the two disasters which remain.

God chooses the pestilence. For three days death makes its trail of destruction through the land from Dan to Beersheba. On the third day the angel of destruction strikes Jerusalem itself. Look, he is standing by the threshing floor of the Jebusite Araunah, high on the hill which looks out over the holy city, and stretching out his hand against it.

'Enough,' cries the Lord, repenting of the disaster that he has brought upon the land. 'Enough. Let your hand fall.'

At the same moment, king David, seeing how the angel of destruction is stretching out his hand against the city, raises his eyes to heaven. 'I have sinned, Lord, but these sheep, the people who live here, what crime have they committed? Stretch your hand against *me and mine!*'

This is another David. No longer the David who wants to save himself and who delights in his power. He is like a priest who prays in humility; like a king who wants to give his life for his people; like a shepherd who has a heart for the sheep.

'Go up to the threshing floor of Araunah,' said the prophet. 'Build there an altar for the Lord.'

David went up as the prophet had commanded him. Araunah saw him coming, went out and bowed before him. 'What brings you here, your majesty?'

'I want to buy your threshing floor to build an altar to the Lord, so that the plague may cease from the people.'

'My Lord the king may take and offer whatever seems good to him. Look, there are the oxen for the burnt offering and the threshing sleds and the yokes of the oxen for the fire. Araunah gives you all this, your majesty. May the Lord your God look graciously upon you.'

'Not at all, Araunah, I shall give you the full price. I do not want to offer the Lord my God a sacrifice which costs nothing.'

David bought the threshing floor for fifty shekels of silver. *And David built there an altar before the Lord and offered burnt offerings and peace offerings. The Lord allowed himself to be entreated for the land, and the plague was removed from Israel.*

The story goes that David's son Solomon built the temple of Jerusalem on the site of Araunah's threshing floor. This lofty place, where king David offered sacrifice and prayer in humility, is to be the place of prayer for all Israel.

56

DAVID DIES

I KINGS 1 AND 2

Israel's prophetic history began with the book of Joshua; now we open the book of Kings, the last part of *The Former Prophets*. If the book of Joshua told of Israel's entry into the promised land, the book of Kings will end with the deportation of the people to distant Babylon. The city of David, which rose to such heights at the heart of these stories, then lay in ruins.

So the story of Israel and Jerusalem is a sorry one. And what about David? Of David too. It's as if the story-teller already wants to depict the downfall of the people in the tarnishing of David. A life which began so brilliantly and flourished so powerfully ends in cold and loneliness.

King David was old and advanced in years, and however many coverings were put on him, he was not warm. His servants said, 'Let us seek a young girl for you, your majesty, to look after you and to lie on your breast, so that you become warm.'

So the king's messengers went in search of the most attractive girl in the land. In Shunem they found Abishag, and they brought her to the king. *The girl was very beautiful and she looked after the king and she served him. The king did not have intercourse with her.*

David is old, old and cold, and even the lovely Abishag cannot arouse any passion in him. The fire is quenched, David is at an end. Is that all that is left of the proud shepherd boy who slew the giant, the singer with his harp, the catlike warrior who escaped Saul, the fiery lover of many women, the ruler who defeated all his enemies, the statesman who brought unity to a divided people, the king who made Jerusalem the royal city, the priest who in rapture danced God's holy ark into the city, and who at the threshing floor of Araunah confessed his sins and pleaded in prayer for his people?

David is now pitiful and alone. Only Abishag is with him, lovely as the spring, to cherish him and offer him the last tenderness. Why isn't

Bathsheba there, the woman with whom he shared his life all those years? Where is Bathsheba?

Bathsheba is downstairs, with Nathan. They're having a crisis meeting. Now that his father is no longer capable, Adonijah, David's oldest still living son, has presented himself as Israel's new king. He has chariots and riders and fifty men who run before him, just like his brother Absalom, who also made an attempt to seize power. Here Adonijah secured the support of no less than Joab and the priest Abiathar. Why hasn't David arranged his succession? Why did he wait?

Adonijah didn't wait. He slaughtered sheep and oxen for a great feast by the spring Rogel: by means of a splendid banquet he wanted to show Jerusalem who would be king over Israel. He invited his brothers and the servants of the king. The only people he didn't invite were his brother Solomon, the prophet Nathan, Benaiah, the head of the royal guard, and the priest Zadok.

Nathan hastened to the palace. He wanted Solomon, Bathsheba's son, and not Adonijah, to ascend the throne. 'Bathsheba, have you heard that Adonijah has proclaimed himself king without David knowing it?'

No, Bathsheba hadn't heard that. Nor was it true. Nathan, the man of God, is making trouble. Does he feel passed over, or does he perhaps fear for his life? 'We must act quickly, Bathsheba; under Adonijah your life and the life of Solomon are no longer safe. Go quickly to David and say, "Did you not swear that my son Solomon would inherit your throne? Why then has Adonijah become king over Israel?" At the moment that you say this to David, I too will enter the room and add my words.'

Bathsheba went to the king in his bedroom. But the king was very old.

There were times when the court whispered, 'Bathsheba went to the king in his bedroom,' but now everything has changed.

'David, once you swore to me that Solomon would inherit your throne. But look, Adonijah has had himself proclaimed king, and at this moment he is holding a great banquet. Joab and Abiathar are there, but Solomon hasn't been invited.'

Did David once promise Bathsheba in the intoxication of love that her son Solomon would succeed him, or is she making this up on the spot?

'You must act quickly, David. If Adonijah ascends the throne, Solomon and I will be in great danger once you have gone to rest with your fathers.'

While Bathsheba was still speaking with David, Nathan came in. 'If I have understood rightly, your majesty, you have ordered that Adonijah shall be Israel's new king. He is holding a great banquet with many guests. "Long live the king," I hear them shouting. However, what surprises me is that neither Zadok the priest nor Benaiah have been invited, nor have I. Did you give orders for this? Why, may I ask, have you not taken us into your confidence?'

David sensed that he had to act. 'As the Lord lives, Bathsheba, your son shall be king after me.'

Bathsheba knelt before David. 'May my lord the king live for ever!'

In haste Solomon was set upon the royal mule and rode to the spring Gihon, right under the palace. There he was anointed king by Zadok the priest. The trumpets were sounded and all the people cried, 'Long live king Solomon!' Afterwards they followed their king with shouts of joy and jubilation up to the palace; *the earth was split with the noise.*

So the festal sounds must certainly have rung in the ears of Adonijah over there at the banquet: his world collapsed. He had ventured and lost. Afraid of being accused of high treason, he rushed to the horns of the altar of burnt offering and held them fast. As long as he clung to the horns of the altar no harm would come to him: that was the Torah of God.

Solomon promised to spare his brother's life on condition that he refrained from any further action.

Then the hour came for David to die. He summoned Solomon. 'My son, I am going the way of all the earth. Be strong. And remember your duty towards the Eternal One: walk in the Lord's way, keep his commandments as this is written in the Torah.'

Had David stopped at these words, he would have made a worthy departure from this life. But there are still some accounts to settle, and David wants Solomon to settle them. The last words of David are full of vengeance. Joab, his faithful general down the years, must pay the penalty. For the wrong he did to Abner and Absalom years ago? Because he took Adonijah's side and along with him might make another attempt to seize power in the future? David also wants Shimei, the stone-thrower, whose life he once spared, to be put to death immediately. *'Let his grey hairs go down to the realm of the dead soaked with blood.'*

Little is left of David's majesty. He dies full of rancour.

Then David went to rest with his fathers. He is buried in the city of David.

Adonijah, Haggith's son, went into the room of Bathsheba, Solomon's mother.

'Do you come with peaceful intentions, Adonijah?'

'Certainly. May I ask you something?'

'Speak freely.'

'You know that the kingship was due to me; all Israel wanted it. But by a sudden reversal it has fallen to my brother. Let it be so. I have only one wish. I truly hope that you will not refuse my request.'

'Speak.'

'Will you ask Solomon to give me Abishag as wife? If you ask, he will certainly grant my request.'

'I shall speak about it to the king.'

Had Bathsheba wanted to spare the life of this son of David, she would never have passed his request on to Solomon. For what is Adonijah asking? Once Abner went into one of the king's concubines to show who held power in the land. Similarly, Absalom went into his father's harem so that all the people should know that David was no longer the lord and master, but he was. And now is Solomon to allow his rival to take the lovely Abishag as his wife? In that case he might as well give him the crown immediately! With his reckless request Adonijah has signed his own death sentence. Benaiah receives orders to carry it out.

Adonijah is the fourth of David's sons to meet his death. The first son, born from David's adultery with Bathsheba, died soon after birth. Amnon, his second son, was killed by Absalom in revenge for the rape of their sister Tamar. Absalom was stabbed with darts, hanging from a branch. Four times a son of David has died. It's as if David has brought down this disaster on himself. He was furious when the prophet Nathan told him about a rich man who seized the ewe lamb of a poor man: 'The man who has done this is a child of death. He must recompense the ewe lamb fourfold.'

Solomon has Shimei, Saul's servant, done away with. Abiathar the priest is deposed and banished. Joab seeks refuge at the horns of the altar, but Solomon nevertheless has him stabbed. So after years of loyal service David's general came to an inglorious end.

There is blood on Solomon's hands. His name means *prince of peace.* It's a name which he still has to make true.

57

THE JUDGMENT OF SOLOMON

I KINGS 3

If in the previous chapter Solomon is depicted as an eastern despot who established his kingship with a hard hand, in the story that now follows we see another Solomon, a pious ruler who on the heights of Gibeon offers his sacrifices to God and then lies down to sleep in the sanctuary, praying that the Eternal One will reveal himself to him in the night.

That night, the Lord appeared to Solomon in a dream: 'Ask what you will and I shall give it to you.'

'Lord, you showed great love to my father, your servant David, who walked before you in faithfulness and righteousness. You have confirmed to him this great love by giving him a son who now sits on his throne.'

With reverence and affection the king first speaks of the man who has gone before him. The world doesn't begin with Solomon; his throne is the throne of his father.

'And now, Lord, you have made me king in place of my father, although I am young. So your servant stands in the midst of this people that you have chosen, a great people, a multitude that cannot be counted. So give your servant *a listening heart* to judge your people, a heart that can distinguish between good and evil.'

It was good in the eyes of the Lord that Solomon had asked for this: 'You have not asked for a long life, or for riches, or for the death of your enemies, but for the capacity of discernment. See, I give you a heart, wise and understanding, as no one has ever had before you and no one will have after you. And what you have not asked me for, I shall also give you: riches and honour. And if you keep my commandments like your father David, I shall grant you a long life.'

Solomon awoke, and look, it was a dream.

Two women came to him, two prostitutes.

'By your leave, your majesty, this woman and I live together in the same house. I bore a child there. Three days later she too brought a child into the world. No one lives in the house but the two of us. In the night this woman's child died; she had lain on it. In the middle of the night she got up, and while I was sleeping she took my child away from me and put her dead child at my breast. Early in the morning I got up to feed my child. He was dead. But when I looked at him more closely, lo and behold, it wasn't the child I bore.

The other woman said: 'That isn't true. My child is the living baby, your child is the dead one.'

'You lie, your child is the dead one and my child the one that is alive.'

Thus the word of the one stood over against the word of the other; there were no witnesses: fathers of prostitutes' children usually live out. What must the king do with them?

> O God, give the king your justice
> and your righteousness to the king's son,
> that he may care for the least.*

'Bring me a sword.'

The king's servant brought a sword. 'Cut the living child in two, give one half to one and the other half to the other.'

The heart of the mother of the living son tightened. 'No, your majesty, no, give her the living child. Give it to her and do not kill it, do not kill it.'

The other woman said: 'Let it be the child of neither of us, cut!'

Solomon knew enough. The woman who was ready to give up her own happiness, her motherhood, for the sake of her child, was the mother. 'Give her the child that lives and do not kill it. She is the mother.'

All Israel heard the judgment that the king had made and was filled with awe. Israel saw that God's wisdom was in him to do justice.

58

THE TEMPLE RISES

I KINGS 8

When David had made Jerusalem the capital of his empire and the religious heart of the land by giving the ark of the Lord a place there, he did not want just to build a house for himself but also a house for God. He spoke about this to Nathan. 'That seems a good idea to me,' said the prophet.*

However, the next day Nathan returned; he had slept on it and in a dream vision from heaven had seen that the Eternal One did not think this a good idea. *I have never lived in a house.*

'And of course that is true, David: the Lord God has never had a house. He went out of Egypt with us in a tent, the wind played through the canvas, and the pegs were loose in the ground, for the next day we went on. If we now give God different housing, won't we also get a different God? The Eternal One is like the wind, you don't know whence it comes and whither it goes. You can't catch God between walls, pin him down with pious words and gestures. We may never imprison God, David, whether in a building, a book, a human being, in stone images or in thought images.'

In other words, Israel was divided over the building of a temple, just as it was at that time over the kingship: there is much to be said for it and much against it, and both the supporters and the opponents are right. First no king was to come, later he came. The temple which David was not to build arose under Solomon.

The God who had never had a house now gets a house. Of course the Eternal One is everywhere, but just as friendship and love also require places and times where one can cherish and preserve friendship and love, so too the covenant between God and humankind requires times and places where this community can be celebrated and deepened.

It is David's son who may build God's house. *Not the blow of a hammer was heard.* It seems like a dream house rising there above the holy city, a prayer in stone. The building is described to us as the silent growth of a miracle. With pious extravagance Solomon made the house of God as attractive as he could, just as a lover gives his beloved the most beautiful jewellery he can find. When the building was finished, the people went in a festal procession to the temple behind the ark, which was carried by the priests high on their shoulders. They also brought all the temple vessels from the tent that David had erected in Jerusalem: the lampstand, the table with the bread, the basins of water. Music rang out from all sides.

The priests reverently set down the ark in the holy of holies, for the Eternal One had said that he wanted to dwell in darkness. The God who makes himself known in Israel is a God who conceals himself.

He is also a God who is not bound to one place. Standing before the curtain, the garment that divides the holy place from the holy of holies, you can just see the curves of the two staves with which the ark is carried. These staves may never be taken out; God is not an unchangeable, an immovable God.

Behind the curtain God dwells, in darkness, and as if that still isn't enough, we are also told that on the day of the consecration a cloud filled the house of the Lord, *so that the priests could not remain there to perform their ministry.*

When the Lord himself appears, a stop can be put to cultic activity. When the Eternal One fills a house or a human heart, all external forms of faith and worship become superfluous.

But the Eternal One never fills a house or a human heart permanently; it is always only just for a while. What remains is the longing. And of the longing prayer is born.

King Solomon enters the temple. He spared neither expense nor effort to build a house for God; the best craftsmen in the land worked on it for seven years. Now his life work is completed; the temple opens its doors. It's a glorious day, the king goes in. People hold their breath; now something is about to happen, now you will hear something, a powerful word from a powerful king. Solomon goes to stand before the altar and stretches out his hands to heaven.

'Lord God, would you dwell on earth? See, the heaven, indeed the heaven of heavens, cannot contain you, far less this house which I have built. Hear then the prayer that your servant offers today before your face. May your eyes be open to this house, night and day, to this place of which you have said, my* *name shall be there. Yes, you shall hear it in the place of your dwelling, in heaven, and you shall give forgiveness.'*

The king as priest. 'O Lord God, I could not have made it more beautiful than I did, but this house is no more than a shadow of your immeasurable glory. This house which we have erected here, a few beams and stones, some cedar wood and gold leaf, cannot of course be your dwelling place. The sea will not fit into an earthenware jar. Your prophet was right: you have never had a house. But Lord, let your name dwell here and hear our prayers. If someone seeks justice in this house, give him justice, O God. If the enemy carries us off, then hear our entreaties and bring us home again. If the heaven remains closed and no rain descends, hear us and give rain on the land that you gave us as an inheritance. If a foreigner comes here from distant lands and he seeks you in this house, then listen to him, for your will is that all the peoples of the earth shall come to know your name. And if because of our sins we are carried off into exile and pray to you in the direction of this land, this city, this house, then hear our prayer in heaven, forgive our sins and give us justice.'

Above all these last words will have spoken to the heart of the exiles in Babylon: centuries earlier king Solomon had prayed for them.

59

THE QUEEN OF SHEBA

I KINGS 10

King Solomon was greater than all the kings of the earth in wealth and wisdom; the whole earth sought Solomon's face to hear the wisdom that God had given him in his heart.

That is Israel's dream. For Israel is never just chosen; Israel is chosen to serve the world of the peoples. Israel is God's testing ground; the field is the world. At the heart of the world lies Israel, and at the heart of Israel lies Jerusalem, and at the heart of Jerusalem stands the temple where God dwells, and from that heart God wants to reach the hearts of men and women, to the ends of the earth, for there too he wants to dwell.

Israel dreams of that in a psalm, a prayer for the king. It is even entitled *For Solomon:**

> *From sea to sea he rules,*
> *from the Jordan to the ends of the earth.*
> *The kings of Tarshish and the coastlands*
> *come to bring him gifts.*
> *The kings of Sheba and Seba*
> *offer him their treasure.*
> *All kings bow before him,*
> *all peoples serve him.*

The prophet Isaiah also sees these beautiful scenes in the distant future. '*A multitude of camels shall cover you; all those from Sheba shall come. They shall bring gold and frankincense, and shall proclaim the praise of the Lord.**

Just imagine. And as you imagine it, then you may see the Queen of Sheba appearing at the gate of the holy city, with precious gifts and the hunger of her heart. *The Queen of Sheba kept hearing about Solomon's sayings and about the name of the Lord, and she came to test him with riddles.*

204

Just like 'the three kings', of whom it is told centuries later that they appeared in Jerusalem in search of the king of the Jews with gold, frankincense and myrrh*, so too the queen of Sheba must have seen 'a star' in her land. Since then she has been seized with a strange unrest, a longing for an unknown God, but one whom she already loves. She has heard of a king, initiated into God's mysteries, a man who can decipher the riddles of life. She saddles her camel and sets out, laden with gold, precious stones and a selection of spices.

The story doesn't tell of a state visit; it's a parable about a queen who hankers after the wisdom that Israel has been given. In it the woman stands for the world of the peoples, and Solomon stands for Israel. May God bless their encounter.

She came to Solomon and told him all that was in her heart. And Solomon explained to her all her words; no word remained hidden from the king, he could explain everything.

The queen revived. All the wisdom and love which the Eternal One has given Israel have become flesh and blood in Solomon. Israel's holy books which bear witness to this wisdom and love – Proverbs, Ecclesiastes and the Song of Songs – were also attributed to him. For the Queen of Sheba all this is a revelation. So much is given to her that in grateful wonderment she exclaims that she had not been told half of the matter. '*What I heard in my land about you and your wisdom is true. I could not believe it until I came and saw it with my own eyes. Praise be to the Lord your God, who had so much delight in you that he gave you the throne of Israel. In his eternal love for Israel he made you king, to do righteousness and justice.*'

And Solomon gave the Queen of Sheba all that she desired.

According to popular belief, that can only mean that the two came together in love. From this a pious legend was born, a dream become reality: the communion between Israel and the people is celebrated here, the love which bids God and human beings together. What is more attractive than that their encounter should be an intimate one and bear fruit?

60

ELIJAH THE TISHBITE

I KINGS 11, 12, 16 AND 17

The wisdom and love given to Solomon radiated into the far distance, but sadly it couldn't last; he too was blinded by power. Moses had already warned against this*: an earthly king who loses sight of the heavenly king begins to over-assert himself, brings up horses from Egypt, seeks his salvation in the accumulation of gold and silver, and surrounds himself with many wives; his heart is no longer with his people or with the God of his people.

Hardly has the Queen of Sheba departed when the narrator takes the king from the golden frame in which he had initially put him. The story began with Solomon's greatness, but it ends with his wretchedness, just as the people will end in wretchedness. Solomon's decline already heralds the decline of the kingdom; one king after another will fall, as the people too falls because it doesn't go the way of the Lord.

The many foreign wives whom Solomon had acquired led him astray into following other gods. His heart was no longer at peace with the Eternal One; he sacrificed to strange gods. And the Lord said to Solomon: 'Because you have not kept my covenant, I shall tear the kingship from you. For the sake of your father David I shall not do this during your lifetime; I shall tear it from the hand of your son.'

And that is what happened: the kingdom which had become a unity under Solomon's father split into two under Solomon's sons. The present-day historian points to the increasing strength of the surrounding peoples as the cause of this spilt, and to the still slumbering opposition between the north and the south. The prophetic story-teller of the time opts for a theological view of the past; he sees the king and his people as it were with God's eyes: *They did what was evil in the eyes of the Lord.* A kingdom that devotes itself only to accumulating treasure and power instead of serving the Eternal One and the neighbour in need brings about its own downfall.

Solomon's son Rehoboam becomes king over Judah, the southern kingdom, with Jerusalem as its capital; a certain Jeroboam becomes king over Israel, the northern kingdom, with Samaria as its capital and with places of sacrifice in Bethel and in Dan, each – would you believe it? – with a golden calf. It's as if we were back in the wilderness and Joshua had never entered the holy land, the land that the Eternal One gave for living in with the Torah and to make a kingdom of God.

Kings come and kings go, and in both the north and the south they do what is evil in the eyes of the Lord. That is true of king Omri: he walked in the ways of Jeroboam, the king of the calves, *indeed he did more evil than all who were before him.*

Historians tell us that this Omri was one of Israel's most important rulers and that in his reign and that of his son Ahab the land had a period of great prosperity. Thus Omri made an agreement with the Phoenician trading cities, and to seal this policy he married his son to the Phoenician princess Jezebel. But once again, this isn't the perspective from which the prophets view these kings. They feel free to demonstrate by Omri and Ahab that a culture goes under if the worship of Israel's God has to give way to the worship of the golden calf.*

Ahab, the son of Omri, became king over Israel. And Ahab, the son of Omri, was king over Israel for twenty-two years in Samaria, and Ahab, the son of Omri, did what was evil in the eyes of the Lord. The least that he did was to walk in the sins of Jeroboam. And he took as his wife Jezebel, the daughter of Ittobaal, the king of Sidon, and he served Baal, bowed down before Baal.

Ahab. *Father's likeness.* A chip off the old block, then, and that promises little good. And what happens? He has Jericho rebuilt. That's turning the clock back. This is a lapse into the time before Joshua, the warrior who destroyed Jericho. Jericho has to fall because in these stories that city stands for a godless world. So in Canaan children's corpses have been found near the houses and under the floors. According to Israel those children were sacrificed to the gods at the building of those houses, magical practices which Israel opposed with all its might.* Therefore it is written in the book of Joshua that anyone who rebuilds Jericho is cursed.

Cursed before the Lord's face be the man
who rises up and rebuilds this city of Jericho.
At the cost of his firstborn he lays its foundation,
*at the cost of his youngest he sets up its gates.**

Now that Israel has reached a nadir in its history, the story-teller recalls the prophetic words of Joshua:

In Ahab's days Hiel of Bethel built Jericho.
At the cost of Abiram, his firstborn son, he founded it,
at the cost of Segub, his youngest son, he set up its gates.

Are these cruel child sacrifices which belong to a distant past? In our day, children are driven over a minefield to spare soldiers. And how many fathers and mothers are prepared to sacrifice their children at the altars of their happiness and prestige?

Cursed be the man who rebuilds Jericho.

It is really high time for this prophetic word to be heard again in Israel, and look, suddenly Elijah is there, quite out of the blue. Elijah the Tishbite. His name means *The Lord is God*. That means that *Baal* is *not* God; a land that makes Baal God is subject to barrenness: '*As the Lord lives, the God of Israel, in whose service I stand, there shall be no dew or rain in these years except through my word.*'

If things go well between heaven and earth, between God and humankind, then the good earth brings forth good fruit, and men and women do good works. The earth which wants to be the earth under heaven is fruitful, just like those who want to live under the kingly rule of God. Not just fruitful in any way, but *at the word of the Lord*. If the word of the Lord is no longer heard, then Baal rules, the god of avarice and possessions, the god who makes human beings walk over dead bodies. Then nothing good will grow any more; everything will be withered and dried up for lack of the heavenly gifts of rain and dew. With the Torah the land becomes the land of promise; without the Torah the land becomes wilderness.

After Elijah has spoken his prophecy of doom, the ground is taken from under his feet. Ahab and Jezebel seek to kill him. A voice tells him that he must go eastwards and hide by the brook Cherith, *which faces towards the Jordan.* Back to the Jordan, where Moses ended and where Joshua began. Back to square one! Back to the question how to live with the Torah in the land which God gives. Back to the wilderness, where God fed his people with manna and quails.

Elijah went and lived by the brook Cherith, which faces the Jordan. And the ravens brought him bread and meat in the morning and bread and meat in the evening, and he drank from the brook.

61

THE WIDOW OF ZAREPHATH

I KINGS 17

'Baal, Baal, send rain.'

But Baal is deaf to the cry of the people. No rain falls, no dew falls, the land of milk and honey withers, the brook Cherith has dried up.

The word of the Eternal One came to Elijah: 'Go to Zarephath in Sidon and settle there. There I shall command a widow woman to give you food.'

In Sidon. Will a widow woman from the pagan land of queen Jezebel have pity on a prophet of Israel's God?

Elijah went. When he arrived at the city gate he saw a woman in black gathering wood. 'Pray bring me some water in this jar, that I may drink.'

The woman went to get it. Elijah called after her: 'Bring me also a morsel of bread.'

She turned round. 'As the Lord your God lives, sir, I would, if only I had bread. I have no more than a handful of flour in the pot and a drip of oil in the jar. I am gathering wood to prepare the last food for my son and for myself. When we have eaten that, death awaits us.'

'Woman, fear not, do as you have said. But first bake a little cake and bring it to me. Then prepare something for you and for your son. For thus says the Lord, the God of Israel: the flour in the pot shall not run out nor the oil in the jar until the day when the Lord shall again make it rain.'

The woman went home and did as Elijah had told her. That is a second miracle in this story: that this widow woman from the pagans did what the prophet told her. Unlike queen Jezebel, that rich powerful woman who seeks to kill Elijah, the poor widow of Zarephath, trusting in the Lord of Israel, has pity on the man of God. She opens her house to him in hospitality. The flour in the pot did not run out, nor the oil in the jar.

The widow of Zarephath has only one child, a precious possession for a mother all on her own in those days: the boy is the provision for her old age. Then – having barely escaped death by famine – the boy falls ill, seriously ill. Life flowed out of him until *there was no breath left in him.* The boy lay motionless in her lap. The mother was inconsolable.

'How are things now with you, man of God? Did you come here to my house to remember my unrightteousness and to make my son die?'

No, the man of God has come here to show up the unrighteousness of Jezebel. We are soon told that *her* sons die. Jezebel is granted no future. But it's different with the life to which the widow of Zarephath gave birth.

Elijah lifted the little corpse from her lap, and carried it carefully upstairs, to the room where he lodged, and put it down on his bed. 'O God, Lord of all life, Lord over death, give us a sign of your loving-kindness and make the breath of life return to this small boy. Cause no evil for the widow who gives hospitality to me as a guest by making her son die.'

In prayer Elijah stretched himself out full length over the child, three times. He embraced the dead child with all his life. 'Lord God, let the soul of this child return within him.'

The Eternal One heard Elijah's prayer; he made the soul of the boy return within him. And Elijah took the child, brought him down from the upper room, and gave him back to his mother. 'Look, your son lives.'

The woman said to Elijah: 'You are truly a man of God. The word of the Lord is trustworthy in your mouth.'

Centuries later the evangelist Luke will make a story about Jesus fit this story about Elijah.* Jesus too meets a widow woman, also at the city gate, and she too has a son, her only one, whom she has lost. It is also written of Jesus that he restored him to his mother, and that story too ends with a joyful recognition that a great prophet has arisen. Again a glimpse of heaven has been caught on earth.

62

ON CARMEL

I KINGS 18

The persistent drought forces king Ahab to scour the land in search of fountains and brooks, and grassy pastures. '*Perhaps we shall find grass to keep our horses and mules alive.*'

The king's greatest anxiety is that the cavalry may come to grief; the prophet's greatest anxiety is that the people may perish.

Ahab goes through the land with his lord chamberlain Obadiah. 'I'll take this way, you take the other.'

The king doesn't know that in secret Obadiah has long been taking 'another way'. His name means *servant of the Lord*. Obadiah may be in the service of Ahab, who serves Baal, but in secret he serves the God of Israel: when Jezebel had the priests of the Lord slaughtered, Obadiah hid one hundred at the risk of his life. He provides them with water and bread in the caves in which they sought refuge. So Obadiah single-handed is keeping prophecy in Israel alive.

'I'll take this way, Obadiah, you take the other.'

It was on this way that Obadiah met Elijah. He went stiff with fright. Has the prophet emerged from his hiding place? 'Is it you, my lord Elijah?'

'It is I.'

The word of the Lord had come to Elijah in the third year of the famine. 'Go, show yourself to Ahab, I will give rain on the earth.'

In the third year. Just like *on the third day*, these words mean that the story is at a turning point, a turning point from death to life, and that God is at work in it. Watch, now something is about to happen. The king of Baal and the prophet of the Lord will meet each other, Ahab in his royal mantle and Elijah in his haircloth coat and with a leather girdle around his loins. Soon the prophet will enter the palace.

But first there is his encounter with Obadiah. 'Is it you, Elijah?'

'It is I. Go and tell your lord, Elijah is coming.'

'What misdeed have I done, that you should have your servant bring this report to Ahab? The king will kill me! There is no people and no land where he has not sought you. He sees you as undermining his authority, a rebel dangerous to the state. And you want me to go to the king to tell him that you are on the way? I can already see it happening. I go to Ahab and meanwhile the spirit of the Lord comes upon you and carries you off, I know not where. The king can only see that you have flown and I shall bleed for it. You know that he isn't bothered over one life more or less.'

Elijah swore to Obadiah that he would show himself in the palace that very day.

'Are you there, you disgrace to Israel?' exclaimed king Ahab.

'I a disgrace, your majesty? How dare *you* say that *I* have troubled Israel? *You* are the one who scorns the commandments of our God and serves Baal. You have brought Israel to the edge of the abyss. No, I am not talking about the drought which is ravaging land and people, I am speaking of what lies behind it: about the apostasy from God, about the righteousness that has departed, the justice that no longer flows like a strong stream. Who is the disgrace here?'

So they stand facing each other, king and prophet – and neither of them will budge an inch. Who is to arbitrate?

'Let all Israel come to Mount Carmel,' proclaims Elijah, 'together with the four hundred and fifty prophets of Baal and the prophets of Asherah who eat from Jezebel's table.'

The children of Israel assembled on Mount Carmel, along with the prophets. Elijah spoke to them. 'How long will you continue to walk lame on both feet, to limp on two opinions? If the Lord is God, then go after him; if Baal is God, follow him.'

Limp. Pesach in Hebrew. Elijah recalls the feast of Passover, when Israel commemorates the exodus from Egypt. 'How long will you go on celebrating Passover ambiguously? You cannot serve both the Lord and Baal.'

The people were silent, alienated from their God and all too ready to seek their salvation with Baal. How can Elijah get the people to say that the Lord is God, the Lord alone?

'I stand here before you as the sole prophet of the Eternal One; the prophets of Baal are four hundred and fifty men. Give us two young bullocks. Let the prophets of Baal choose one bullock, cut it in pieces and put it on the logs, but bring no fire. I shall prepare the other bullock and put it on the wood, and I too shall bring no fire. Then you shall call to your god and I shall call to the God of Israel. The god who answers with fire shall be God.'

The whole people answered, 'That is good.'

Two steers were slaughtered, bull calves which, if they aren't sacrificed, will grow up into symbols of power. The god who consumes this bull with fire will be God. It is the God who once spoke in fire with Moses and summoned him to free his people from the tyranny of Egypt. Elijah believes in this God.

The prophets slaughtered the steers and cried out the name of Baal from morning to noon: 'Baal, answer us!'

No answer. The prophets danced round the altar that they had made. They *limped*. The prophets were celebrating Passover, but with a deaf, dumb god. Nothing happened; from morning to noon nothing happened.

Elijah mocked: 'You must cry out a bit louder! Isn't he a god? Perhaps he's meditating; perhaps he's gone to relieve himself; perhaps he's on a journey; perhaps he's having a doze and must be woken up!'

The prophets of Baal cried louder, and after their custom they castigated themselves with swords and darts; their god wants to see blood. 'Baal, give answer.'

Baal gave no answer.

Elijah came forward and spoke calmly to the people: 'Come closer.' He set up again the altar of the Lord which had been torn down. He took twelve stones, according to the number of the sons of Jacob. So Elijah built an altar to Israel's God, with twelve stones restoring the unity of a divided people. He also dug a ditch round the altar, with enough room for two measures of seed. A new people of God will rise from the dead.

Elijah got the wood, cut the bull in pieces and put it on the wood. 'Fill four jars with water and pour that over the burnt offering and over the wood.' They did so. 'Do it a second time.' They did it a second time. 'Do it a third time.' They did it a third time. How will this sacrifice ever burn?

And it happened at the evening hour of the burnt offering…

Elijah came forward and turned his face to Jerusalem, the city of God, where at this moment the evening sacrifice was being offered in the temple. Our times are in the Lord's hand. At the moment when on Mount Zion the fire for the evening sacrifice was being kindled, on Mount Carmel Elijah lifted his eyes to heaven: 'Lord, God of Abraham, Isaac and Jacob, let it be known this day that you are God in Israel and that I am your servant and have done everything in your name. Answer me, Lord, answer me, that this people may know that you alone are God.'

Then the fire of the Lord descended and consumed the burnt offering, the wood, the stones and the clay; the flames even swallowed up the water that was in the ditch. The whole people saw it and threw themselves to the ground: 'The Lord is God, the Lord is God.'

Elijah spoke to them: 'Seize the prophets of Baal, let none of them escape.' They seized them. Elijah had them taken to the brook Kishon and slaughtered them there.

This story, too, ends with the same violence with which some fairy stories end, and which children enjoy so much. It's theatre, sacred theatre on Mount Carmel. A war of liberation rages here, a life-and-death struggle which everyone has to wage with his or her Baals. Those who choose Baal will perish by Baal. Those who choose the Eternal One will have to make short work of Baal. There will never be peace between God and Baal. Baal promises life, but he leads to death. The Eternal One liberates from death and leads to life. He gives rain.

Elijah spoke to king Ahab: 'Go, eat and drink, for I can already hear the noise of the rain.' Ahab went to eat and drink.

Elijah climbed Carmel. Not a cloud could be seen in the sky. He bowed to the ground, his head between his knees. He prayed. Elijah said to his servant, 'Climb up and look out to sea.'

The boy climbed up, looked out to sea and returned. 'There is nothing to be seen, sir.'

'Go back, my boy, and look again carefully.'

'I see nothing.'

When the boy had climbed up the seventh time, it happened. 'Look, sir, a cloud as small as a man's fist is rising from the sea.'

'Go, my boy, and tell Ahab to harness his chariot and depart quickly, before the rain falls and the wheels of his chariot get stuck.'

From one moment to the next the sky grew black with clouds and wind, and a heavy squall came down. Ahab rode to Jezreel. *And the hand of the Lord was upon Elijah, he girded his loins and outran Ahab, to where one comes into Jezreel.*

That's how it is in Israel. It isn't the king who shows the way, but the prophet.

63

THE VOICE OF SILENCE

I KINGS 19

Eli-jah, his name is his programme: 'There is only one God (*El*) and that is the God of Israel (*Jah*). Any other god who offers himself shall not be your God.'

Someone who – faithful to the Torah – wants to allow only the God of Israel to be God will inevitably be brought into conflict with those who do not want that, the Ahabs and the Jezebels. Elijah has fought this fight, and with God at his side has won a glorious victory. Why is he now so empty and so downcast? After all, Ahab has come off worst; Baal has failed him at the crucial moment, and the king has returned to his palace in humiliation. Yes, but Jezebel is adamant and will not give an inch. In a fury she exclaims that she will not rest until the death of the prophets of Baal has been avenged and Elijah has been killed. And the people again finds itself in the grip of fear and forgets the marvellous sign on Carmel.

Elijah is overcome with weariness. What is he to do now? Why keep on dreaming of a tomorrow that never dawns? The powers of darkness are always stronger. How did Moses cope with that in his day? How did he manage, clinging to his vision of peace and righteousness? Elijah is at the end of his tether.

There is little left of the God's indefatigable champion who swore to convert king and people from their errors. 'Back,' he then cried, 'back to Moses, back to the beginning and to why God began it all. Let's not fall into slavery again. The Eternal One has saved us from that. Why do you constantly lose sight of that? Why do you forget how the storm wind arose and parted the sea and brought us liberty? Why do you forget that God made a covenant with us, high on his holy mountain? The earth quaked, fire descended from heaven, awe seized us, for we knew that God was there. Don't you remember that any more?'

But now Elijah himself doesn't remember it any more. He no longer wants to fight or resist; he wants to disappear into nothingness. In deep dejection he goes to Beersheba. After a day's journey into the wilderness he sits down under a broom tree. Let God now serve *him* and rescue his servant from the intolerable burden of this life. '*It is enough,*' he says. '*It is enough, now let me die.*' Israel has again forsaken the God of the fathers; the people is again bowing to the gods of the queen. What shall the prophet – who must be the voice of God – still proclaim in a world which seeks his life?

Elijah lay down to sleep under the broom tree in the hope of never waking up again.

But look, an angel touched him, '*Arise, eat.*'

Elijah opened his eyes, looked around, and lo and behold, at his head was a loaf of bread, baked on glowing stones. There was also a jar of water. He ate and drank and lay down again.

The angel of the Eternal One came a second time, touched him and said, '*Arise, eat, the way is enough for you.*'

The angel had clearly heard Elijah sigh that he had had enough. 'Enough, Elijah? The way is enough for you! As long as the Eternal One doesn't call you, there is still a way to go. Take the food, drink the drink, eat for the journey, for the way is long.'*

Elijah arose, ate and drank and, having regained his strength, journeyed forty days and forty nights until he came to the holy mountain of God.

A remarkable journey. Elijah went back in his memory to Moses, his great model. He didn't make this journey because he was so pious, but because the angel had aroused in him the longing to become pious again. He travelled back in time, back to Moses, back to the beginning and why God began it all. A pilgrim, on the way to the mountain where the Eternal One once revealed himself. A journey of forty days and forty nights.

Elijah lay down to rest in the cave where God had *passed by* Moses.* 'Lord, led me see your glory,' Moses had asked then. Moses had to go and stand in a cleft in the rock. '*When my glory passes by, I shall cover that cleft in the rock with my hand until I have passed by. Then I shall take away my hand. You shall be able to see me from behind.*'

'What brings you here, Elijah?' said a voice in the night.

'O Lord, I have been so zealous for you. The children of Israel have forsaken your covenant, torn down your altars and killed your faithful with the sword. I alone am left and now they also seek my life.'

'Come outside, Elijah. Go and stand on the hill before the face of the Lord.'

The prophet may not hide himself from God in the cave. 'Outside! Go and stand on the mountain, the mountain of the Torah. Go and stand before the face of the Eternal One.' Israel lives with the Eternal One face to face, or it doesn't live at all. God doesn't want to give up the experiment Israel. 'Come outside, Elijah.'

Will the Eternal One now pass by Elijah, as he once passed by Moses?

And behold, the Lord passed by. First a powerful storm wind arose, which rent mountains and shattered rocks. But the Eternal One was not in the wind. Hardly had the storm subsided, when the earth shook to its foundations, but the Eternal One was not in the earthquake either. Then fire flashed from heaven, but the Eternal One was not in the fire.

One by one the prophet sees his images of God shattered; the former signs of God's liberating presence no longer work.

Then Elijah heard the voice of a pulverizing silence, the voice of an overwhelming, ominous silence. How can a person stand it? Elijah wrapped his face in his prophet's mantle, went outside, and continued to stand at the entrance to the cave.

Again the voice rang out. 'What brings you here, Elijah? Return upon your way.'

The Lord wants Elijah to return to the land that lies behind him, the land where now the voice of prophecy is no longer heard. Retrace your steps, Elijah. I want you to anoint Hazael king over Aram; I want you to anoint Jehu king over Israel; and I want you to anoint Elisha, the son of Shaphat, in your place. Whoever escapes the sword of Hazael shall fall by the sword of Jehu, and whoever escapes the sword of Jehu will be killed by Elisha. Only a remnant of the children of Israel will remain, seven thousand in number, all the knees which have not bowed to Baal, all the mouths which have not kissed him.'

God has changed. He is no longer in the signs of his liberation: not in the storm, not in the earthquake, not in the fire. Now that the children of Israel have forsaken the covenant and seek to kill the man of God, God can only be there in silence.

'Retrace your steps, Elijah.'

Back to the bloody battlefield, where on earth the battle against Baal must be fought, and also against the children of Israel who bow their knees to Baal and whose mouths kiss him. A people that opts for Baal will perish by Baal. Elijah still has a way to go. Then his work will be taken over by Elisha. His name sounds almost like that of Elisha. They are brothers in prophecy: with his name Elijah proclaims that *Eli* is *Jah* and no one else, Elisha that he is a God *who liberates*. With his name, Elijah's successor bears the promise of liberation into the future.

Elijah retraced his steps.

Elisha, the son of Shaphat, was ploughing in the field with his servants, twelve teams of oxen in front of him. It seems that all the tribes of Israel are assembled here. Elisha was with the twelfth team, the tribe of Israel where *he* belongs.

Elijah passed by him.

Just as the Eternal One passed by Moses in the cave, just as the Eternal One passed by Elijah there, so now Elijah passed by Elisha. *And he cast his prophet's mantle on him.*

For Elisha it was as if God himself was passing by. He abandoned his oxen and hastened after Elijah. 'Let me kiss my father and my mother, then I will follow you.'

'Turn round,' said Elijah. 'Have I not cast my mantle over you?'

Turn round. What God said to Elijah, Elijah says to Elisha. 'God wants you, Elisha, to go the way that I too must go.'

Elisha turned round. He will not bid farewell to his father and mother; he will follow Elijah and thus his Lord. He slaughtered the team of oxen with which he had been ploughing, prepared the flesh on the wood of the plough, and gave some of it to all the people on the land to eat. So he broke the bonds with his family and with his tribe. From now on he will belong to all Israel, and is to feed all the people.

Elisha arose, followed Elijah, and served him.

From now on he will plough elsewhere.

64

NABOTH'S VINEYARD

I KINGS 21; II KINGS 1

Naboth was at work in his vineyard, which adjoined the summer residence of king Ahab.

'What an attractive vineyard you have, neighbour,' said Ahab, who was walking on his estate. 'I would very much like you to give me that vineyard; I want to make it into a vegetable garden. I will give you a better vineyard elsewhere in exchange, or, if you prefer, I will give you its value in silver.'

A *vegetable garden.* Anyone who knows the Torah must immediately think of the land of Egypt, the land that you *must drench as a vegetable garden.* By contrast Canaan is a land *which drinks water from the rain of heaven, a land which the Lord God cares for.**

in Israel's stories the promised land is often depicted as a *vineyard,* in which people see life as a gift from God. The *vegetable garden* stands for a land in which people have set up on their own account, independently of the heavenly Owner. 'Naboth, I want to make your vineyard into a vegetable garden.'

So that's what this Ahab has been doing all these years! Exchanging Israel's God for Baal and taking the people back to the paganism of Egypt. The question is what his neighbour Naboth, the Jezreelite, thinks about it.

'The Lord forbid that I should give you the inheritance of my fathers.'

Ahab is talking about a *vineyard* and Naboth is talking about an *inheritance.* For hasn't the land been given to Israel by the Eternal One as an inheritance? And if that is the case, you can't do business with it. *'The land is mine, you are sojourners and guests on it.'** Israel must remain faithful to the Eternal One and to the inheritance of the fathers; it isn't to bow before Baal, the god of the land in which the strongest have the power and the rich enrich themselves at the expense of the poor. *'Woe to him who adds field to field until there is no more room and he only has possessions in the* *land,'* warns the prophet.* In the midst of all those who collaborate with Baal, the Jezreelite Naboth remains faithful to the God of the fathers.

Ahab, offended by Naboth's refusal, goes home in a sulk to lie on his bed, his face to the wall.

'What's the matter, Ahab, why are you so out of sorts, why won't you eat anything?' asked Jezebel.

'I asked Naboth the Jezreelite for his vineyard. I offered him a better vineyard in exchange, or a sum of money. But he said, "I will not give up my vineyard."'

Ahab is twisting Naboth's words. Naboth didn't say that he didn't want to give him his *vineyard*. What he said was, 'The Lord forbid that I should part with my *inheritance*.' The king, who must be the guardian of God's holy Torah, refuses to initiate his Phoenician wife into its mysteries. And *she* knows a great deal. Jezebel hears a quite reasonable proposal for an exchange or a purchase. What's wrong with that? She regards Naboth's refusal as an unprecedented insult. She doesn't understand why Ahab is so downcast. He should have had the rebellious peasant put to death immediately. 'Ahab, who is really master in Israel? Get up and eat, cheer up, I will see to it that you get that vineyard.'

The queen wrote letters in Ahab's name to the elders of Jezreel, instructing them to put their fellow-townsman to death. She sealed the letters with the royal seal. A show trial was held, in which two false witnesses declared under oath that Naboth had cursed God and the king. *God and the king.* For Jezebel there is no difference between blasphemy and *lèse-majesté*. So corrupt was the justice of the land that Naboth was condemned to death with no reprieve. So a smallholder fell victim to big capital.

Jezebel came in person to report the good news. 'Ahab, get up, Naboth the Jezreelite has been stoned, Naboth is dead. Inherit the land which he refused to give you for money.'

Inherit the land. Words once spoken by the Eternal One, no, not to the rich but to the poor, to slaves, who had escaped from the tyranny of Egypt, and crossed the Jordan like down-and-outs. 'Inherit the land.' *Those* are the words that Jezebel speaks.

On his high horse, Ahab went to Naboth's vineyard to inherit it. Jezebel waved him off. She had a strange husband, king of a peculiar people. He had almost allowed himself to be bamboozled by a simple peasant who refused to understand that a request from the king amounted to an order. A good thing that she had intervened.

The word of the Eternal One came to Elijah the Tishbite: 'Arise, go to Ahab the king of Israel. Look, he is in Naboth's vineyard in order to inherit it. Say to him: Have you murdered and also inherited? Thus says the Lord, As the dogs have licked the blood of Naboth, so too shall the dogs lick your blood!'

Elisha arose and went. Look, there he is in Naboth's vineyard, to give a voice to the man whose voice has been silenced.

'Have you found me, my enemy?'

'I have found you, for you have sold yourself to what is evil in the eyes of the Lord and you have caused Israel to sin. Thus says the Lord: I shall bring doom upon you, I shall sweep away your descendants, I shall exterminate from your house all those who piss against the wall, and dogs shall devour Jezebel on the walls of Jezreel.'

And it happened that when Ahab heard these words, he rent his garments. He sat there in sackcloth and ashes; he fasted, he did penance. God saw it. And the word of the Lord came to Elijah: 'Have you seen how Ahab has humbled himself before my face? Therefore I shall not make this evil come in *his* days. I shall make this evil come in the days of his *son*.'

Unfortunately Ahab again succumbed to evil and the end of the sorry tale was that he met his death on the battlefield from a stray arrow. His chariot dripped with blood and dogs lapped it up.

And how did things go with Ahaziah, his son? *Ahaziah went the way of his father and the way of his mother, he offended the Lord.*

But anyone who offends the Lord and seeks his salvation among the idols ultimately finds the only thing that you can find among the idols: death. At least that is the view of the prophetic story-teller, as is also evident from the next story.

One day king Ahaziah fell though the trellis of the window of a room high in his palace and became ill. Uncertain whether he would recover from his illness, he sent messengers to the priests of Baal-zebub in the land of the Philistines.

That god is really called Baal-zebul, *Lord enthroned on high*, but the narrator mockingly turns his name into Baal-zebub, *Lord of the flies*.

Meanwhile the angel of the Lord said to Elijah, 'Go to the messengers of king Ahaziah and say to them, "Is there no God in Israel that you turn to Baal-zebub?"'

The messengers of Ahaziah found the messenger of God on their way. 'Why do you turn away from the Eternal One? Return and say to the king: Thus says the Lord, the bed that you climb into you shall never come down from. You shall die, die.'

The messengers returned to the king: 'You've been quick about that.'

'A man crossed our path and told us to return. Thus says the Lord, he said, the bed that you climb into you shall never come down from. You shall die, die.'

'What did that man look like?'

'He wore a hairy garment, and his loins were girt with a leather girdle.'

The king was terrified. 'That must have been Elijah, Elijah the Tishbite.'

Not long after that he died.

Thus this sorry story about the son of queen Jezebel is a mirror image of the joyful story about the son of the widow of Zarephath. Both women come from pagan Sidon, the one a princess of good fortune, the other a needy widow. Both of their sons fall sick.

Elijah *goes up* the stairs to his *upper room* with the sick boy from Zarephath, there to raise him from the *dead*; the boy will *come down living, according to the word of the Lord.*

Elijah tells the sick king's son who in Samaria has *fallen* from his *upper room* that he will *never come down alive* from the bed that he *went up into*; he will find *death* there, *according to the word of the Lord.*

The woman from Zarephath saved the prophet's life; Jezebel hounded the prophets to death.

65

ELIJAH GOES TO HEAVEN

II KINGS 2

Elijah is approaching the hour of his end; soon he will no longer be in the land of the living. Will prophecy also disappear from the land with his departure?

And it happened that when the Eternal One was going to make his servant Elijah ascend to heaven in a storm wind, Elijah left Gilgal. Elisha went with him. Elijah said, 'Remain here, Elisha, for the Lord has sent me to Bethel.'

Elijah thinks it better to bid farewell in Gilgal. He wants to prevent Elisha expecting his master to transfer the office of prophet to him. Only the Eternal One can make a person a prophet. 'Remain here.'

But the love of this pupil for his teacher cannot bear such a hidden death, a dying in solitude. 'As the Eternal One lives and you yourself live, I shall not forsake you.'

So the two went to Bethel. And look, sons of the prophets, followers of Elijah, came to meet him from Bethel. They took Elisha aside and asked, 'Do you know that today the Lord will take your master from over you?'

'I know,' said Elisha, 'be silent.'

Elijah said: 'Remain here, Elisha, the Lord has sent me to Jericho.'

'As the Eternal One lives and I live, I shall not forsake you.'

So the two went to Jericho. Sons of the prophets from Jericho came to meet them. 'Elisha, do you know that today the Lord will take away your master from over you?'

'I know,' said Elisha, 'be silent.'

Elijah said, 'Remain here, Elisha, the Lord has sent me to the Jordan.'

'As the Eternal One lives and you live, I shall not forsake you.'

So the two went on together, to the Jordan, to the bank of the river, to the border of the land of the living.

They went the way of Joshua, the way of the man who brought the

Torah into the land, but at that time in the opposite direction. With his end before his eyes, at the bidding of the Eternal One Elijah goes from Gilgal to Bethel, from Bethel to Jericho, from Jericho to the Jordan. He has to go back to the wilderness, where Moses died and Joshua began. It's as if the entry has to be undone. Must prophecy leave the land? What then will remain of Israel? What is the Torah without the prophets?

When they arrived at the Jordan, the fifty sons of the prophets who had accompanied Elijah and Elisha stopped. They saw from afar how Elijah took his mantle, rolled it up and put it in the water. The water gave way and Elijah and Elisha went between it to the other side.

And it happened that when they had crossed over, Elijah said to Elisha: 'Make me a wish. What can I do for you before I am taken from you?'

Elisha said, 'Let a double portion of your spirit come upon me.'

That is what the firstborn in Israel received, a double portion.* So Elisha is really asking, 'Let me be your firstborn, I want to continue to honour you and remember you as my father.'

Since the hour of his calling, when he left his father without bidding him farewell, Elisha has seen Elijah as his father. 'Let me be your son, prophet in Israel.'

'It is not for me to say that to you, Elisha; it lies in the hands of God. It will happen if you see me when I am taken from you. If you do not see it, it will not happen.'

Only if the Eternal One allows Elisha to share in the mystery by which Elijah lived will he be able to be his son. If he doesn't see it, he won't be a seer, a prophet. If he has eyes to see how Elijah is taken away from the earth, that is a gift of God.

And it happened that while they were going, walking and talking, look, a chariot of fire and fiery horses separated the two of them. Elijah went up to heaven in a storm wind. And Elisha saw it!

Elijah is taken up to heaven in a chariot by the fire by which he lived, borne up by the breath of the Eternal One. And Elisha? Elisha sees it! The Lord has appeared to him. Elisha has become a seer, a prophet. What would he have to tell over there in the land if he hadn't seen the land on the other side? A new prophet has arisen. Elisha will be Elijah's son.

'My father, my father,' he exclaimed, 'you are Israel's armed forces.'

The power of Israel lay in the power of prophecy. Israel's armaments are the voice of the prophet.

And Elijah saw him no more. He took his garment and tore it in two. Then he put on the mantle of Elijah which had fallen from him. He turned round and continued to stand on the bank of the Jordan. He took the mantle of Elijah and put it on the water. 'Where is the Lord, the God of Elijah?' Like Elijah he smote the water, and the water gave way and Elisha crossed over.

The Lord confirms what Elijah did to Elisha when he cast his mantle over him and called him from behind the plough. Just as the Eternal One did with Moses when he stretched out his staff over the sea, just as the Eternal One did with Joshua when he crossed through the water of the Jordan with the ark, so the Eternal One has done with Elisha. Prophecy returns to the land! The history which began with the exodus of Moses and the entry of Joshua now begins again.

The sons of the prophets from Jericho saw Elisha from the other side and said: 'The spirit of Elijah rests upon Elisha.' They prostrated themselves before him. 'See, sir, your servants, fifty men, strong, bold folk. Let us go out and look for your master; perhaps the spirit of the Eternal One has taken him up and cast him down somewhere on the mountains or in a valley.'

'You need not look,' said Elisha. But when they continued to urge him mournfully, he said, 'Go on and look then.'

The sons of the prophets hadn't seen what Elisha saw. They should have listened to Elisha, who has seen it, but they don't. Then they have to work it out for themselves.

After three days they returned. They hadn't found the dead man.

'Did I not tell you?'

Elijah is nowhere to be found, any more than the grave of Moses is to be found. The Eternal One has taken good care of him. Anyone who wants to honour Israel's prophets should honour the word of God that Moses received in the wilderness, that Joshua bore through the Jordan, and that Elijah proclaimed throughout the land with so much fire.

Together with Elijah, Elisha has gone from Bethel to Jericho and from Jericho to the Jordan. Now Elisha returns as a prophet through the Jordan to the land. He goes to Jericho and from there to Bethel. So he literally treads in the footsteps of his great predecessor.

A new prophet treads the soil of Israel. And what he has to do there is told us in a nutshell: in two parables, each with a theme that will later be developed at length. In Jericho Elisha demonstrates the *healing* power of the prophetic word, and in Bethel its *devastating* power.

The well in Jericho is polluted; the dirty water causes miscarriages and death. This well is like Israel, the spiritual well which has also become unclean and which produces catastrophe.

'Bring me salt,' said Elisha.

They brought him salt. Elisha threw the salt into the spring. 'Thus says the Lord, I shall make this water sound again; no death or miscarriage shall result from it again.'

True prophecy is like salt: it purifies teaching and life. *And the water became pure again, to this day, according to the word that Elisha had spoken.*

In Bethel Elisha is mocked by boys: 'Go up, bald head.' The prophet cursed them in the name of the Lord, and two bloodthirsty she-bears came up from the wood and tore the boys to pieces.

A grim tale which relates how the children of Israel who mock God and his prophets will perish: they will be punished by the bloodthirsty Hazael and Jehu – instruments in God's hand.

As it was in the time of Elijah, so too it will be in the time of Elisha: in Israel the prophet is a matter of life and death.

66

BRING ME A MINSTREL

II KINGS 3

Three kings go out with their armies through the wilderness: Joram, who has become king of Israel, the northern kingdom, after the death of his father Ahab; Jehoshaphat, the king of Judah, the southern kingdom; and his vassal, the king of Edom. They're going to fight against Mesha, the king of Moab, who after Ahab's death refused to go on paying tribute to Joram. Jehoshaphat proved ready to accompany king Joram and his vassal from Edom on this punitive expedition. *'I shall go with you. You and I, your people and my people, your horses and my horses, we are one.'*

They want to invade Moab from the south, where king Mesha doesn't expect such an attack, but for the moment an attack is out of the question, for after seven days' journey through the wilderness the water is used up. The men and the horses are perishing from thirst.

As always in times of disaster, the question arises, Why? Joram presumes that the Lord is the one who is thwarting them and wants to deliver them up to Moab. 'We've fallen out of favour, don't you think, Jehoshaphat?'

Jehoshaphat is silent. He thinks it dangerous to identify God and nature in this way, for in that case how does God differ from Baal? Joram may have pulled down the idols of his father Ahab and his mother Jezebel, but the old thought-patterns are still standing. 'Jehoshaphat, don't you also think that the Lord is against us?'

Jehoshaphat doesn't know. What does a man know of God? 'Isn't there some prophet here through whom we may enquire of the Lord?'

'Elisha lives here, your majesty,' say one of Joram's servants, 'the prophet who served Elijah for years.'

'Let's go to Elisha; the word of the Lord is with him.'

They come to the prophet's hut, but to begin with he doesn't seem prepared to say a single word from the Lord. Joram is simply told crossly that he must go to his father's and mother's prophets of Baal and leave Elisha out of it.

But Jeshoshaphat the king of Judah insists, and Elisha feels that his longing for God is genuine: 'Joram, were it not for the sake of Jehoshaphat, I wouldn't think you worth a glance. Well then, bring me a minstrel.'

And it happened that when the minstrel played on the strings, the hand of the Lord came upon Elisha.

Something began to vibrate in his soul; the evil which kept him from other people and God was dissolved in the sounds of the music. Elisha was receptive to the word of the Lord. 'Dig ditches in the valley.'

An absurd command of Elisha's. Dig ditches in the wilderness. Just as foolish as what Noah once had to do: build an ark in the yard behind his house. 'Dig ditches, for soon you will not be able to hold the water.'

Israel's God can give water even in the wilderness. And so infectious was Elisha's faith, that although there wasn't a breath of wind or a cloud in the sky, the kings immediately began to dig ditches.

It's an old truth: life is what you believe. Those who expect nothing get nothing. Those who expect little also have a thrifty God and receive little. Those who expect everything stammer something, sooner or later, like, 'The Lord is my shepherd, I shall lack nothing, my cup overflows.'*

The next morning, just when the food offering was being made in the temple, look, water came and drenched the earth.

The Moabites heard that the kings had come out against them for battle. All the men who could hold a weapon stationed themselves on the frontier. The sun rose over the water and coloured it as red as blood.

'Just look,' they exclaimed, 'that's blood! The kings have certainly killed one another, each has turned against the other! Come on, Moab, off to the plunder!'

Unprepared for a battle, they suffered a devastating defeat from the three kings.

67

DEATH IN THE POT

II KINGS 4

Elijah and Elisha: their names are similar and the legends which go the rounds about this 'father' and 'son' also show great affinity, as the four stories which now follow tell us. They are stories about life and death.

The wife of one of the sons of the prophets seized Elijah and cried out: 'Your servant, my husband, is dead. You know that he was a godfearing man. And now the creditor has come to take away my two children as slaves.'

The Torah indeed commands that widow and orphan must be protected, but for the hard-hearted man at the door, business is business. Unless he is paid rapidly in hard cash, her children will become his slaves. Then the woman will have nothing and no one. In her despair she turns to Elisha. 'In God's name, help me!'

His name means *God is a help*.

'What can I do for you? What do you have in the house?'

The woman does *not* have gold and silver in the house. As a good pastor, the prophet asks what she *does* have in the house, for she will have to make do with that.

'Your servant has nothing in the house, sir, except a little jar of oil.'

'Go, ask your neighbours and acquaintances for vessels, empty vessels, a lot of them. Then close the door of your house behind you and your sons, pour oil into those vessels, fill them to the brim, and set aside those that are full.'

The woman and her sons collect empty vessels for oil that they do not have in the house. The neighbours shake their heads: what kind of folly is this? It's like digging ditches in the wilderness for water that isn't there.

When she gets home again, the widow woman shuts the door on herself and her sons. The boys bring the vessels and she fills them one after the other from her little jar until all the vessels are full to the brim.

'Quick, another vessel.' The little jar keeps on pouring.

'There aren't any more vessels, mother.'

It seems that the limit doesn't lie with God's fullness but with the space a person has available to receive this fullness. And when this is used up... *Then the oil stopped flowing.*

The woman hastens to Elijah. 'Go,' he says, 'sell the oil, pay your debts and live with your sons on what is left over.'

The second legend also tells of a woman: not a poor woman but a well-to-do woman, a Shunammite. On his journeys through the land Elisha used to stay with her and her husband. He was a welcome guest. One fine day they even had a separate room for him made on the roof, the prophet's upper room, with a bed, a table, a chair and a lampstand.

Moved by so much hospitality, Elisha wanted to express his gratitude. The woman might make a wish, but she had none.

'Can I perhaps put in a word for you to the king or the army commander?'

'That isn't necessary, sir, I live in the midst of my people,' the woman replied self-confidently.

What could he do for her, then? 'Do you know anything?' he asked Gehazi, his servant.

'They have no child, sir, and her husband is old. It's a great sorrow.'

'Call her.'

Gehazi called the woman; she stood in the doorway. 'Did you call me, sir?'

'Around this time, in a year, you shall embrace a son.'

'Oh no, my lord, you man of God, don't delude your handmaid.'

A year later she gave birth to a son. When the child had grown up, one day he went to his father, who was in the field with the reapers. There he suddenly fell ill. 'My head, my head!'

'Take him to his mother quickly,' the father said to one of his servants. That same noon the boy died in her arms, the child that heaven had given. But surely that cannot be! The mother took the dead child in her arms, carried him upstairs and put him on the bed of the man of God. She said nothing about the boy, not even to her husband. 'Give me a servant and an ass, I must go quickly to the man of God. After that I shall return.'

The husband didn't understand why his wife had to go to the prophet so urgently. 'Today isn't new moon or sabbath, is it?'

'Just be patient.'

But to the servant she said, 'Quick, quick! Drive the ass on without stopping!'

Elisha sat on Mount Carmel and saw the Shunammite woman approaching from afar. He sent his servant Gehazi to meet her. 'Is it well with you? Is it well with your husband? Is it well with your child?'

'It is well.'

Gehazi is told no more.

When she reached the man of God on the mountain, the woman embraced his feet. Gehazi wanted to intervene, send her away, but Elisha restrained him. 'Her soul is bitterly sorrowful, I don't know why. The Eternal One has kept that from me.'

The woman said, 'Did I ever ask my lord for a son? Didn't I tell you that you mustn't deceive me?'

Elijah sent Gehazi to Shunem. 'Gird up your loins, take my staff in your hand and go. Greet no one on the way, do not stand on ceremony, travel on as quickly as you can and put your staff on the boy's face.'

However, the woman didn't go with Gehazi; she remained with the prophet. She wanted the man of God and no one else to accompany her. *'As the Eternal One lives and as you live, I shall not forsake you.'*

These are the very words that Elisha said to Elijah when death was about to part them.

Elisha arose and followed the woman to Shunem.

Gehazi had put the staff on the boy's face but in vain; the spirits of life hadn't returned. 'The boy has not awoken, sir.'

Elisha went into the house, and look, the boy lay dead on his bed. Elisha closed the door; only he and the boy were in the room. Elisha prayed to the Eternal One and went to lie on the boy, his mouth on the boy's mouth, his eyes and his hands on the boy's eyes and hands. He continued to lie on him like this. The boy's body became warm. After that he went downstairs, walked up and down in the house, went up again and once more lay on the boy. Then the boy sneezed seven times and opened his eyes. Elisha called Gehazi. 'Summon the Shunammite.'

Gehazi called her. 'You can carry away your son. He lives.'

The woman fell at Elisha's feet. After that he took her son and went away. Elisha and Gehazi left the house to return to Mount Carmel.

The boy grew up and thrived. His mother could tell fine stories about the love of God which overcomes death. And the boy always remembered that little room upstairs, with that chair, that table, that lampstand and with the bed on which he came back to life.

Famine broke out in the land; the prophet and the sons of the prophets had almost nothing to eat.

'Put the big pot on the fire,' said Elisha to the cook, 'and cook vegetable stew for the sons of the prophets.' Another servant went into the field to gather plants. He found a wild vine and picked its fruits, his lap full; they looked edible. When he got back, he cut the fruit in pieces and put them in the stewpot. The cook filled it to the brim, but hardly had the men tasted it when they cried out, 'Man of God, death is in the pot.' The food was inedible.

'Get flour,' said Elisha.

He put a handful of flour in the pot. '*Ladle it out for the people, for them to eat.*'

And lo and behold, there was no longer anything bad in the pot.

Yet another story about famine has been handed down to us.

A man came to Elisha with twenty barley loaves and fresh wheat. The prophet was supported by the pious people like a mendicant friar. Elisha immediately wanted to share what he'd been given. '*Give it to the people, for them to eat.*'

'Twenty barley loves for one hundred men, how do you think that will go round?' his servant asked him.

'Give it to the people to eat, for thus says the Lord: eat and survive!'

Man shall not live by calculation, but by faith and hope and love.

The servant gave them the bread and they ate and they had some over, according to the word of the Lord.

Sharing is multiplying. Provided that you continue to break bread, there is enough for everyone.

68

THE HEALING OF NAAMAN

II KINGS 5

Naaman the commander of the king of Aram was a great man in the sight of his lord.

The warrior hero often returned to his land as a victor, laden with booty. He has given his wife a Hebrew serving girl, captured during a campaign in Israel. Naaman has riches and fame. See how proudly he walks through the streets of Damascus; he walks like an immortal. Then fate strikes: Naaman becomes a leper. Disaster for him and his house, everyone laments. Except for the slave girl from Israel: 'My lord your husband must go to our prophet in Samaria; he will be able to make him better.'

The young thing knows of a mysterious power which could cure the commander of his leprosy. In this story she stands for lady Israel, called to bear witness to God in the world of the peoples.

'Your majesty,' Naaman said to his ruler, 'my wife has heard from our serving girl from Israel that a prophet lives in her land from whom I can find healing.'

'That's good news, Naaman. I shall give you a letter of commendation to the king of Israel, along with ten talents of silver, six thousand shekels of gold and ten outer garments.'

Not a letter of commendation for Israel's *prophet* – the king of Aram thinks that a prophet is in the service of the king.

'With this letter I send you my commander Naaman. Be so good as to cure him of his leprosy and accept these gifts as a sign of my gratitude.'

Israel's king tore his garments. How could *he* decide on life and death? 'Am I God, that I have power over life or death? Of course the king of Aram is looking for a pretext to attack us.' In his fear he neglected to do what a good king should have done: to send the unfortunate Naaman to the man of God. A serving girl lives in distant Aram who understands more about that.

Fortunately Naaman's arrival didn't remain hidden from Elisha: 'Why, your majesty, have you rent your garments? Let this man come to me, that he may know that there is a prophet in Israel.'

Elisha's sons of the prophets didn't believe their eyes when they saw the stately procession of Aramaean carriages and horses riding past, and Naaman didn't believe his eyes when he saw the simple hut in which the man of God lived. He was too proud to go in, and Elisha didn't come out; he sent Gehazi, his servant. Does the prophet know who he has before him? 'My master says that you must go to the river Jordan and wash in it seven times. Then your body will be healthy again; you will be clean.'

Naaman must perform a ritual. He has to bathe in the water of the holy river and do so in a holy sequence. He must immerse himself in the Jordan and thus in Israel's history. Where the Eternal One has made a new beginning with Israel, he wants this man from the pagan world to make a new beginning. 'Wash in the Jordan.'

That was too much for a great man like Naaman. Or rather, it was too little. He's being treated like a small boy. He has to put aside his pride and arrogance, his uniform and his royal accoutrements. Then he must go down into the Jordan, a ditch compared with the Abana and Pharpar, the broad rivers of Damascus. Naaman had imagined a different kind of reception: the prophet coming out with great ceremonial, solemnly invoking the name of his God and meanwhile waving his hands over the white patches on his skin. Insulted, Naaman turned round and gave his drivers orders to return to his own land.

'I don't think that he's going to the Jordan,' said Elisha's servant when he got back.

'That's a shame,' said Elisha.

But Naaman did go! In this story, in which kings fall short and subjects bring about salvation, it is Naaman's servants who put their master back on the right track. One of them speaks. 'My father, if the prophet had asked something great of you, you would certainly have done it. Nothing would have been too much for you. Why then is this simple thing too little? You are willing to spend gold and silver on a cure; is it too much to ask you to make a few dips in the Jordan? A child can do it!'

Naaman heard the wisdom in the words of his servant. Now he understood what the prophet required of him: he was to become like a child. He went down and immersed himself seven times in the Jordan, confidently surrendering to the mystery of Israel.

And Naaman's body became sound again like that of a small boy. He was clean.

The great man who had become like a small boy hastened back to Elisha with his followers. 'See, now I know that there is no other God on the whole earth than the God of Israel. May your servant offer you a gift?'

'The Lord forbid that I should accept your gifts.'

Naaman urged Elisha, but he was not to be persuaded.

'Give me then a load of earth from your land, as much as a pair of mules can carry. I shall never again offer sacrifices to the gods, but only to Israel's God.'

Naaman has gone through the Jordan; he has become part of Israel, incorporated into the people of the Torah, and to express his abiding bond with the land of promise he wants to take a load of earth from that land back home. 'May the Lord, your God and my God, forgive me if I enter the temple of the god Rimmon with the king of my land. The king then leans on my arm, so I too must bow to Rimmon.'

From now on Naaman will have to live in two worlds, and that can't be done without compromising. He asks the man of God in advance for forgiveness.

'Go in peace.'

Naaman went.

Gehazi looked on, gnashing his teeth. His master has just let Naaman go, with all his silver and gold! That rich Aramaean dearly wanted to hand over his gifts, but the prophet preferred to remain poor! Gehazi ran after the coach. Naaman saw him coming, stopped and jumped down from the carriage. 'Is all well?'

'All is well. We suddenly have guests, two sons of the prophets, and to tell the truth we have nothing in the house. Now my master asks whether you can perhaps give us a talent of silver and two sets of upper garments.'

'I shall give you two talents of silver and the clothes besides.'

Naaman was glad that he could still do something; he felt bad that all his wealth was still on the beasts of burden. And Gehazi was glad that he could relieve him of some of the burden. When he got home he hid his treasures, and cheerfully returned to Elisha's dwelling.

'Where have you come from, Gehazi?'

'I? I haven't come from anywhere, sir.'

'Wasn't I with you in the spirit, Gehazi, when a man jumped from his carriage for you? Did you think it necessary to enrich yourself? Naaman's leprosy shall come upon you and upon your descendants, for ever.'

Gehazi went away, as leprous as snow.

Naaman was a great man in Aram. He came to Israel, became like a little boy and was cleansed.

Gehazi was a little man; he let go of Israel, he wanted to become great, and he became unclean.

Whether he later found healing, just like Naaman, the story doesn't say.

69

THE BLIND AND THOSE WHO SEE

II KINGS 6

The king of Aram was at war with Israel. He laid an ambush, but Elisha, God's seer, saw with the eye of his spirit where he had camped and warned his ruler, so that he could take measures not to be caught unawares. That happened many times, and the king of Aram smelt treachery and summoned his commanders. 'Which of you constantly betrays our position to the enemy?'

'None of us, sire; it is Elisha the prophet who sees and hears everything with his divine gift. Even what you whisper in your bedroom doesn't remain hidden from him.'

'Where does that man live? I shall send troops to silence him.'

'He is in Dothan, sire.'

It was a dark night when Aram's troops besieged the city. Early in the morning one of Elisha's servants discovered their horses and chariots; they were surrounded. 'What must we do, sir? We can't get out in any direction.'

'Do not fear,' said Elisha. 'Those who are with us are more than those who are with them.' However, fear and dismay did not depart from his servant's eyes. 'Lord, open his eyes that he may see,' the prophet prayed.

The Lord opened the servant's eyes: he saw, and look, the hill was full of fiery horses and chariots. The God who once took the great Elijah up to heaven in a fiery chariot and fiery horses now also encircled Elisha and his men.

The king of Aram went down to occupy Dothan and kill the man of God. Elisha lifted his hands to heaven. 'Lord, strike this warrior people with blindness.'

The Lord smote the warrior people with blindness.

The servant of the prophet who had recently been blind was given sight, and the warriors who had seen were struck blind. 'Who are you looking for?' asked Elisha.

'We are looking for Elisha.'

'Elisha? He's in Dothan.'

'Isn't this Dothan?'

'No, this isn't Dothan, you're on the wrong track. Let me go before you and bring you to the person you seek.'

Elisha led the warriors smitten with blindness to Samaria, Israel's fortress. Unsuspecting, the Aramaeans walked behind him like the rats of Hamelin behind the pied piper. They went through the city gate. Then, in the heart of the city, before the palace, they stopped. 'Lord, I pray you, open their eyes that they may see again.'

The Lord opened their eyes, the spell disappeared, they saw, and look, they were in the middle of Samaria like rats in a trap.

Israel's king visibly enjoyed that moment. Justice at last. No Aramaean would escape. 'Shall I slaughter them, my father, shall I slaughter them?'

'No, you shall not,' said Elisha, his father. 'You do not kill prisoners of war. Given them bread and give them water, so that they may eat and drink. Then let them return home.'

On the square in front of the palace a meal was arranged for friend and foe. The circle of evil had been broken. *The marauding bands of Aram did not show themselves in the land again.*

So great had become the number of sons of the prophets who surrounded Elisha that they had to look out for larger accommodation. 'Let us go to the Jordan, sir, and there saw beams and planks to build a house and live in it.'

'Go.'

'Sir, be so good as to go with us.'

'All right, I shall go with you.'

Elisha went with them. They arrived at the Jordan. And look, one of the sons of the prophets was cutting a tree with an axe; the head flew off and fell in the water.

'Oh, sir, the iron of my axe has fallen in the water. And this axe is not mine; I borrowed it from someone.'

'Where did the iron fall?,' asked the man of God.

The son of the prophet showed him the place.

Elisha cut off a piece of wood, threw it in, and made the iron rise to the surface. 'Take it.'

The man stretched out his hand and took it.

It began with Elisha cleansing the polluted well of Jericho with salt. Then the prophet showed that nothing is impossible for the one who trusts God, against all the odds. Then lepers are cleansed, the blind see, wood sinks, iron floats. Then water begins to flow in the wilderness and oil continues to flow out of a small container. Then there is bread for all, war turns into peace, death into life.

In a man who puts all his trust in God, unsuspected powers rise to the surface.

70

THE SIEGE OF SAMARIA

II KINGS 6 AND 7

But the circle of evil was not *permanently* broken through. The circle of evil never is; it always has to be fought against. *And it happened that Benhadad, the king of Aram, assembled his whole army, went up and besieged Samaria.*

The king of Aram besieged Samaria for so long that the people risked dying of hunger. The provisions shrank, the price of food rose, and what food! An ass's head cost eighty silver pieces and a clump of dove's droppings five.

Every day the king of Samaria went the rounds on the walls of the city. He tried to instil courage into his people, but they were at the end of their tether. Wouldn't it be better for him to stop doing the daily round? The attitude of the citizens began to become threatening here and there, as if they thought that the king was to blame for all the disasters. He read hatred and envy in their hollow eyes, and it wasn't difficult for him to guess their thoughts. 'There's still food in the palace. They don't have it so bad in the palace; we should make him a plate of rubbish.'

A woman detached herself from the people and screamed to him, 'Help us, your majesty!'

'If the Lord doesn't help you, where can I get help from? From the threshing floor, or from the wine press?'

Silence fell. What next? The king couldn't help, but by God he couldn't go on either. The only thing that he could do was to stand and listen. 'Woman, what is it?'

'The woman standing next to me, your majesty, said to me, "Let's eat your son today, then we'll eat mine tomorrow." That's what we did: we cooked and ate my son. But when I asked her the next day where her son was, so that we could eat him, it proved that she had hidden him.'

Filled with dismay, the king tore his royal robes. In a world in fragments, that garment was also torn in fragments. *The people saw him pass by on the wall, and see, under his cloak he wore a mourning garment, on his bare skin.*

There he went, the king who under his stately royal garment had this piece of sackcloth, his mourning garment. And where he went, the voices fell silent. It wasn't his intention that the citizens should see it, but now they did. They were moved. A man who seemed to live on the other side of their suffering was still one of them. He said nothing more, only made a gesture, and that gesture was comforting. Outwardly their ruler seemed the unbroken bearer of power and dignity. He went proudly before his people. Inwardly he was torn by the same suffering as they were. When his royal garment still clad him, only God knew the sorrow that this king bore in secret. Now they all knew.

The hunger went on and on, and in the end the king too was at the end of his tether. His faith had gone, and in his despair he heaped reproaches on the prophet. Hadn't Elisha once said that they shouldn't go into battle, but that it was better for them to endure a siege, or does the king see the siege by Aram as a sign of God's anger, and does he let *his* anger over it descend on the head of the man of God? 'Have that prophet's head cut from his body!' The king sent his adjutant to carry out the sentence.

Elisha felt disaster approaching and ordered his people to shut the door before the king's adjutant reached his house. But the man was already inside. 'Look at the evil that has come upon us from the Eternal One. What can we still hope from the Eternal One?'

But Elisha said: 'Thus says the Lord, tomorrow at this time a measure of fine meal will cost a shekel in the gate of Samaria and two measures of barley also.'

The man of God is certain of it: there will be enough food for everyone, and at normal prices.

'Do you want me to believe that?' said the adjutant. 'Even if the Almighty made windows in heaven, such a thing couldn't happen.'

The adjutant didn't yet know the story of the floating axe.

Elisha said: 'You shall see it with your own eyes, but you shall not taste it.'

Four lepers sat at the gate of the city. The men were starving to death. 'Why are we still sitting here? We can enter the city where hunger reigns, and we will doubtless die there. But we're also dying here. So let's go over to the camp of the Aramaeans. If they leave us alive, we shall live, but if they want to kill us, then we shall die.'

The four lepers had nothing to lose. In the evening twilight they got up and went to the camp of the army of Aram. How strange, not a person to be seen! How could that be?

They didn't know that the Eternal One had made the trees in the forest behind the hill rustle and that the king of Aram and his men out of sheer fright had heard this noise as the approach of chariots and horses, a great army. Panic in the camp. 'The king of Israel has hired the kings of the Hittites and the Egyptians to attack us.' Head over heels they ran for their lives, leaving behind them all their possessions.

The four lepers went into the tents and satisfied their hunger with food and drink. They also satisfied their hunger for silver and gold by plundering. They hid their treasures.

And then they realized: *'This is a day of good news and we are keeping silent!'*

Up to the gate, where they told the guards the great news. At first the king couldn't believe the report; he feared an ambush. 'Send out two chariots on reconnaissance, your majesty, with the horses that we still have. It may be that the observers die, as so many of us have died. It may also be that they are left alive. We shall see.'

It wasn't long before the warriors returned at the gallop. 'We're free! We're free!'

The starving citizens thronged outside through the gate, plundered the camp and returned laden with provisions. The king's adjutant, who the day before had exclaimed mockingly that the prophet's word would never be fulfilled, was appointed by the king to watch the gate. While he was gazing at the abundance of food with his own eyes, he was trampled on by the frantic people so that he died. 'You shall see it but never taste it,' Elisha had foretold.

And it happened: a measure of fine meal cost a shekel, two measures of barley also.

71

ANOINT TWO KINGS

II KINGS 8, 9 AND 13

Once the prophet Elijah had received three tasks from God: 'I want you to anoint Hazael king of Aram, I want you to anoint Jehu king of Israel, and I want you to anoint Elisha prophet in your place. Whoever escapes the sword of Hazael shall fall by the sword of Jehu, and whoever escapes the sword of Jehu shall be killed by Elisha. Only a remnant of the children of Israel shall survive, seven thousand in number, all the knees which have not bowed to Baal, all the mouths which have not kissed him.'

Elijah carried out the last task; it was for Elisha to anoint these two kings.

Also the king of Aram? Why does the Eternal One give a prophet in *Israel* the task of anointing *Aram's* ruler? What has the man of God to do with the succession in Damascus?

According to the prophetic story-teller, *everything*, since he sees the king of Aram as an instrument in God's hand to strike Israel because of the wickednesses committed by Ahab and Jezebel. The doom that is to come upon Israel is a judgment from God.

Ben-hadad, the king of Aram, was sick when Elisha arrived in Damascus. 'Your majesty, the man of God has come into the city.'

The king summoned his adviser Hazael.'Go to the prophet, take a gift with you, and ask the Lord through him whether I shall recover from my sickness.'

With many precious gifts, loaded on forty camels, Hazael went to Elisha. 'King Ben-hadad has sent me to you. My lord asks you whether he will recover from his sickness.'

'Go to your Lord and tell him, "You shall recover, yes, recover." But know well that the Eternal One has shown me that your Lord will die, yes, die.'

Elijah has seen in the spirit that the king's days are numbered. But Hazael must keep this harsh truth hidden from his lord.

The man of God saw more, and so gruesome were the scenes which passed before his eyes that he couldn't keep back his tears.

'Why are you weeping?'

'Because I know the evil that will come upon the children of Israel, Hazael. You will burn their fortresses with fire, kill their young men with the sword, smash their infants to pieces and rip open their pregnant women.'

Elisha wept with dismay on seeing the images of the approaching disasters. Hazael saw things otherwise: 'Do you think that I, your worthless servant, am capable of doing something so great?'

Paganism cannot manifest itself in a more shameless way. Hazael saw the brute force of violence that he would unleash – if the prophet's word was fulfilled – as *something great.*

'The Lord has shown you to me as king over Aram.'

In pronouncing these words Elisha has proclaimed Hazael king of Aram and fulfilled his task. Hazael returned to Damascus.

'What did the man of God say?' Ben-hadad asked him.

'That you will recover, your majesty, recover!'

The king needn't be afraid that he will die of his sickness.

The king will die of something else. The next day Hazael again entered his bedroom, soaked a coverlet in water and pressed it down on the king's face so that he suffocated. Hazael became king of Aram in his place.

Now the third task awaited Elisha: anointing the army commander Jehu king over Israel. Rather than go himself, he entrusted this dangerous task to one of his disciples. 'As soon as you have anointed Jehu king, get out of there as fast as your legs will carry you.'

The young prophet met Jehu in the midst of leading the army and asked for a conversation with him in an inner room of the house. There he poured oil on Jehu's head. 'Thus says the Lord, the God of Israel. I anointed you king over the Lord's people. You shall smite the house of Ahab, and avenge the blood of the prophets that clings to Jezebel's hands. The whole house of Ahab will perish, and Jezebel will be devoured by the dogs on the field of Jezreel. No one shall bury her.'

Hardly had the son of the prophet spoken these words when he opened the door of the room and made his escape. Jehu returned to his fellow-soldiers. 'What was that *meshuggah* on about?'

'Oh, just gossip, you know that kind of fellow.'

'You're lying. What did he say?'

'He said, "Thus says the Lord: I anoint you king over Israel."'

The men hastened to spread their outer garments before him and blew the trumpet. 'Jehu has become king, king over Israel.'

King Joram, Ahab's son, was unaware of any danger. Recovering from the wounds he had incurred in a fight with Hazael, the king of Aram, he was remaining in Jezreel. Jehu set course with his men for Jezreel; the watchman on the gates saw him approaching in a cloud of dust.

'Send a rider to meet them,' commanded Joram. 'Ask, Is it peace?'

The rider spurred his horse. 'The king asks you, Is it peace?'

'Peace?' replied Jehu, 'What peace? Join my following!'

The watchman on the tower saw that the rider didn't return. 'The rider isn't returning, sire.'

A second rider is sent out. 'The king asks you, Is it peace?'

'Peace?' replied Jehu, 'What peace? Join my following!'

'The second rider isn't returning either, sire. If you ask me, it's Jehu who is tearing towards us like a madman.'

'Harness my chariot.'

Joram went to meet Jehu and encountered him on the land of Naboth the Jezreelite. 'Is it peace, Jehu?'

'What peace? What is peace as long as the whoredom and magic arts of your mother Jezebel flourish?'

Joram turned the reins and sought to flee, but Jehu drew his bow right back and hit Joram between his shoulder blades; the arrow pierced his heart and, fatally wounded, he hung over the back of his chariot. 'Pick him up,' said Jehu to his charioteers, 'and throw him on the land of Naboth the Jezreelite. Didn't the Eternal One swear that on this field he would avenge Ahab's crime?'

In the palace of Jezreel, queen Jezebel is informed of her son's death. She made up her eyes, arranged her hair, and sat in front of her high window. Regally she has lived, and regally she will die. She has never understood why Israel's prophets regarded her zeal for Baal as whoredom, seductions which the people of God must resist powerfully. Nor has she ever seen why the same prophets accuse her and her husband of carrying out a policy in which the small landowners become the victims. She has lived in the midst of an alien people, and on alien soil she will die.

Down below she sees Jehu coming through the gate. 'Is it well with Zimri, the murderer of his lord?,' she shouts from the window.

She could hardly be more sarcastic. Jezebel is talking to Jehu about Zimri. When she was still a princess, a certain Zimri had murdered his defenceless predecessor, but he hadn't lasted long as king; within seven days he, too, was dead. 'Is all well, Zimri? Is all well with the cowardly murderer? Do you want to play king for one week?'

Jehu looked up at her window. Jezebel's servants stood in the other frame. 'Who is on my side?' Jehu cried out to them. Two or three of them gave a sign. 'Throw that woman down.' The courtiers threw her down, and her blood splashed against the wall and the horses. Jehu seized the reins and drove his chariot over her lifeless body.

The country's new king arranged a feast; he ate and drank, while outside the dogs feasted on Jezebel's remains.

When Jehu was clearly in a slightly better mood after the meal, he ordered Jezebel's body to be buried. She might be accursed, but after all she was the daughter of a king. However, Jehu's servants found nothing but her skull, her feet and the palms of her hands. 'There is no more left of her, your majesty.'

Then Jehu remembered the word of the Eternal One spoken by the mouth of his servant Elijah the Tishbite. 'On the piece of land of Jezreel shall the dogs devout the flesh of Jezebel; the remains of Jezebel shall be as refuse on the field of Jezreel.'

Jezebel is accursed, and accursed she will remain. *No one may ever be able to say. 'This is Jezebel.'*

The pious popular tradition judges Jezebel more gently. Why were the palms of her hands preserved? Because she had clapped her hands at wedding feasts, sharing the joy of the lovers. And why were her feet spared? Because she used them to accompany funeral processions, sharing in the sorrow of the mourners. So Jezebel wasn't utterly corrupt.

72

ELISHA DIES, PROPHECY LIVES ON

II KINGS 8 AND 13

Seven years previously, Elisha roused the dead child of the Shunammite woman to life in the little room that the woman had made for the prophet. Moved by so much hospitality, the man of God had then asked her whether he might perhaps put in a good word for her with the king. At the time the Shunammite woman had declined: 'I live in the midst of my people.'

But for seven years she hasn't lived in the midst of her people. On the prophet's advice, she had fled from famine to the land of the Philistines. Now she thought the time had come for her to return, but to her horror her house proved to be occupied by someone else, and he refused to leave the place that he had illegally appropriated. Should Elisha now be her spokesman to the king? No, she can cope on her own. Indignant, she hastened to the palace. 'Give me justice, your majesty,' she exclaimed, 'give me justice.'

At that very moment the king was speaking to Gehazi, Elisha's servant. *'Tell me, Gehazi, all the great things that Elisha has done.'**

'In Shunem Elisha raised a dead person, sire. Look, there's the woman whose son he raised to life.'

The woman approached. 'Give me justice, your majesty, my house and home have been taken from me and again hunger is staring me in the face.'

'In truth, your majesty, this is the woman of whom I spoke, the Shunammite, and that is her son.'

The woman told her story. Not long afterwards she left the palace, accompanied by a servant on the orders of the king. 'See that this woman gets her property back, and also the produce of the field from the day that she left the land to today.'

248

Elisha was sick with the sickness of which he was to die. King Joash, son of Jeoahaz, grandson of Jehu, came to visit him. He wept, for how was Israel to go on when Elisha was no more? *'My father, my father, the armed forces of Israel!'*

Those were the very words that Elisha exclaimed in desperation when he had to bid farewell to the dying Elijah. Prophecy makes Israel Israel; without a prophet, the people and its king are powerless. 'My father, my father, how will it be with us when you are no longer there?' Just as the father comes before the son, so in Israel the prophet comes before the king.

Elisha said: 'Take a bow and arrows.' The king took a bow and arrows. 'Put your hand on the bow.' The king put his hand on the bow, and Elisha put his hands on those of the ruler. As if he wanted to say, 'Now I am going hence, from now on you must be Israel's chariots.'

'Open the window to the east.'

Joash opened the window. Over there lay Aram, where the unscrupulous Hazael wielded the sceptre. 'Shoot!' said Elisha. The king shot. 'It is the arrow of liberation which God gives you, the arrow of liberation from the power of Aram. You shall smite Aram until it is destroyed. Take the arrows.' The king took them. 'Strike them on the ground.' Joab struck them on the ground, once, twice, three times. Then he stopped.

'Why do you stop?' asked Elisha in a fury.

Joash did what anyone else would have done. Third time lucky. But that's wrong; the king mustn't do what everyone else does. More may be expected of a king. 'You should have struck five or six times; then you would have inflicted a devastating defeat on Aram. Now you will smite Aram three times.'

Elijah died and was buried in a rock tomb.

The new year dawned, the harvest was in, and so the hordes of Moab again came rushing in to plunder Israel's barns. And it happened that just when they were burying a man, look, another band of invaders approached. Helter-skelter, the bystanders threw the body of their dead man into the neighbouring rock tomb of Elisha and made good their escape.

The man touched the bones of Elisha and again came to life and stood up on his feet.

Israel is like this dead man, now that the prophet is dead: powerless and abandoned by everyone. But you only need to be touched by prophecy and you revive. The power of prophecy extends beyond the bounds of death.

73

KING HEZEKIAH

II KINGS 18 AND 19

Kings came and kings went, but one after they did *what was not good in the eyes of the Lord*. The Torah was trampled under foot in the land. Was that what the Lord God given the land for? For the prophetic story-teller it isn't surprising that finally the Assyrians came to drive Israel out of the land again. He can only see the fall of Samaria and the subsequent exile of the northern kingdom as a divine punishment. *They did not listen to the voice of the Lord; they had not listened to all that Moses had commanded them, nor had they done it.*

The anxious question now arises whether Jerusalem, too, will fall, and the inhabitants of Judah, the southern kingdom, will also be carried off into captivity. God grant that this will not happen. God grant the people a king who does what is good in his eyes.

And it happened that Hezekiah, the son of Ahaz, the king of Judah, became king in Jerusalem. The name of his mother was Abi, the daughter of Zechariah. He did what was right in the eyes of the Lord, just as David, his father had done.

At last a good king. David was his spiritual father and Abi his mother, *The Lord is my Father*. Zechariah, *The Lord remembers*, was his grand-father. So this Hezekiah has good credentials. His name was at the same time his vocation. *My strength is the Lord*. In great trust in God he broke with the idols and destroyed the high places. He obeyed the Lord and did what Moses had commanded. As a second David he slew the Philistines and rebelled against Sennacherib the king of Assyria by refusing to pay any more taxes.

Wasn't that over-confidence? Only recently Assyria had overwhelmed Samaria and deported the ten tribes of the northern kingdom. In anger, Assyria would soon stand at the gates of Jerusalem. What happened then?

Two stories go the rounds about that. One story tells how Hezekiah, seeing that Sennacherib, the king of Assyria, had occupied all the fortified cities of Judah and was advancing on Jerusalem, offered submission and declared himself ready to pay many talents of gold and silver if Sennacherib would spare the holy city.

The second story – that we also find in the book of Isaiah* – tells how Sennacherib sent a courtier to persuade Hezekiah to surrender. *The man stood in front of the watercourse from the uppermost pool, by the street which leads to the fuller's field.*

At that very spot, years earlier the prophet Isaiah had prophesied to king Ahaz, Hezekiah's father: '*See, the young woman shall become pregnant*' – he was referring to Ahaz's wife Abi – '*and bear a son, and she shall give him the name Immanuel, God with us.*'* Then Hezekiah was born.

'I have come with a message for Hezekiah,' said the courtier to the three delegates whom Hezekiah had appointed: his lord chamberlain, his recorder and his chancellor. The courtier doesn't say that Hezekiah is *king;* for this Assyrian Hezekiah has already ceased to be king.

'You have a messenger for our ruler?'

'That I have,' said the courtier, actually in Hebrew. 'Thus says Sennacherib, the great king of Assyria. What kind of trust is it that you cherish? Do you think I am just speaking empty words, using threatening language that I will not carry out? In whom do you trust, that you dare to rebel against me? On the support of Egypt? Just look at reality. What is the Pharaoh of that land but a broken reed? If you lean on him he breaks in your hand.'

The courtier looked around; the people on the wall kept silent. 'Do you trust in the Eternal One? This Hezekiah of yours claims that. But was it not Hezekiah who destroyed the high places of the Lord and ordered Judah to offer sacrifices only on the altar of Jerusalem?'

The courtier is lying; Hezekiah simply purged the high places of all idolatry!

'My king will make a wager with you: he will give you two thousand horses if you have riders for them! Thus says my lord, the great king of Assyria. Do not think that I have come up to destroy Judah without the Eternal One. It is truly the will of God that I stand before your gates. I am only an instrument in his hand and I shall not leave one stone upon another. What do you want, your own God is against you!'

Hezekiah's delegates shuddered. What this huckster of paganism is saying with his lying propaganda is calculated to confuse people. He doesn't fear to take the holy name of God upon his lips, and in Hebrew at that; the people on the wall don't miss a word of what this demagogue says! The chamberlain is afraid that they will be hoodwinked by this crafty theology: God is almighty, therefore he is the cause of everything that happens, thus he is always on the side of the strongest! The chamberlain tries to avert the evil: 'Allow me to interrupt you for a moment. I would ask you to speak Aramaic with me and not Hebrew; the people on the wall can understand your every word.'

'It is precisely because of the people that I have come. Is it not precisely the people on the wall who are driven by hunger to eat their own dung and drink their own piss?' And once more Sennacherib's servant raised his voice, so that everyone could hear him: 'Listen to the word of the great king, the king of Assyria. Do not let yourselves be deceived by Hezekiah; he cannot save you. Do not believe his so-called trust in God. Do not think that the Eternal One will save your city. Why should the people of Assyria and the people of Israel not be a blessing to each other? Let us together form one people and restore law and order. Then each one of you will eat of his own vine and his own fig tree, then each one will drink the water from his well, until I come to take you to my land, a land like yours, a land of grain and new wine, a land of bread and vineyards, a land of olives, oil and honey. So you shall live and not die.'

It's as if you're hearing the great Moses speaking about the promised land! This deceiver stands everything that is sacred to Israel on its head: injustice is called justice, subjection is depicted as a reconciliation rich in blessing, exile as a deliverance.

Assyria's courtier fires a last poisoned arrow from his bow. 'The Eternal One will save us, cries your king. A false hope! How many people have we already trodden under foot? Did their gods save them? Did the gods save Samaria? And do you believe that the Eternal One will save Jerusalem?

There was silence. No one spoke a word. What was there to say against such a torrent? The man of Assyria spoke anti-language, non-language. It sounded like the language of Canaan, but he said precisely the opposite.

The chamberlain, the recorder and the chancellor returned to Hezekiah, their clothes torn as a sign of mourning. 'Blasphemies, your majesty, vain use of the holy name of our Lord.'

Hezekiah listened, arose from his throne, tore his royal garments, covered himself with a sack and went into the house of God. He sent his chamberlain, his recorder and the elders of the people with a message to the prophet Isaiah: 'Thus says Hezekiah. This day is a day of distress, punishment and shame. Jerusalem is like a woman in the pains of childbirth: her child has come to the mouth of the womb, but she has no more strength to give it birth. Perhaps the Lord has heard the words of the man whom the king of Assyria sent to scorn the Eternal One, and perhaps the Lord will not leave his words unpunished. Isaiah, please send up a prayer for the little flock which still remains of Israel.'

Isaiah heard the lament of Hezekiah's servants. 'Say to the king: Thus says the Lord, do not fear the blasphemy of Assyria's king. Truly, terrible tidings will come to him and make him return to his land. There in his own land I shall fell him with the sword.'

Sennacherib increased the pressure on besieged Jerusalem still further and sent another message to Hezekiah, in the form of a letter: 'Do not let your God deceive you. You trust in that God, you believe that Jerusalem will not fall. Have you then never heard of all those lands which Assyria has conquered? And do you think that you will escape? I ask you, have the gods of those lands ever had one helping hand stretched out to them? And their kings, too many to mention, what has become of them?'

Hezekiah sped to the house of God. There he spread out the letter before the face of the Lord. 'Lord God of Israel, will you please read this? You who are enthroned on the cherubs, you alone are the God of all the kingdoms of the earth, you who have made the earth and the heaven. Then incline your ear and hear, open your eyes and see what Sennacherib has written, *all those words that he sent to taunt the living God.*'

Just as David trusted in the Eternal One and went out to meet Goliath, *who came to taunt the living God,** so too this son of David – besieged by gigantic paganism – trusts in the Eternal One. 'I know, Lord, that the Assyrians have swept away peoples and lands and thrown their gods in the fire. But they were not gods at all, they were the work of human hands, gods of wood and stone, gods that you can destroy. I pray you, Lord, save us from the power of this man, that all the kingdoms of the earth shall know once and for all that you are God.'

The Eternal One will not allow his own land and people to be swept away by Assyria. Otherwise the Sennacheribs of all times and places would be able to scorn the God of Israel with impunity. 'Incline your ear, Lord, open your eyes!'

The Lord inclined his ear, opened his eyes and spoke through the mouth of Isaiah his prophet: 'Thus says the Lord, the God of Israel, to Sennacherib, the king of Assyria: virgin Jerusalem, the patroness of the holy city, despises you, she mocks you, the daughter of Zion shakes her head at you. Who have you taunted and shamed? To whom did you raise your voice and proudly direct your gaze? To the Holy One of Israel! I have heard you say, "I am the one who in the north with many chariots ascended the heights of the mountains, the flanks of Lebanon, where I uprooted its great cedar trees, the choicest of its cypresses. I went down to the south, to the land of Egypt, where I dried up the delta of the Nile with the soles of my feet."* I have heard you say it. As if *you* were the Lord of history, not I. You were no more than an instrument in my hand. I know your sitting down, your coming and going, and your fury against me; your arrogance ascends to my ear. Therefore I shall do with you as you do with those whom you defeat: I shall put my hook in your nose, my bit between your lips. So on a rope I shall lead you along the way that you came.'

'Were these the words of the Eternal One?' asked Hezekiah.

'Yes, sire. And this shal be a sign for you: this year you shall eat what grows of itself, and the second year its produce. In the third year, however, you shall again sow and reap and plant vineyards and eat of their fruit.'

The appearance of the enemy has made it impossible to cultivate the land. But there is a prospect of better times. When Elisha's work is done, God will preserve a little remnant: 'The little flock of Judah which is still there will again dwell in peace and bear fruit.'

These were words which years later also rang like music in the ears of the exiles in Babylon.

'Fear not, Hezekiah, for thus says the Lord: I shall protect Jerusalem against the king of Assyria. He shall return the way he came without having set foot in the city. I shall save you for my sake and for the sake of David, my servant.'

And it happened in that night that the angel of the Lord went out and slew one hundred and eighty-five thousand men in the camp of Assyria.

Sennacherib and the few men remaining to him returned to Nineveh.

And it happened that when Sennacherib was prostrating himself in the temple of Nisroch, his god, his sons killed him with the sword.

Even in distant Nineveh Sennacherib wasn't safe from Israel's God. Nisroch couldn't save him, any more than he could save himself.

74

THE HEALING OF HEZEKIAH

II KINGS 20

Hezekiah became seriously ill. Was the king dying?

The king was dying. Isaiah the prophet came to tell him in person. 'Thus says the Lord: do what still remains to be done as ruler over this house, for you shall die, you shall not remain alive.'

Hezekiah turned his face to the wall.

He turns away from the man who announces disaster to him. He turns to his God, not in surrender but in protest: 'Is this your will, Lord? Let me yet live!' Hezekiah is too sick to go to the house of the Lord, as he used to do in time of need, but he can still pray in his own house. 'Remember, Lord, how I constantly went my way before your face in dedication and faithfulness and did what was good in your eyes.'

Hezekiah wept. He wept a great deal.

And it happened that hardly had Isaiah left the middle courtyard when the word of the Lord came to him: 'Go back, say to Hezekiah the ruler of my people: Thus says the Lord, the God of David your father, I have heard your prayer, I have seen your tears. Look, I heal you; on the third day you shall go to the house of the Lord.'

Isaiah returned. 'The Eternal One has spoken to me once again, your majesty. You shall be healed and on the third day again you shall go to the house of the Lord.'

There is still time for Hezekiah.

'What will be the sign of that?' he asked.

'Can you see the shadow there on Ahaz's staircase?'

Hezekiah's father Ahaz had built that staircase there, the king who did what was not good in the eyes of the Lord. The decline after David had continued in Ahaz's days; with the monarchy it had gone further 'downstairs'.

'Do you see the shadow on Ahaz's staircase? Do you see the shadow that comes down on the steps with the setting of the sun? What would you like? Should the shadow go ten steps forward or ten steps backwards?'

'Backwards! In God's name, backwards!'

Isaiah the prophet called to the Lord and the Lord made the shadow which came down on the steps of the staircase of Ahaz go backwards, ten steps.

Hezekiah revived.

Merodach-baladan, the king of Babylon, heard of Hezekiah's healing and sent a delegation with letters and gifts.

Hezekiah was delighted at the arrival of the delegation, and he proudly showed them his treasures: the silver, the gold, the spices, the best oil and his whole arsenal of weapons. There was nothing in his house and in his kingdom that Hezekiah did not show them.

Isaiah came to the palace. 'Who were those men?'

The prophet feels anxious. How often has he warned the kings of Judah about the kings of the lands round about! Surely Hezekiah won't be so naïve as to fall into the trap! 'Where did those men come from?'

'They came from a distant land, from Babylon.'

'What did they see in your palace?

'They saw everything in my palace, everything. There is nothing among my treasures that I did not show them.'

'How could you have done that? The moment that you show such people your precious treasures, you've lost them. Hear the word of the Lord: See, the days are coming when everything that is in your palace, all the treasures that your fathers have collected to this day, will be taken away to Babylon. Nothing of them will remain. And your sons, the descendants that you fathered, will be eunuchs at the court of the king of Babylon.'

Because of Hezekiah's prayer God liberated Jerusalem; because of his prayer he found healing in the face of death. *Those* were the treasures that Hezekiah had accumulated in his lifetime, and one might have expected that since he was no longer attached to things transitory he would have wanted to show *those* treasures. Does the king realize that, at long last?

Hezekiah said to Isaiah: 'The word of the Lord which you have spoken is good. There shall be peace and truth for the days of my life that remain to me.'

He would die purified. Hezekiah would enter into no other alliance than with the Lord.

75

IN EXILE

II KINGS 22-25

After Hezekiah things kept on going downhill in Israel. Other kings appeared. They did what was evil in the eyes of the Lord and their subjects followed them. It could not be long before Jerusalem was destroyed, the temple plundered, the people taken away prisoners. In the eyes of the prophetic story-tellers the Eternal One must make an end of the sorry story which had begun so promisingly with Joshua's entry into the land.

Did nothing at all go right, then, in those days? After Hezekiah, wasn't there one king to whom the exiles by the rivers of Babylon could look up, a genuine son of David?

And it happened in the eighteenth year of king Josiah that the king sent his scribe Shaphan to the house of the Lord.

The temple was in decay, and Joshua ordered Shaphan to put in hand the restoration of the house of God with the money that had been collected. He was a king who did what was good in the eyes of the Lord. *He walked wholly in the ways of his father David, and did not depart from them, to the right or to the left.*

Shaphan returned from the temple with a scroll in his hand. 'Look, your majesty, what the high priest gave me. He found this scroll in the house of the Lord. Shall I read it out to you?'

And it happened, when the king heard the words of the book of the Torah, that he rent his garments.

If what is written there is of God, if this is the word that the Eternal One gave to Moses, the word that Joshua received to give form to in the land, and if what Shaphan is reading out from it is true, that Israel's king is called on constantly to read in this book and live by it,* then Israel has been found wanting and then Israel's rulers have failed; then it is appropriate to do mourning and show penitence and where possible avert the

258

evil. The book with which Joshua entered the land*, how could it have been forgotten?

The book lay living buried under rubble
it called from between the temple foundations.
Sometimes old men who came there heard
the fiery voice they knew of old.

It was found. Priests who read it
did not understand the letters that they spelt.
An old woman could still explain the meaning.
They brought it to Josiah. He was dismayed

by what he heard: centuries-old unaccustomed
pure truth: old commandments
never done which should save the poor
and establish righteousness on earth,

by so many treasures which had been lost
by so many indications from the distant past
he was dismayed, by so many words of love
*swept away, the life of light for men.**

And it happened that when the king heard the words…
'Shaphan, go to Huldah the prophetess, and consult the Lord for me and for the people about the words of this book which has been found. The Lord's anger must be great, because we have not listened to the words of this book.'

Huldah, a prophetess. Now that the story-tellers are on the point of completing their prophetic work, they can't help thinking back to the beginning. The first prophetic figure that they brought on stage – it was the time of the judges – was a woman, Deborah. The story-tellers want to finish their composition by also making the last prophet in the land a woman. 'Say to your king: Thus says the Lord. See, I am bringing disaster on this place and on its inhabitants, for they have forsaken me; they have offered sacrifices to other gods, they have insulted me with the work of their hands. My anger against this place has been kindled, an anger which will not be quenched. But you, O king, shall die in peace. Your eyes shall not see the disaster on this place.'

The downfall of city and land was inevitable. God saw no other way – that was the only way in which the prophets could read the history of the land and people. But before they make us witness the collapse of Israel, they first want to tell of king Josiah, the one shining figure who rediscovered the Torah and was indefatigably zealous for the Lord.

The king sent out messengers and they gathered all the elders of Judah and Jerusalem to him.

Together with the people of the city and the land, great and small, they assembled in the temple square and in the hearing of them all king Josiah read out from the book of the covenant which had been buried alive in this house of God for years and years. And Josiah made a new covenant before the face of the Lord: 'The Lord alone shall we serve. From now on we shall live obedient to the words of the covenant, as that is written in this book, heart and soul.'

'Amen,' said the people.

The king added deed to word: idols were removed, consecrated poles were ground to dust, high places razed to the ground. Away with paganism! The horses which the kings of Judah had consecrated to the sun had to leave the field, sacred stones were smashed to pieces, priests were slain on their own altars.

It's a misunderstanding to think that pagans aren't believers; they're believers in a terrifying way. Pagans believe in the power of nature, in the power of the strongest; they bow before the god of numbers, they worship blood and soil. Only those who have heard the words of the book of the covenant know with the prophetess Huldah that those gods lead irrevocably to destruction. 'Away with those gods, the Lord alone shall we serve.' They're idols. That doesn't mean that they don't exist; it means that they can't exist for a true Israelite.

Don't think that Israel is preaching religious intolerance here. By means of stories, here a perplexed people is reflecting on its banishment from the promised land. Those who do not live with the Torah find themselves far from home. The exiles are emphasizing the need to break with gods who – as their history teaches them – lead only to slavery and servitude.

After making a clean sweep of the temple and then having had a great spring-clean throughout the land, Josiah returned to Jerusalem. *The king now commanded the people: 'Celebrate Passover to the Lord your God, as it is written in the book of the covenant.' For no Passover had been celebrated from the days of the judges who judged Israel and during all the days of the kings of Israel and the kings of Judah. But in the eighteenth year of king Josiah this Passover was celebrated before the Lord in Jerusalem.*

They celebrated Passover as the people celebrated Passover with Moses on the night when they departed from the slavery of the Egyptian captivity. They celebrated Passover as Joshua and his people celebrated Passover when they had entered the land. There is still hope for the exiles in Babylon if they rediscover the words of the Eternal One and break with the gods. The people that knows of liberation and celebrates Passover unanimously may live in the expectation of a new entry into the land.

Not long after Josiah's death – his eyes would not see the disaster that God brought upon Israel, as Huldah had prophesied – Nebuchadnezzar the king of Babylon came up and besieged Jerusalem. When the famine had become intolerable, Israel's warriors with their king Zedekiah made a breach in the wall by night and broke out. They were pursued and routed by the enemy; Zedekiah was captured and brought before Nebuchadnezzar. Sentence was quickly passed. Zedekiah's sons were killed before his very eyes, and that was the last thing he saw on earth, for immediately afterwards his eyes were gouged out. Israel's last king perished as Samson, Israel's last judge, had perished. And like Samson he was bound with two bronze chains. In this way Zedekiah was led off to Babylon. The temple treasures were plundered, the house of God set on fire, the walls of the city levelled. The upper class of the people and the able-bodied men in the country, the craftsmen and the smiths were deported; Nebuchadnezzar left the poor behind to cultivate the fields and vineyards. The produce was for the treasure chest of Babylon; the king's officials would see that those poor remained poor.

It 's cruel. But thank God it's not the end. Like king Josiah, the people too can rediscover the faith in exile.

ABOUT THE BIBLE

The Bible (from the Greek *biblia,* meaning 'books') is a library in itself, comprising a varied collection of books – sixty-six in all – written during a period of more than a thousand years (900 BC-AD 130). Most of the texts underwent a long development, and in the form in which we know them today they are the result of an age-old process of growth. The book consists of two main sections.

Christians call the first section the Old Testament; it comprises the thirty-nine sacred books of the Jewish faith, written in Hebrew. The second section is called the New Testament, and comprises the twenty-seven sacred books of Christianity, written in Greek.

The First, or Old, Testament is referred to by Jews as the 'TeNaKh', an acronym consisting of the T of Torah (Law), the N of Nebi'im (Prophets) and the K of Ketubhim (Writings), the main divisions of the book.

The Torah (called 'Pentateuch' in Greek) comprises the first five books of the Bible and describes, primarily in narrative form, the *way* to live. *Instruction, guidance,* is a better translation of the word Torah than law. Because Moses was thought to be the author, these books are also called the *books of Moses.*

In the Nebi'im, the prophetic writings, the people of God are summoned to follow the Torah. The Nebi'im are subdivided into the 'Former Prophets' (Joshua, Judges, Samuel, Kings) and the 'Latter Prophets' (Isaiah, Jeremiah, Ezekiel and the twelve minor prophets). In an unguarded moment Christianity called the 'Former Prophets' 'the historical books', thereby wrongly giving the impression that these stories are historical and not prophetic in character. It is especially because of this that in my retelling of the Old Testament I have preferred to follow the division of the TeNaKh.

In the Ketubhim we find a more individual reflection on the Torah. These writings offer a richly varied collection of prose and poetry (including Psalms, Job and Proverbs), as well as the five *megilloth*, the scrolls read publicly in the synagogue during Jewish days of remembrance (Ruth, Song of Songs, Ecclesiastes, Lamentations, Esther).

The Second or 'New' Testament consists of four Gospels (Matthew, Mark, Luke and John), the Acts of the Apostles, a number of letters and the Book of Revelation. The Gospels and Acts were written some time after Jesus' death (AD 60 – 100), and bear witness to the faith of the first Christian community. They are not 'historical' texts in our sense. The letters, written by various authors, are among the oldest books of the New Testament. The Book of Revelation was written as a work of the Christian resistance, intended to offer comfort to persecuted believers in a language accessible only to the initiated.

TRANSLATOR'S ACKNOWLEDGMENT

Translating Nico ter Linden's remarkable books has presented enormous problems. In retelling the stories of the Bible he uses a special kind of Dutch, at times colloquial, at times archaic, and often reflecting the original Hebrew. This interplay of various levels of Dutch is one of the appeals of the books, but is sometimes all but impossible to reproduce in English. In addition, he makes use of Dutch hymns and children's hymns, Dutch traditional songs and other indirect allusions, which again cannot be translated directly; sometimes it is possible to introduce English equivalents to retain the effect, sometimes this cannot be done.

I wish to acknowledge here the interest and concern shown in the English translation by Nico ter Linden himself, but more particularly the painstaking work and the help of Dr Henk Aertsen, Senior Lecturer in the English Department of the Free University of Amsterdam, who has checked out the translation and has been a sure guide through the minefield of sub-meanings as well as correcting errors and misunderstandings. Without him the translation would have been much inferior, and he deserves my deepest gratitude. Any errors that remain are mine.

John Bowden

BIBLIOGRAPHY

General

M.A. Beek, *Wegen en voetsporen van het Oude Testament,* Delft 1957

K. Bouhuijs and K.A. Deurloo, *Dichterbij de profeten,* Amsterdam 1968 (especially for Chapters 40 and 44)

M. Buber, *Bücher der Geschichte,* Cologne 1956

M. Buber, *Königtum Gottes,* Berlin 1932

K.A. Deurloo, *Dichterbij de profeten,* Amsterdam 1968 (especially for Chapter 65)

J.P. Fokkelman, *Vertelkunst in de bijbel,* Zoetermeer 1995 (especially for Chapters 14, 15, 31, 55 and 56)

J.A. Kwint, *Preken,* unpublished

E. Whitlau (ed.). *Tenachon,* Hilversum 1987 (especially for Chapters 15 and 28)

Joshua

Amstelkerk preaching team, *Exegetische notities over Jozua,* unpublished

M.A. Beek, *Jozua,* Nijkerk 1981

P.A.H. de Boer (et al.), in *De intocht, Phoenix Bijbelpocket no. 7,* Zeist 1963

K. Bouhuijs and K.A. Deurloo, in *Postille 25,* The Hague 1973

K.A. Deurloo, *Jozua,* Kampen 1981 (an unbeatable commentary from which I have taken a lot, sometimes word for word. I also made grateful use of it in the translation)

J. de Groot, *Jozua,* Groningen 1931

H.W. Hertzberg, *Josua, Richter, Ruth,* Göttingen 1973

H. Renckens, in *Werkschrift jrg 3 no.1,* Amsterdam 1982

N.A. Schuman, in *Schrift 107,* Heilig Landstichting 1986, especially for Chapters 5 and 6)

Judges

H. Abma, *Profetie en poëzie*, Kampen 1989 (especially for Chapters 8, 16 and 22)

M. Bal, in *Schrift* 151, Heilig Landstichting 1994

H. Blok (ed.), *Geen koning in die dagen*, Baarn 1982 (I have borrowed much from this exegesis, sometimes word for word)

P.A.H. de Boer (et al.), in *De Richteren, Phoenix Bijbelpocket no.8*, Zeist 1963 (especially for Chapters 8 and 9)

A.G. van Daalen, *Simson*, Assen 1966

E. Drewermann, *Den eigenen Weg gehen*, Munich 1995 (especially for Chapters 10, 15 and 16)

H.W. Hertzberg, *Josua, Richter, Ruth*, Göttingen 1973

J.D. Martin, *The Book of Judges*, Cambridge 1975

P.J. van Midden, *Koningschap en broederschap*, Amsterdam dissertation 1998 (especially for Chapters 10-14)

T.J.M. Naastepad, *Simson*, Kampen n.d. (especially for Chapters 19, 20 and 22)

N.A. Schuman, *Verbonden voor het leven*, Delft 1988 (especially for Chapters 18 and 21)

Societas Hebraica Amstelodamensis, *Richteren, een vertaling*, Haarlem 1982 (I have followed this translation a good deal)

J.A. Soggin, *Judges*, London 1981

I and II Samuel

Amstelkerk preaching team, *Exegetische notities*, unpublished

W. Brueggemann, *First and Second Samuel*, Louisville 1990 (especially for Chapters 44, 46, 53 and 55)

K.A. Deurloo (ed.), *Sjofele koning*, Baarn 1984 (especially for Chapters 37, 42, 43, 44 and 45)

E. Drewermann, *Das Köningreich Gottes in unserer Seele*, Munich 1996 (especially for Chapter 50)

J.C.M. Engelen, *I Samuel 1-15*, Kampen 1982 (especially for Chapter 29)

J.P. Fokkelman, *Narrative Art and Poetry in the Books of Samuel*, Volume I, *King David*, Assen 1981; Volume II, *The Crossing Fates*, Assen 1986; Volume III, *Throne and City*, Assen 1990; Volume IV, *Vow and Desire*, Assen 1993 (chapter by chapter I have made grateful use of this splendid study)

F.O. van Gennep, *School voor koningen,* Baarn 1976 (especially for Chapters 29, 30, 37, 39, 40 and 42)

J. de Groot, *I en II Samuel,* Groningen 1934

A. Jobsen, *David,* Kampen 1992 (especially for Chapters 34, 36 and 53)

J. Koopmans, *Toen stelde de Heere zich daar,* The Hague 1945

T.J.M. Naastepad, *Het geheim van Rachel,* Antwerp 1965 (especially for Chapters 26, 31, 44 and 53)

— , translation in *De eerste lezing no 13,* Voorburg 1987

H. Oosterhuis, in *Werkschrift 2e jrg no. 2,* Amsterdam 1981 (especially for Chapters 31, 33 and 53)

N.A. Schuman, *Messiaans en menselilk,* Kampen 1988 (especially for Chapters 27, 42, 44, 45, 47 and 53)

K.A.D. Smelik, *Saul,* Amsterdam 1977

J. Soetendorp, translations in *Phoenix bijbelpockets* no 9, Zeist 1964

W. van der Spek, *1 Samuel,* Zoetermeer 1996 (especially for Chapters 27, 30 and 31)

— , *De Messias in de Hebreeuwse bijbel,* Gorinchem 1992

I and II Kings

Amstelkerk preaching team, *Exegetische notities,* unpublished (especially for Chapters 64 and 66)

B.E.J.H. Becking, *De ondergang van Samaria,* Utrecht dissertation 1985

A.G. van Daalen, in *Amsterdamse cahiers* 1, 2, 3, 4 and 5, Kampen 1980-1984

J. Gray, *I and II Kings,* London 1985

G.H. Jones, *I and II Kings,* London 1984

P. Kevers (ed.), *Elia,* Leuven 1996 (especially for Chapters 62, 63 and 64)

D. Monshouwer, translation in *De erste lezing no.16,* Voorburg 1988

M.J. Mulder, *Koningen,* Kampen 1987

T.J.M. Naastepad, *Elia,* Kampen nd (especially for Chapter 64)

M.J.W. Schopenhauer, *Preken uit Werselo 1975-1976,* unpublished

K.A.D. Smelik, in *Amsterdamse Cahiers no 6,* Kampen 1985

— , *1 en 2 Koningen,* 's-Hertogenbosch 1993 (especially for Chapters 60, 74 and 76)

W. Veen, *Hizkia,* Kampen 1996 (for Chapters 73, 74 and 75 I have made abundant use of this study, sometimes word for word, and also of the translation)

T. Veerkamp, *De vernietiging van de Baäl*, Amsterdam 1996 (especially for
    Chapters 62, 63, 64, 65, 68, 71 and 72)
K. Waaijman, *De profeet Elia*, Nijmegen 1985 (especially for Chapter 64)

I am most grateful to the Keizerskroon Foundation, which has made it
possible for me to devote myself entirely to writing this work.

OTHER SOURCES, SOURCES OF QUOTATIONS, NOTES

Chapter 1

P. Kevers, *Schrift 133*, Heilig Landstichting 1991

H. Renckens, in *Werkschrift jrg 3 no 1*, Amsterdam 1982

A.L.H.M. van Wieringen, *Heraut jrg 128 no 9*, Nijmegen 1997

p. 1   G. Santayana

p. 2   They were called the Former Prophets, not because they played their role at an earlier time in Israel but because they are printed in the Bible before the Latter Prophets: Isaiah, Jeremiah, Ezekiel and the twelve Minor Prophets. See 'On the Bible', p.ooo.

p. 2   Numbers 32.

Chapter 2

N.J. de Jong-Dorland, *Postille 40*, The Hague 1988

p. 5   Numbers 13

p. 6   Exodus 15

p. 6   Deuteronomy 4.39

Chapter 3

p. 8   Ecclesiastes 1.6-8

p. 10   Isaiah 32.15 and 41.18

Chapter 4

T.J.M. Naastepad, *Uw redelijke eredienst*, Amsterdam 1980

H.G.L. Peels, *Postille 41*, The Hague 1989

L. van Reijendam-Beek, *Heraut jrg 28 no.9*, Nijmegen 1997

p. 12   Martin Luther King

p. 13   Exodus 19.12, 13

p. 14   Exodus 23; Leviticus 25

p. 14   Leviticus 25

Chapter 5

p. 16   It is open to question whether foundation sacrifices were offered in ancient Canaan. It could also be that young children who died of a sickness were buried close to their homes. Child sacrifices are in evidence for Phoenicia and above all Carthage.

p. 16   Jonah 4.11

Chapter 6

p. 18   Genesis 12. 6

p. 18   Genesis 31 and 35.4

p. 19   Joshua 10

Chapter 8

p. 24   Joshua 11

p. 24   Psalm 19.11

p. 25   Psalm 124.1-2

p. 26   Judges 3.31

Chapter 9

G. van Hemert, in *Werkschrift jrg 1 no. 4*, Amsterdam 1981

K. Waayman, in *Speling jrg 35 no. 3*, Nijmegen 1983

G.A. de Vries, in *Postille 49*, Zoetermeer 1997

E. van Wolde, *Schrift 158*, Heilig Landstichting 1995

Chapter 12

H. Altena, in *Postille 16*, The Hague 1964

J. Nieuwenhuis, *Te pas en te onpas*, Kampen 1991

Chapter 13

p. 43   Numbers 32.27-32

Chapter 14

p. 45   Deuteronomy 17.16 and 17

Chapter 15

J. Holman, in *Schrift 123*, Heilig Landstichting 1989

J.H. de Wit, in *Postille 48*, Zoetermeer 1996

Chapter 16

Huub Oosterhuis, *Werkschrift 7e jrg no 6*, Amsterdam 1987

J. Smit en H. Stroeken, *Lotgevallen*, Amsterdam 1993

W. Straatman-Wortel, *Schrift 164*, Heilig Landstichting 1996

P. Trible, *Texts of Terror*, Philadelphia and London 1984

H. Zorgdrager, *HN*, 23 October 1993

p. 51   A remark by Voltaire about God, '*Pardonner c'est son métier.*'

p. 54   About Sarah and Raguel, for example, in the apocryphal biblical book of Tobit. See Eugen Drewermann and Nico ter Linden, *Het verhaal van Tobit, Tobias en de engel*, Hilversum 1988

Chapter 17

p. 55   Psalm 133

Chapter 18

K.A.D. Smelik, *Simson*, Kampen 1992

p. 57 Numbers 6

p. 59   Judges 5.13

Chapter 21

p. 71   II Kings 25

Chapter 22

K.A. Deurloo, *Waar gebeurd*, Baarn 1981

p. 75   See *The Story Goes* I pp.68f.

p. 75   Joshua 2.1

p. 76   See *The Story Goes* I, p. 202. In the Hebrew Bible the letter n is added, which makes it no longer Moses but Manasseh – this is in order to spare Moses this shame.

Chapter 24

p. 82   Luke 1.36-55

Chapter 25

E. Drewermann, *Wat ons toekomt*, Zoetermeer 1993

Chapter 26

K.A.D. Smelik, in *Amsterdamse cahiers* no.I, Kampen 1980

p. 88   Deuteronomy 8. 3 and Matthew 4.4

Chapter 29
p. 99   Psalm 72. 4

Chapter 30
p. 101   I Samuel 10. 8

Chapter 31
K.A.D. Smelik, in K.A. Deurloo and B.J. Diebner, *YHWH-Kurios-Antitheism*, Heidelberg 1996
p. 104   Exodus 17. 8-16. See *The Story Goes* I, pp.226f.
p. 104   Esther 3.1. Haman is an Agagite, a son of Agag, king of the Amalekites
p. 104   Deuteronomy 25.17-19

Chapter 32
R. Venema, in *Bekirbenoe 32e jrg* no 11, Amsterdam 1990

Chapter 33
K.A. Deurloo, *Waar gebeurd*, Baarn 1981
p. 113   II Samuel 21.19-21. The narrator takes over the words printed in italics into his story of David and Goliath.

Chapter 34
p. 117   J.C. de Bruïne
p. 117   II Samuel 5. 6-16
p. 118   II Samuel 6.17

Chapter 35
p. 119   I Samuel 23.17

Chapter 36
K.A. Deurloo, *sermon 28.10.1990*, unpublished
p. 124   The Dutch National Anthem, sixth verse

Chapter 40
p. 137   Psalm 14.1

Chapter 42

p. 143   I Samuel 21.13

p. 143   I Samuel 27.1-12

p. 146   Matthew 20.1-16

Chapter 43

p. 148   Muus Jacobse, *Het oneindige verlangen*, Nijkerk 1982

Chapter 44

J. Fokkelman, *Vertelkunst in de bijbel*, Zoetermeer 1995

J.M. Hasselaar, *In de waagschaal jrg 1969*, Amsterdam 1969. 103.

Chapter 45

H. Oosterhuis, *Werkschrift 2e jrg* 1102, Amsterdam 1981

p. 156   Dietrich Bonhoeffer, 'Powers of Good', from Letters and Papers from Prison, London 1971, 400

p. 156   A notion from the Talmud

Chapter 46

T.J.M. Naastepad, in *Mededelingen Van der Leeuwstichting 54*, Amsterdam 1980

H. Oosterhuis, in *Werkschrift 2e jrg* no.2, Amsterdam 1981

K.A.D. Smelik, in *Amsterdamse cahiers 4*, Kampen 1983

p. 157   Psalm 24

Chapter 47

p. 161   A. Roland Holst

p. 162   Job 33.15-17

Chapter 48

K.A. Deurloo, Op *bergen en in dalen*, Baarn 1988

Chapter 49

p. 168   I Samuel 8. 11-18

p. 168   Psalm 51.1-4,19

Chapter 50

M.A. Beek, *David en Absalom*, Amsterdam 1972

P. Trible, *Texts of Terror*, Philadelphia and London 1984

Chapter 52

M.A. Beek, *David en Absalom*, Amsterdam 1972

Chapter 53

M.A. Beek, *David en Absalom*, Amsterdam 1972

K.A. Deurloo and K. Bouhuys, *Taalwegen en dwaalwegen*, Amsterdam 1967

J. van der Wiel, in *In de waagschaal*, Amsterdam 1969

p. 184   Vondel, *Gysbrecht van Aemstel*

Chapter 55

p. 192   I Chronicles 21

p. 193   A. Herzberg, *Tweestromenland*, Amsterdam 1950

Chapter 56

K.A.D. Smelik, *Schrijt 103*, Heilig Landstichting 1986

Chapter 57

K.A. Deurloo, in A.I. van der Woude (ed.), *New Avenues in the Study of the Old Testament*, Leiden 1989

p. 200   Psalm 72.1 and 13

Chapter 58

p. 201   II Samuel 7

Chapter 59

W. Barnard, in *Woord en Dienst jan.1973*, The Hague 1973

p. 204   Psalm 72

p. 204   Isaiah 60.6

p. 205   Matthew 2.1-12

Chapter 60

T.C. Frederikse, *Postille 33*, The Hague 1981

R. Zuurmond, *Postille 27*, The Hague 1975

p. 206   Deuteronomy 17.16, 17

p. 207   See *The Story Goes* I, p. 257

p. 207   See the note on Chapter 5, p. 16

p. 208   Joshua 6.26

Chapter 61

K.A.D. Smelik, in *Amsterdamse cahiers no 10*, Kampen 1989
A. Wessels, *En allen die geloven zijn Abrahamsgeslacht*, Baarn 1989
p. 211   Luke 7. 11-17

Chapter 63

p. 217   Muus Jacobse, *Liedboek voor de kerken*, hymn 11
p. 217   Exodus 33.12-23

Chapter 64

K.A.D. Smelik, in *Amsterdamse cahiers no.10*, Kampen 1989
p. 220   Deuteronomy 11.10
p. 220   Deuteronomy 25. 23
p. 221   Isaiah 5. 8

Chapter 65

E. Drewermann, *Tiefenpsychologie und Exegese*, Olten 1988
p. 225   Deuteronomy 21.17

Chapter 66

p. 229   Psalm 23

Chapter 67

B.J. Oosterhoff, *Postille 23*, The Hague 1971

Chapter 70

M.A. Beek, *Maskerspel*, Bussum 1955

Chapter 71

K.A.D. Smelik, in *Analecta Bruxellensia 2*, Brussels 1997

Chapter 72

p. 248   In a previous story Gehazi was a leper, but that doesn't deter the story-teller. He needs the prophet's servant in this story to tell the king about 'all the great things that Elisha has done'.

Chapter 73

p. 252   Isaiah 36-39. Kings speaks of three Assyrian delegates, Isaiah of one.

p. 252   Isaiah 7.3 and 4
p. 254   I Samuel 17.26, 36

Chapter 74
J.J. van Es, sermon of 19 January 1995, unpublished

Chapter 75
K.A. Deurloo, *Amsterdamse cahiers no 3*, Kampen 1982
K.A. Deurloo, *Joshua*, Kampen 1981
J. van Dorp, *Josia*, Utrecht dissertation 1991
J. van Dorp, *Amsterdamse cahiers no.8*, Kampen 1987
p. 258   Deuteronomy 17. 18-20
p. 259   Joshua 1. 8
p. 259   Huub Oosterhuis, *Nieuw Bijbels Liedboek*, Baarn 1986